"Now that mindfulness and somatic approaches are the rage in psychotherapy, it is important to appreciate that they arose, at least in part, from Eugene Gendlin's *Focusing*. In this engaging and scholarly book, Ann Weiser Cornell provides a deeper understanding of the Focusing process and explains how to usefully integrate it into many other therapy approaches."

—Richard Schwartz, PhD,
developer of Internal Family Systems Therapy

"An instant classic. Read it. And then read it again. Ann Weiser Cornell has written a masterpiece—with ease, conviction, clarity, and natural grace, she makes a huge contribution by clearly articulating specific aspects of what it means to use Focusing in clinical practice, and how to do so in a way that rings true to clinicians. As she promises in the subtitle, this book deepens our understanding of 'the essence of change.' Kudos!"

—Diana Fosha, PhD, developer of AEDP,
author of *The Transforming Power of Affect* (2000),
and co-editor of *The Healing Power of Emotion:
Affective Neuroscience, Development & Clinical Process* (2009)

FOCUSING IN
CLINICAL PRACTICE

A NORTON PROFESSIONAL BOOK

FOCUSING IN CLINICAL PRACTICE

The Essence of Change

ANN WEISER CORNELL

W. W. Norton & Company

New York • London

For information about permission to reproduce selections from this book,
write to Permissions, W. W. Norton & Company, Inc., 500 Fifth Avenue,
New York, NY 10110

For information about special discounts for bulk purchases, please contact
W. W. Norton Special Sales at specialsales@wwnorton.com or 800-233-4830

Manufacturing by R.R. Donnelley, Harrisonburg
Production manager: Leeann Graham

Library of Congress Cataloging-in-Publication Data

Cornell, Ann Weiser.
    Focusing in clinical practice : the essence of change / Ann Weiser Cornell.
— First edition.
        pages cm.   "A Norton Professional Book."
    Includes bibliographical references and index.
    ISBN 978-0-393-70760-1 (hardcover)
    1. Therapist and patient.   2. Clinical competence.   3. Core competen-
cies.   I. Title.
    R727.3.C684 2013
    616.69'6—dc23

2013007250

ISBN: 978-0-393-70760-1

W. W. Norton & Company, Inc., 500 Fifth Avenue, New York, N.Y. 10110
www.wwnorton.com
W. W. Norton & Company Ltd., Castle House, 75/76 Wells Street, London
W1T 3QT

2   3   4   5   6   7   8   9   0

For Gene Gendlin, mentor and friend

CONTENTS

ACKNOWLEDGMENTS

Many people helped me with conversations about their work with clients and their views on therapy, including Michelle Bendowski, Karin Bundschuh-Müller, Frans Depestele, Nancy Eaton, Lakme Batya Elior, Glenn Fleisch, Ken Frank, Elena Frezza, Mary C. Howard, Carol Ivan, Joan Lavender, Karen Levin, Bret Lyon, Noga Maivar, Dave Potter, Jane Quayle, Elke Schaettgen, and Susan Stephens. Elmar Kruithoff deserves a special mention. I am eternally grateful to the Focusing Institute, without whose existence I might never have met most of these special people, and to the whole Focusing community.

I had a team of close discussants who were willing to talk to me regularly and comment on early drafts: Helene Brenner, Shulamit Day, Elmar Kruithoff, Larry Letich, Lauren Mari-Navarro, and especially Carol Nickerson, whose weekly conversations with me about the book were a source of great support.

I also benefited from conversations with fellow authors and noted theorists: John Amodeo, Helene G. Brenner, Robert Elliott, Diana Fosha, Eugene Gendlin, Mike Hellwig, Sue Johnson, Lynn Preston, and Margaret S. Warner.

Lauren Mari-Navarro, Kevin Sachs, and Judy Schavrien each read the manuscript and helped me catch mistakes and speak in a clearer voice. Their help was invaluable. The mistakes that remain are all mine.

My boundless gratitude and appreciation go to my brilliant and creative staff, Shannon Crossman, Brittany Dean, and Maggie Hurley, who make it possible for me to have both a business and a life, and Elizabeth Kaye, my Focusing-oriented leadership coach.

I bless the fabulous baristas at Philz Coffee in North Berkeley: Andie, Angela, Anna, Anthony, Bijan, Caroline, Catherine, Celsa, Christian, Daniel, Darren, two Dereks, Dylan, Eric, Ilya, Jamie, Kate, Kathryn, Katie, Kyle, Lucky, Petra, Rachel, Sadie, Samantha, Tess, Zach—sorry if I missed someone! You knew my name, remembered my goat milk, and made it possible to write this book in a great atmosphere.

I'm grateful to my book-writing software for the Mac: Scrivener, by Literature & Latte, which allows the ducks to be put in a nice neat row.

My appreciation to my editor at Norton, Andrea Costella Dawson, who had the idea for this book and never wavered in her vision of a "concise road map to Focusing" for clinicians.

My working partnership with Barbara McGavin illuminates my life and has built a place to stand, to reach beyond where I ever could have reached alone.

Gene Gendlin, I can never say enough about what your life and being have meant to me.

Finally, my undying thanks to my daughter Mika, my nieces Corinne and Nicole, and my nephews, Christopher, Jon, Josh, and Kip, who are a constant source of delight and great pride, and Joe McBride, cheerleader, in-house editor, and soulmate, whose abundant love and generous good humor have never failed me.

—Ann Weiser Cornell

Introduction

A DOORWAY IN A MOMENT

I learned Focusing 40 years ago, and it probably saved my life. I learned it for my own personal growth, in a series of meetings on Sunday nights in a community church in Chicago. There was no book about it then; no one knew it was going to become something used by hundred of thousands of people in more than 50 countries, in psychotherapy (Amodeo, 2007; Friedman, 2007; Gendlin, 1996; Purton, 2004), counseling (Purton, 2007), coaching (Madison, 2011), self-help (Cornell, 1996; Gendlin, 1981), and community wellness (Omidian & Lawrence, 2007), with applications in creativity (Rappaport, 2009), business (Ikemi, 2007), health (Klagsbrun, 1999, 2001; Summerville, 1999), trauma release (Armstrong, 2010; Grindler Katonah, in press), spirituality (Hinterkopf, 2004), addiction (Tidmarsh, 2010), chronic pain (Bärlocher, 1999; Frezza, 2008; Müller & Feuerstein, 1999), working with children (Stapert & Verliefde, 2008), adolescents in residential treatment (Parker, 2007), parents and babies (Boukydis, 2012)—and much more. It was just something that this guy Gene Gendlin was teaching for free and that my friends and I practiced with each other.

I fell in love with Focusing, and eventually, after life took many turns, I became a professional Focusing teacher and practitioner. I became well known in the Focusing community as an innovator and articulator of the method. Since the 1980s I have traveled to 19 countries doing training, wrote the second most widely used book about Focusing, worked with clients, and trained and supervised other practitioners. In my clients, and in the clients of my students, I saw powerful, moving, life-changing experiences, and was always somewhat puzzled that this remarkable process was not better known. More than half the time, when I told people what I did, I was met with blank stares. "What is Focusing?"

Focusing is better known now, but it still feels like a well-kept secret—even though it inspired much of the somatically oriented, mindfulness-based work being done today. In October 2010, when Peter Levine received the Lifetime Achievement Award from the U.S. Association for Body Psychotherapy, he recommended Gene Gendlin from the stage to be the next recipient of the award, citing Gendlin's seminal contributions to his work, Somatic Experiencing. Focusing was also incorporated by Ron Kurtz (1997) into his Hakomi Therapy, which led to sensorimotor therapy (Ogden, Minton, & Pain, 2006), and Focusing forms an essential part of Greenberg, Elliott, and Rice's Emotion-Focused Therapy for Individuals (Elliott, Watson, Goldman, & Greenberg, 2004). In fact, anyone working experientially today owes a debt to Gendlin's research in the 1950s into this client process that is an essence of change, and to his creation of Focusing, a way to facilitate that process. As we will see, the Focusing process incorporated and integrated, over 50 years ago, many of the processes and methods that seem like fresh discoveries today, notably mindfulness, the adaptive power of affect, a somatic orientation, client self-regulation, and the importance of the present moment.

But there is something that sets Focusing apart from every other way of working with clients and understanding change, and even the theorists who have deliberately incorporated Focusing have mostly missed this essential, paradigm-shifting concept.

It is possible to get great results from bringing Focusing to clients and yet not know the fundamental reason why this work is an important essence of change. But just think what will happen if we do understand it, and can really get behind it and support what brings change to our clients (and ourselves). That is my purpose for you: that you grasp what makes Focusing uniquely powerful as a way of supporting your clients in the change they need, and that you have the tools to bring this work to your clients in the ways that fit for them and for you.

HOW IT ALL BEGAN

When a young philosophy student named Eugene Gendlin forged a research partnership in the 1950s with the legendary Carl Rogers at the University of Chicago, the result was a startlingly new way of understanding—and facilitating—the human change process.

Eugene Gendlin was born in Austria in 1927. At age 11, young Gene watched his father make intuitive choices, trusting one person and not trusting another, that enabled their Jewish family to escape the Nazis, when many other families were blocked from leaving the country and later were sent to their deaths. When Gene asked, "Papa, how did you know you could not trust that person?" his father tapped his chest and said, "I follow my feeling." In 1994 Gendlin told an interviewer, "I was surprised then and also often asked myself later what kind of feeling it is which tells you something. Sometimes I tried to find such a feeling within myself, but I could not. But that I started to look for it had its effect in the end" (Korbei, 2007).

Flash forward to 1952: Gene was a graduate student in the Philosophy Department of the University of Chicago, studying with the terrifyingly brilliant Richard McKeon, reading especially the existential phenomenologists Heidegger, Sartre, and Merleau-Ponty. Gene was wrestling with a philosophical question that seemed to him at the very center of human life: how an experience that comes before words becomes an idea framed in words. He wasn't satisfied with any of the answers he was given by the philosophical tradition; none of them seemed to engage with the obvious fact that meanings can be present before the words that describe them.

Gene knew from his own self-inquiry that there is a kind of experience that a person speaks from. But he needed examples. He wanted to be around people who were articulating their own experiences and were interested in other people articulating theirs, especially when they were saying something new, something they had never said before.

This sounds like something that happens in psychotherapy, so it seems obvious—in retrospect—that Gene Gendlin would find himself at the doorstep of Carl Rogers, who was heading the University of Chicago Counseling Center and overseeing an energetic group of psychology graduate students. They had a psychotherapy practicum, which, in keeping with Rogers's ideas, did not require a psychology background. Even so, young Gene was the first applicant to the program who came from philosophy. He remembers Rogers leaning toward him and asking, "But are you obtuse about people?"

I understood that that was his concept about philosophers, that they were obtuse about people. And I said no, I didn't think so, because people talk to me all night and I listen to them. I found myself being a listener but without any way to help, and I was eager to learn how. He liked that. About two weeks later, I realized that I actually came because *I* needed it. (personal communication, 2012)

So Gendlin joined the group around Rogers, both as a therapist trainee and as a client. He became a psychotherapist, eventually honored four times by the American Psychological Association, including receiving the first Distinguished Professional Psychologist of the Year award from the Clinical Division. But he never stopped being a philosopher and has received honors in that field as well. His philosophy "begins where the existentialist philosophers left off, namely with the problem of just how symbols (thoughts, speech, other symbols) are related to, or based on, concrete experiencing" (Gendlin, 1973, p. 320).

The next thing that comes to the person to feel and say is not necessarily what follows logically from what was last said. Rather it follows from the feeling of what was said. . . . Imposing interpretations and schemes on oneself is useless, but allowing one's next authentic step to form is, along with brave choices, the way to live one's real possibilities forward. (Gendlin, 1973, p. 319)

Gene's input changed the type of research being done by the Rogers group and ultimately caused Rogers to reformulate his theory of the human change process, described in *On Becoming a Person*, in which he gave credit to Eugene Gendlin (along with two others) "whose demonstrated ability to think in new ways about [psychotherapy] has been particularly helpful, and from whom I have borrowed heavily" (1961, p. 128).

The result of that collaboration was a way of viewing the process of change in psychotherapy that is dependent on two key interdependent factors: how the therapist is with the client, and how the client is with her own "experiencing." The therapist created an atmosphere of empathic, close attention to the client, along with an acceptance of the client as a person. Facilitated by this atmosphere, the client—supposedly—moved in therapy through a series of stages of greater and greater attentiveness to immediately feeling in the present moment, where change happens. The question was: Did clients actually move through stages of being more and more present to themselves in the course of therapy? This was a question for research—the research that led to the creation of Focusing.

THE RESEARCH BEHIND FOCUSING

Determined to discover what in the therapist-client process correlated with therapeutic change, and in particular if clients progressed through stages of experiencing during the therapy process, the researchers, led by Gendlin, taped psychotherapy sessions and sorted them by outcome, successful versus unsuccessful. They developed a Process Scale (later the Experiencing Scale) for use in rating clients' ability to be in contact with and speak from directly felt experience (Gendlin & Zimring, 1955; Klein, Mathieu, Gendlin, & Kiesler, 1969).

> Thus, there is only one question and one measurable dimension: to what extent do the individual's words and actions refer to, or freshly phrase his ongoing felt experiencing, and to what extent are they rather "mere" words, not involving and carrying his felt experiencing any further? (Gendlin, Beebe, Cassens, Klein, & Oberlander, 1968, p. 220)

The research showed that clients who "freshly referred to ongoing felt experiencing" during the therapy sessions tended to have significantly more positive therapy outcomes than clients who merely talked about their problems or their emotions.

What disturbed Gendlin and his fellow researchers was that the success or failure of therapy could be predicted from the first session. In other words, it looked as though therapy did not change clients' ability to be in experiential contact, even though this experiential contact was the key factor in change, and that therefore a significant subset of clients were "doomed" from the start to be unable to be helped by therapy (Gendlin et al., 1968).

Clients who already had an ability to freshly contact immediate experience succeeded in their therapeutic goals; others did not. This finding, if true, meant to Gendlin that something needed to be added to therapy in order to include all clients in the benefits of therapy. Since the ability to be in contact with and speak from directly felt experience was what tended to correlate with successful therapy, he began to develop a way of teaching this ability, which he called Focusing. Further research showed that clients who were taught or facilitated in Focusing steps tended to do better in therapy than those who were not.[1]

FELT SENSING: THE ESSENCE OF CHANGE

At the core of Gendlin's research was the discovery of a new type of experience that he named a *felt sense*. A felt sense is a freshly forming, whole, bodily sense of some life situation—not the same as a simple emotion or thought. The felt sense is the least understood aspect of Gendlin's work, and the aspect that has the greatest transformative power.

People have been getting felt senses since long before Gendlin named them, yet he was the first to name them. Understanding the nature of a felt sense requires at least a preliminary grasp of the philosophical questions of experiencing and symbolization that are Gendlin's life work, and that starts with the nature of "experiencing."

"Experiencing" is a directly felt, here-and-now process of felt meaning. It is not simply "interoception," the feel of the body from inside, because experiencing has intricate implicit meaning. We do have an inward sense of our bodies, such as whether we are tense or calm—and at first glance it might seem that experiencing is simply this inner feeling. But experiencing is actually more than feeling; it is where we find what we mean (Fisher, 2002).

> Yet, upon further reflection, we can notice that only in this direct sensing do we have the meanings of what we say and think. For, without our "feel" of the meaning, verbal symbols

---

1. Hendricks discusses thirty-nine research studies finding that that "Focusing or EXP level can be increased by training or specific therapist interventions" (2001, p. 226).

are only noises (or sound images of noises). For example, someone listens to you speak, and then says: "Pardon me, but I don't grasp what you mean." If you would like to restate what you meant in different words, you will notice that you must inwardly attend to your direct referent, your felt meaning. Only in this way can you arrive at different words with which to restate it. (Gendlin, 1964, pp. 108–109)

Experiencing can be referred to directly, as when we say, "I can't put *this* into words very well." It's often when we have trouble articulating something we think or feel that we are most aware of this dimension of experiencing. Especially in those moments when there is "something" that we are aware of—"this"—and when no way of saying it so far has succeeded in capturing it, we are in touch with the "direct referent" of experiencing.

This is what the to-be-successful clients were doing, in the research—they were referring directly to their experiencing. The raters, listening to the tapes, could tell from how the clients spoke—"Uh . . . I'm not sure how to say this. . . . It's right here. . . . It's not exactly anger. . . ."—that they were in touch with something immediate, real, and hard to describe. Furthermore, when a description finally fit, there was evident relief: "Oh, it's not anger, it's feeling both trapped and helpless. That's what it is. Whew!"

A felt sense is a fresh, immediate, here-and-now experience that is actually the organism forming its next step in the situation the person is living in. A felt sense is experiencing forming itself, and it can be sensed. Felt senses form because we deliberately invite them to form. We say, with genuine curiosity, "How am I right now?"— and wait for the answer. We wonder inwardly, "What is it about this that bothers me so much?" and wait to feel what comes.

The pause, the inner intention of asking, enables a felt sense to form. Of course it is not necessary to have all this conceptual apparatus for felt sensing to happen, since anyone can have a felt sense without knowing the term. When a felt sense forms there is always some kind of pausing, some kind of turning toward "something." What we then find may be murky, unclear, vague, and not feel like much—but the fact that it formed is already the beginning of our life moving forward in new and fresh ways.

There will be much more about this in Chapter 1.

THE SIX-STEP VERSION OF FOCUSING

In 1978, 6 years after I met him, Gene Gendlin wrote the book *Focusing*, his offering of the Focusing process to the general public. When *Focusing* was picked up by Bantam Books in 1981, excitement about the process spread rapidly by word of mouth. To date, over half a million copies have sold of the "little paperback with the stones on the cover," which has never gone out of print.[2]

In order to offer Focusing to the general public, Gendlin systematized the process into six steps. When I had learned Focusing from him in 1972–1974, he was experimenting with many different ways of teaching the process, but in order to simplify the process for his book, he chose this six-step form, starting with Clearing a Space, followed by Getting a Felt Sense, Finding a Handle, Resonating the Handle, Asking, and Receiving. Because of the popularity of the book, those particular six steps became identified with Focusing, even though Gendlin himself acknowledged they were only one way of teaching the process. No single form can encompass Focusing, or work for everyone. I was one of the earliest to develop and publish other ways to present Focusing (Cornell, 1993).

Psychotherapists who heard about Focusing were naturally excited about the implications of the work and wanted to apply it in client sessions immediately. But the little book *Focusing* with its six steps was intended as an introductory self-help book, not as a guide to clinical practice. Therapists who tried to apply the six steps directly with clients often found themselves frustrated or coming quickly to the apparent limitations of the process. If Gendlin's six steps are seen as a kind of "manual" of Focusing applied to clinical settings, they quickly fail to encompass the complexity of working with a variety of types of client process and client readiness. At the time there were no further resources for clinicians about Focusing. Even so, a number of psychotherapists did adopt Focusing as a methodology. One early adopter was Neil Friedman (1982, 1987, 2007),

---

2. Although the second revised edition does have a new cover . . . and I miss the stones!

whose books about bringing Focusing into psychotherapy and combining Focusing with other methods are classics in the field. Later Gendlin (1996) wrote an excellent book for clinicians, *Focusing-Oriented Psychotherapy*, which I highly recommend.[3]

Gendlin never intended the six steps in his first book to encompass Focusing. I remember he said at the time, "The six steps are a rope across the territory. When you know the territory, you don't need to hang onto the rope." In addition, Focusing, like any living process, has evolved, and there is general consensus among Focusing practitioners today that the six steps originally proposed are only one way to teach or describe the Focusing process.

Readers who assume that Focusing is the six steps defined by Gendlin in 1978 will be pleasantly surprised to discover that there is a much vaster world of possibilities for bringing Focusing to clients, allowing us to be responsive and flexible in a way that will fit a much larger number of clients.

THE PLACE OF FOCUSING IN THE CURRENT PSYCHOTHERAPY CONVERSATION

In recent years there has been increasing interest in psychotherapy circles in a number of developments including mindfulness, somatic orientation, the present moment, relationality, the importance of acceptance and empathy, and the insights from attachment theory and self-regulation. Each of these areas is being pursued and often developed separately—and yet all are found, in some form, integrated in Focusing and developed further. I'll discuss each of them, along with the ways that Focusing brings in a somewhat different perspective.

---

3. For those who are curious about how the present book differs from Gendlin's, I can briefly say that his is a manual for how to do Focusing-Oriented Psychotherapy, whereas my intention is to offer a concise guide to bringing Focusing into any form of clinical practice. Others who have written helpfully about Focusing and psychotherapy include Armstrong (1998), Depestele (2004), Fleisch (2008), Geiser (2010), Grindler Katonah (in press), Ikemi (2010), Jaison (2004), Leijssen (2007), Madison (2001), Nickerson (2009), Preston (2005, 2008), Purton (2004, 2007), Rappaport (2009), and Tidmarsh (2010).

Somatic Orientation

Bringing a somatic orientation to therapy has been growing in popularity since the 1970s. Ron Kurtz (1997) created the Hakomi Method, which he also called "Body-Centered Psychotherapy." One of his students, Pat Ogden, went on to create sensorimotor therapy (Ogden et al., 2006). Ogden was also influenced by Peter Levine (1997, 2010), whose powerful method of working with somatic processes for releasing trauma called Somatic Experiencing is now widely taught. Levine has stated, "There's no therapy that can't be made better by referencing the body" (Yalom & Yalom, 2010).

Focusing was an important influence on these somatic pioneers, the "felt sense" having been adopted from Gendlin by both Kurtz and Levine. Focusing is well known for being a somatic process, for bringing the bodily dimension into therapy (Kurtz, 1997; Levine, 1997). But actually, what Focusing offers goes further than "somatic" in the usual sense. What Focusing adds to the world of somatic orientation in therapy is the possibility of inviting felt senses, which, it is important to note, are more than body sensation, as I discuss at length in Chapters 1 and 3.

Mindfulness

In recent years there has been a surge of interest in mindfulness as a supportive adjunct to healing of all kinds. Naturally, psychotherapists have become interested in mindfulness as a process to bring into therapy, both for client and therapist, although we find "mindfulness" being defined in many ways, as in this passage from Daniel Siegel:

> One way of conceptualizing mindfulness is that it is intentionally focusing attention on moment-to-moment experience without being swept up by judgments or preconceived ideas and expectations (see Kabat-Zinn, 2005). . . . Another way of defining mindfulness is in avoiding premature closure of possibilities that often come with a "hardening of the categories" (Cozolino, 2002) by which we filter and constrain our perceptions of the world. . . . And even in our everyday use of the word *mindful*, we have the connotation of being thoughtful, considerate, and aware. . . . In each of these three ways, a mindful therapist brings an awakened mind to focus on things as they are with

care and concern, to literally be present in awareness with what is happening right now. (2010, location 136)

Inviting the client to bring a "mindful" quality of awareness to present experiencing, including body sensation, is increasingly a key factor in many modalities. Notable examples of bringing mindfulness into psychotherapy include Dialectical Behavioral Therapy (DBT) and Acceptance and Commitment Therapy (ACT), both part of the group of practices termed "third-wave behavioral therapy." Mindfulness also forms part of somatic approaches like Hakomi Therapy (Kurtz) and Sensorimotor Therapy (Ogden).

Kabat-Zinn defines mindfulness as "paying attention in a particular way; on purpose to the present moment, and nonjudgmentally" (1994, p. 4). Linehan (1993) defines mindfulness as a combination of the "what" skills of observing, describing, and participating and the "how" skills of a nonjudgmental attitude, focusing on one thing at a time, and being effective. In a sensorimotor approach, mindfulness entails orienting and attending to the ebb and flow of present internal experience. (Ogden et al., 2006, p. 193)

In all these cases of the use of mindful awareness as a part of a psychotherapy modality, mindfulness is not used alone, but rather to set the stage or form the frame for the processes of inner work that are the therapy itself. The same is true of Focusing.

From its inception, Focusing has included the set of attitudes and behaviors known today as mindfulness. Focusing is facilitated when clients can bring nonjudgmental attentiveness to their own immediate felt experiencing (Bundschuh-Müller, 2004). Just as in the other therapeutic methods that include mindfulness, Focusing incorporates mindfulness and then goes further. "Mindfulness" is a good description of the quality of attentiveness that is the optimal environment for the forming of a felt sense. It is the forming of the felt sense itself, and the further attending to it, that is the Focusing process.

The Present Moment

The most eloquent modern advocate of the importance of the present moment in psychotherapy is the child psychiatrist Daniel N. Stern (2004) in his excellent and rewarding book *The Present Moment in Psycho-*

therapy and Everyday Life, although an understanding of the importance of the present moment goes back a long way in the history of psychotherapy. Wilfred Bion wrote, "Psychoanalytic 'observation' is concerned neither with what has happened nor with what is going to happen, but with what is happening," (1967, p. 271) and famously exhorted us to approach our clients with neither memory nor desire (1967).

In Focusing, the lived, experienced, present moment is key to therapeutic change. Psychotherapist and client are present in and attending to the texture and quality of how it feels to be here, right now. Change happens from now forward, and that includes change in how the past functions in the client's life.

> One experiences the present with one's past as implicit in one's body. Both are changed together if there is change and growth. It may sound odd that the past is changed in the present, but it is, insofar as the past functions now. This presently implicit past is very different from one's life history or telling about it. It is what one directly finds in the moment now, as one senses into the implicitly rich and complex experiencing of how one lives in one's present situations. (Gendlin, 1973, p. 334)

Gendlin's concept of "experiencing" is a key to understanding how Focusing contributes to the process of change, and experiencing is a profoundly present-moment occurrence. "Experiencing occurs in the immediate present. It is not generalized attributes of a person such as traits, complexes, or dispositions. Rather, experiencing is what a person feels here and now, in this moment" (Gendlin, 1961, p. 234).

Being in need of change can feel like being at a dead end, locked into endless repetitions of the problem in only slightly different forms. But from the present moment forward it is also possible for something new to happen, for new possibilities to open and new behaviors to emerge. The Focusing process invites a particular kind of attention to present experiencing and the freshly forming felt sense, and makes powerful use of the present moment as a key element of that attention.

Empathy

In the earlier years of psychotherapy, the therapist's empathic connection with what the client was going through did not seem to have a high priority, taking a back seat to analysis and interpretation. But today there is broad consensus across all the major modalities of psychotherapy that a respectful, empathic contact with the client will further the goals of therapy. Heinz Kohut's passionate advocacy of "experience-near" empathic attunement and Carl Rogers's development of empathic reflection are two of the most well-known parents of this movement.

Judith Beck of Cognitive Therapy: "Most patients respond quite positively to direct expressions of empathy" (2011, p. 65). Russ Harris of ACT: "When we give our full attention to another human being with openness, compassion, and curiosity—that in itself is therapeutic" (2009, p. 51). Patricia DeYoung of Relational Psychotherapy: "In my experience as both client and therapist, I've become convinced that empathy creates a better context for growth and change than explanation or confrontation does" (2003, p. 40).

Empathy is never mere rote repeating. Robert Elliott and colleagues put it like this: "The therapist follows the track of the client's internal experience as it evolves from moment to moment. Following does not, however, mean mechanically paraphrasing the client's words. Instead, it refers to the therapist's trying to remain empathically attuned to the client's immediate inner experience and checking his or her understanding of this" (2004, p. 5).

Diana Fosha points to the power of empathy as "being in the patient's world, and the patient's feeling it and knowing it."

> In the presence of such a presence, the patient's world unfolds. This presence—equal parts knowing and wanting to know, being there and wanting to be there—makes it possible for people to talk about parts of themselves that are painful and hidden and frightened and frightening and dangerous and disorganizing. (2000, p. 29)

In Focusing, empathy is key in two ways. A close empathic contact from therapist to client enables the client to attune to subtle, freshly arising qualities of his immediate experience. Reflections are offered not primarily to "check understanding" (Rogers, 1986a) but to support the client in inwardly checking, with the assumption that not-yet-described, emerging elements of experiencing will come forward (Gendlin, 1984).

In addition, there is an inner relational process in which empathy is crucial. The client is supported by the therapist to be empathic toward his or her own experiencing process, in a kind of "self-listening" that furthers the emergence of change. The therapist's empathy supports and furthers the client's inner empathy.

Relationality

There is no longer any doubt that the dimension of relationality in the therapeutic dyad is a key to the effectiveness of the process of psychotherapy. Paul Wachtel (2008) eloquently puts forth the case that relationality is at the leading edge of current psychoanalysis. Self psychologists Stolorow and Atwood's (1992) concept of "inter-subjectivity" explodes the myth of the isolated individual mind. Other methods putting the therapeutic relationship at the center of the matter include ACT: "None of this will be effective if you don't have a good relationship with your client. In ACT, we aim to be fully present with our clients: open, authentic, mindful, compassionate, respectful, and in touch with our own core values" (Harris, 2009, p. 41) and existential psychotherapy:

> Therapists must convey to the patient that their paramount task is to build a relationship together that will itself become the agent of change. . . . Above all, the therapist must be prepared to go wherever the patient goes, do all that is necessary to continue building trust and safety in the relationship. (Yalom, 2002, pp. 34–35)

Although Focusing seems to be defined by the client's inner contact with experiencing, bringing Focusing into therapy is actually a radically relational approach, as Lynn Preston points out:

> I often quote Gendlin as saying that we don't focus inside ourselves but inside an interaction. . . . Focusing is a self responding, but the self that is being responded to is not an entity, a package of things. It cannot be reduced to an internal process. It is larger than its traits, perceptions, the way that it organizes experience, its issues or problems. Gendlin uses the term "person " to talk about this larger open relatedness that a self is. He speaks of the person as "the one who looks out from behind the eyes." This more that a person is, is not static but always becoming. It is a unique and individual articulation of life pro-

cess. A person cannot be separated from culture, language, temperament etc., but is always more than these. (2005, p. 6)

Gendlin began his book on Focusing-oriented psychotherapy with this comprehensive declaration: "Many methods and strands of psychotherapy are integrated in this book. Each is uniquely valuable in certain respects, *provided the client-therapist relationship is given priority over anything else*" (1996, p. 1, italics mine).

"Interaction is first," Gendlin writes elsewhere. "Even before we think and speak, the living body is already one interaction process with its situation" (2004b, p. 6). In therapy that situation, of course, includes primarily the therapist. Focusing is defined as a client manner of experiencing, but there is no way that that manner of experiencing is not uniquely impacted by the presence and manner of experiencing of the therapist.

Attachment and Self-Regulation

Attachment theory has been growing in recognition and usefulness to psychotherapists in recent years, ever since the pioneering work of Bowlby (1988), Ainsworth (1969), Main (1999), and Fonagy, Gergely, Jurist, and Target (2002) helped us to understand the importance of secure attachment between caregiver and child and its implications for a person's ability to self-regulate emotional states (Wallin, 2007). What was originally research with children has been applied now to adults as well. The work of Sue Johnson (2008) called Emotionally Focused Therapy is based on the profound insight that attachment needs underly the dynamics of adult intimate relationships. Diana Fosha's AEDP carries an understanding that emotional processing and attachment are profoundly interwoven: "Attachment, as both phenomenon and construct, refers to the fundamental human need to form close affectional bonds; it is at the foundation of our psychological life" (2000, p. 33).

Attachment is connected to self-regulation of emotional states and the ability to recover from trauma. Rothschild writes: "As Schore (1996) describes, quite soon after birth the caretaker and infant develop an interactional pattern that is central to the process of affect regulation. They learn to stimulate each other through face-to-face contact, which enables the infant gradually to acclimate to greater and greater degrees of stimulation and arousal" (2000, p. 23). Many have pointed out (Fosha, 2000; Wallin, 2007) that the relationship between therapist and client has the potential to remediate and fill in the "missing" attachment experiences that were not there as they should have been between parent and child.

In Focusing, the client is supported to "be with" (rather than "being") emotional experience. This "being with" is an inner relationship that has the qualities of a secure attachment bond. Carol J. Sutherland Nickerson (2009, 2012) points out how the stages of Focusing correspond to the stages of attachment, bonding, and trust between parent and infant. Focusing is supported by an inner relationship of awareness, contact, attentiveness, and empathic connection, in which the "I" of self can be with the "it" of felt experience in a process that has qualities of safety, trust, and compassion. The client's inner relationship is in turn held and mirrored by the relationship with the therapist.

Working With Parts

A number of methods have arisen to pursue the insight that human beings have "ego states" or "parts," not just in the extreme case of dissociative identity disorder but in the course of ordinary life, and that doing psychotherapy with an awareness of parts can be effective, especially when clients experience inner conflict. One of the most widely influential of these methods preceded Focusing: the two-chair work of Gestalt therapy (Perls, Hefferline, & Goodman, 1951). Elliott and Greenberg (1997) have included "two-chair" work, adapted from Gestalt therapy, as one of the methodologies in Emotion-Focused Therapy (formerly Process-Experiential Therapy).

> Multivocality (multiple internal voicedness) is an essential part of being human and should be regarded as a therapeutic resource, to be nurtured and valued. . . . Therapists can benefit their clients by helping them to discover and use the variety and conflict that exists within them. (Elliott & Greenberg, 1997, p. 225)

In 1972, Hal and Sidra Stone began developing Voice Dialogue, a method for strengthening what they call the Aware Ego by dialoguing with parts of the self. "This Aware Ego is not a self, it is a 'you' that is not dominated by any self or set of selves" (1993, p. 19). One of the most prominent methods today of doing psychotherapy through working with parts is Internal Family Systems Therapy (IFS), developed by Richard Schwartz (1995), a process quite compatible with Focusing (see Chapter 9).

In Focusing, working with parts is implicit in Gendlin's emphasis on the importance of an "I-it" relationship between self and felt experience. "Focusing is this very deliberate thing where an 'I' is attending to an 'it'" (Gendlin, 1990, p. 222). "The client and I, we are going to keep it, in there, company" (p. 216).

> She has compassion for this part of her which feels that it gets "tromped on." . . . Her "self" is not this "part" nor any other part of content. Rather, she is the one who senses it, can speak for it, understands it, and senses its all goodness. The self is not any specific content. (Gendlin, 1996, p. 35)

The ability of the client to "be with" felt emotional experience has been an aspect of Focusing from the beginning, and in fact was what the researchers heard happening in the clients who were going to have successful psychotherapy (Hendricks, 2001; Purton, 2004). Once a distinction is made between "I" or "self" and "this" or "it," this opens the way to the possibility of an inner relational dialogue in which the "I" listens to what the "it" is revealing. But in Focusing, the "it" is not considered an entity. It is an emergent process and may change to the point of dissolution without fighting for "its" identity.

MY OWN JOURNEY WITH FOCUSING

Thinking back to the evening of my introduction to Focusing, in October 1972, I have a vivid memory of sitting in the library of the community church in the Hyde Park neighborhood of Chicago, a room meant for perhaps 40 packed with nearly 100 people, on the floor, sitting on tables, leaning against the walls—and Gene Gendlin, perched on a table at one end of the room, teaching Focusing in a relaxed, conversational style. He seemed like a likable guy, and I was drawn to his friendly demeanor. But when he said, "Now go to the place in your body where you have feelings," I had no idea what he was talking about. Coming from an alcoholic Midwestern family where we had dealt with feelings by ignoring them, I literally had no referent for what he was saying. I remember peering around the room to see if other people seemed to be getting what was so mystifying to me. Their eyes were closed, and some were crying. Crying! I felt like an odd bird.

When I tried Focusing, my body felt "blank," empty, nothing there . . . even though, looking back, I remember having lots of feelings. They were mostly feelings of worry, anxiety, shame. *Will I be able to do this? Will I look good? Will I be liked? Or will I fail and fall on my face and be rejected?* I didn't recognize those experiences as "feelings." They were more like the wallpaper of my existence, always there and never to be examined.

Luckily, I was good at something that first night, and felt welcomed and approved, at least enough to keep coming back. Driven by a sense that I had found something I needed, I threw myself into learning this strange skill, meeting as often as possible with Focusing "partners" to exchange turns at being the "Focuser" and being the "Listener." (A form of active listening was taught as the way to be a partner to a person who was Focusing. That was what I was good at.) At first I found the process frustrating, but I was motivated to stay with it by seeing the changes in my friends. One day, in a memorable peer Focusing session that I recount in my article "How I Met Focusing" (2004), I experienced a significant shift in a problem with social awkwardness, when feeling "too big" in social situations emerged as connected to a painful childhood rejection. This was the first of many positive changes I experienced personally from using Focusing as a self-help skill during my turbulent 20s.

If any of us in the Focusing/Listening community at that time had any idea that Focusing would someday become known outside of our little circle, I certainly did not. Focusing was a process that helped me find and know myself, and got me on track for a rewarding life of genuine feelings within real relationships. I would be forever grateful—and it never occurred to me then that Focusing would be any more than that for me.

FOCUSING EVOLVES FURTHER

Meeting Gendlin and learning Focusing as a young graduate student at the University of Chicago transformed my life. At first those changes were personal. Exchanging Focusing sessions with peers enabled me to shift significant issues with social anxiety, identity, self-expression, relationships with men, and access to emotions. Sometimes I try to imagine what my life would have been like if I had not found Focusing at age 22. It's not a pretty picture. I suspect I might not even be alive, since two people in my immediate family died early from the effects of alcoholism. I certainly wouldn't have the ease and joy in living that I now have every day.

It wasn't until I left my first career when I was 28 and was looking for the right next thing, and reconnected with Gendlin, that Focusing became a professional avenue for me. As luck would have it, my search for next steps was happening at the same time that Gendlin's (1981) book *Focusing* was blossoming in popularity, and I was one of the people he asked to help him teach the workshops that were being requested. That began our collaboration as colleagues, which continues to this day.[4]

As soon as I started helping Gene teach Focusing workshops, I began to think about how the teaching of Focusing could be elaborated—a process he encouraged. By 1984 I was teaching my own Focusing workshops, as well as working with clients and, eventually, creating books, manuals, and audio material for my own Focusing training programs. My interaction with students and my longing to create clarity and simplicity for them led me to keep evolving and refining the teaching of Focusing until it became somewhat different from what I had first learned. Rather than six steps, I first had five steps and four skills (Cornell, 1993) and later four movements (Cornell & McGavin, 2002).

---

4. I was trained and worked as a psychotherapist in the early 1980s with James Iberg and Margaret Warner at the Chicago Counseling Center, a descendent of the Center that had been run by Carl Rogers in the 1950s. When I moved to California in 1983, I decided to center on training and facilitation rather than doing psychotherapy. Today I create training programs to teach Focusing to individuals, run Focusing trainings for psychotherapists and other healing professionals, and conduct individual sessions to facilitate people in Focusing. In writing this book, I also drew on my many years of training therapists and co-training with them, and on the interviews I conducted with Focusing-oriented therapists in which they generously shared their experience, expertise, and client vignettes. Although this book is primarily for the clinician doing psychotherapy, there are clear applications of Focusing to many kinds of facilitated sessions, including coaching, spiritual counseling, and career counseling.

In 1991, visiting Britain, I met Focusing teacher Barbara McGavin, and we began a collaboration that has been extremely rich and rewarding for both of us. Barbara and I developed Focusing further, with enough distinctions from the original method that we eventually named our method Inner Relationship Focusing. Inner Relationship Focusing is still Focusing, as Gendlin himself recognizes, and it follows all the principles he set forth in his work. It also adds certain emphases and directions.

Today many people in the Focusing world are working with Inner Relationship Focusing, and many of those who are not have at least been influenced by it. There is a stimulating and productive diversity in the world of Focusing. All share the essential understanding that Focusing is defined as the process of a person attending in an open, accepting way to a felt sense.

INNER RELATIONSHIP FOCUSING

During the years I was "apprenticing" with Gene Gendlin, assisting him with workshops and meeting with him, I heard him respond to scores of questions from new students. There was one question he was often asked, and one answer he invariably gave, that later grew in my work with Barbara McGavin into a polar shift in what lay at the heart of our facilitating Focusing.

Gendlin would tell people that Focusing requires "a friendly attitude" toward what comes up. Typically someone in the group would ask him, "But what if I can't be friendly to it?" Gendlin would rotate his finger toward himself in a kind of returning-to-an-earlier-place gesture, and say, with a grin, "Then see if you can be friendly to *that.*"

I was struck by this notion that "not being friendly" was a "that" which could in turn be attended to. As I began to teach Focusing and work with clients, I became aware of how often people had difficulty allowing a felt sense to come because they were in a reactive state in relation to their own experiencing: afraid of it, impatient with it, trying to figure it out, trying not to feel it. I realized that if I could help my clients experience these reactive states as a "that" inside of them, instead of as an "I," they were more likely to access a state from which change could happen.

The concepts of identification and disidentification were key. When people are identified with an emotional experience, they lack the differentiation from it that would enable them to sense into it. Disidentification is not dissociation, and it is not even distance. It is company.

> I go around the world with a tattered poster that I call "The Three Guys." The guy on the left has a red cloud around his whole body, and he says, "I am angry." The guy on the right has a red cloud behind his back, not in his body, and he says, "I am not angry." (I demonstrate this by clenching my teeth, tapping my foot, and growling "I am not angry!") The guy in the middle has a red cloud around his belly, labeled "something," and nearby, connected with an arrow of relationship, the word "I." He says, "I'm sensing something in me is angry." Only in the middle case will "the anger" get a hearing, have some company, be able to make steps. Because someone is there, the "I," keeping it company. (Cornell 2005a, pp. 44–45)

Studying what experienced clinicians such as Gene Gendlin actually said when responding to clients, I noticed a form of language that facilitated the client in disidentifying from felt experience while still staying in contact with it. I began to teach this form of language to my trainees, calling it "presence language" (see Chapter 5). By this time, Barbara McGavin and I had begun to try to name the state of awareness of a person who is able to be present with all kinds of emotional and reactive experiences without being caught up in them. We went through "Larger I," "Larger Self," and "Presence." Today, influenced by the work of Richard Schwartz and Cesar Millan,[5] we call it "Self-in-Presence."

Inner Relationship Focusing is an approach to Focusing that emphasizes the importance of the person being able to be Self-in-Presence in order to have genuine felt senses and not merely to be in repetitive reactive states. This approach has turned out to

---

5. I point to the work of Cesar Millan (2007) with a smile, but it is quite true that Barbara McGavin and I were inspired by this "dog whisperer" who trains not dogs but dog owners. When the dog owner can be in a state of "calm-assertive energy," dogs calm down. This can be an evocative and helpful metaphor for emotional regulation.

be especially powerful when working with clients facing long-standing issues such as addiction, depressive states, and severe self-criticism. It is the approach taught in this book.

CLARIFICATION: FOCUSING IS NOT THE ONLY WORTHWHILE PROCESS

As a person passionately enthusiastic about Focusing, I can sometimes sound as though I think Focusing is the only process people need, and that without Focusing, failure looms. In fact I don't believe either of those propositions.

I am in awe of the remarkable psychotherapy being done in every modality and school of therapy of which I am aware. Human beings do change and grow in a diversity of settings, and with a variety of types of support and intervention. I would never want to be read as suggesting that my way is better than any other.

I would, however, like to say three things:

1. A type of Focusing awareness comes naturally to many clients, and is at least part of what helps people change whether we or they are conscious of it or not. Let's become conscious of this process and encourage it so its effectiveness can be even greater.
2. The felt sensing process, with its ability to tap into the essence of change, is worth a look. There are many instances of clients moving from "stuck" to "flow" through pausing and allowing a felt sense to form. Since this process can be added to any modality of therapy, it takes nothing away and has much to offer.
3. Focusing in itself does not make up a complete therapeutic modality. You need to be doing something as an overall frame—even if that is an eclectic mix that you brought together from a number of sources—and then include Focusing. This is another reason for clinicians of any modality to become interested in and explore how your modality can be enhanced by Focusing.

A Focusing moment is a "doorway," a moment in process when there is a potential to experience more than is already known and to break through old, frozen, stuck patterns. You can learn to recognize the Focusing moments that are already happening, and encourage them. You can also learn to invite and facilitate Focusing moments when they are not already happening. This process of orienting to Focusing moments can be integrated smoothly into any other process or modality. You won't need to stop doing anything that is working for your clients. You'll be enhancing that work, making it even more effective and supportive.

THE PROCESS OF THIS BOOK

In Chapter 1 I begin with an example of Focusing, and from it I draw out the characteristics of Focusing and review the theoretical and philosophical underpinnings that help explain how Focusing works. I introduce some odd-sounding concepts such as "implying," "stopped process," and "carrying forward" that we will need to understand the kind of change process on which Focusing rests. At the end of Chapter 1, there is another example of Focusing, and I talk about how the forming of a felt sense in Focusing is actually the person's next steps of change already happening.

After soaring in Chapter 1 at an exalted philosophical level, in Chapter 2 we come back to earth with the grounded, practical questions of how to get started bringing Focusing into psychotherapy, how to lay the foundation for using Focusing with clients including a Focusing-oriented assessment for a first session, how to talk to clients about what we do, and how to talk to colleagues about what Focusing is and why we want to do it.

In Chapter 3 we engage with the heart of Focusing: the felt sense. I talk about what makes a felt sense different from an emotion and other kinds of experiences, and how to recognize a felt sense when it occurs naturally. When our clients get felt senses spontaneously, as many do, we can nurture that process by a certain kind of responding called the "empathic prompt." In Chapter 4 we discover what to do when clients do not get felt senses spontaneously, and we learn how to help clients move from stories or emotions to felt senses.

There is a certain kind of inner environment needed for felt senses to form, and that is the quality of self-attention that we call Self-in-Presence. In Chapter 5 I show how to support the client in being the strong, calm self that overwhelmed, reactive states need in order for a felt sense to form.

There is more to Focusing than getting felt senses, and Chapter 6 shows how to facilitate clients in going further. In Chapter 7, I show how to work with more challenging types of client process such as intellectualizing, resistance, and the inner critic. For those who wonder how Focusing might be helpful with the more extreme types of client issues, Chapter 8 gives examples of bringing Focusing into work with clients struggling with trauma, addictions, and depression.

In Chapter 9 I give examples of combining Focusing with 10 of the more commonly practiced current psychotherapy modalities, so the reader can get a feel for how to bring Focusing into his or her own practice. Finally, Chapter 10 covers what might be the most important use of Focusing of all: when the therapist is Focusing. I show how being a therapist who is Focusing can enhance the work of psychotherapy in a number of ways, including being more available to the client as a genuine person, accessing intuitive moments, and being able to do self-care before and after challenging client sessions.

FOCUSING IN
CLINICAL PRACTICE

Chapter 1

THE ESSENCE OF CHANGE

"Focusing" is a particular process of attention that supports therapeutic change, a process that has been linked in more than 50 research studies with successful outcomes in psychotherapy (Hendricks,
2001). Facilitating Focusing in our clients can enable natural and
adaptive change in body, mind, and behavior. The rest of this book
offers practical support in bringing Focusing into your clinical practice, no matter what modality of psychotherapy you follow. But first,
we'll have a look in this chapter at what sets Focusing apart, what
makes it unique, what gives Focusing its particular power. To do so,
I will give an example of Focusing and then introduce some new
concepts for understanding the process of change.

What change is, and what brings change, are key questions for all
clinicians. Our clients come to us faced with life situations that feel
burdensome and unshiftable, struggling with emotional states that
are sometimes out of control and frightening in themselves. They
have anxiety, or flashbacks to traumatic memories, or they are shut
down, hemmed in by defenses that have been their best way of getting by until now. They may be finding some measure of relief in
addictive or obsessive behaviors that nevertheless are problems in
themselves. Their lives may be mostly on an even keel except for one
troublesome area that somehow underlies the whole system, or they
may feel close to a frightening disintegration, hanging on by their
fingernails. Some may experience emotional overwhelm, others a
puzzling lack of emotion, and others a persistent sense of worthless-

ness and shame, dogged by an inner critic. Some are quite self-aware and able to talk at length about their own contributions to their issues, while others aren't even sure they have a problem at all, as in: "My spouse wanted me to see you. . . ."

Often we see our clients change, and nothing is more deeply satisfying than being a part of and a witness to someone's life becoming better. In some mysterious way our own willingness to be present for our clients, to bring our own selves up to the line every day, makes a difference for these often courageous, often struggling people.

> As therapists, we go to work each day prepared to engage not only with the satisfying experience of facilitating developmental steps, but also with the awesome task of participating with whatever suffering, brokenness, and trauma is presented to us. Is this not because we believe, that no matter what has gone wrong, how dark the road, how desolate the lived experience, people have the ability to heal, to change and grow? And even more surprising, that we, therapists, can meaningfully participate in this renewal? (Preston, 2005, p. 22)

When I interviewed psychotherapists for this book, I asked them, "What drew you to Focusing? What made you want to bring Focusing to your clients?" I heard from them about wanting to empower clients, to offer them a self-aware, self-regulating way of being, one they could continue to bring to their lives outside of and beyond psychotherapy. Most people also mentioned how valuable Focusing had been to them personally. As one clinician said, "My life with Focusing for the last few years has been so tremendous in terms of what it opened up, how I've changed my sense of self, how I've opened up my way of being in the world, that it makes me trust that there really is something about this that will work with others." Most of all, though, people spoke about the theoretical power of the Focusing concepts. Preston writes about this first encounter with Focusing:

> I immediately felt like I had come home—like I had found the missing link that, as a young therapist, I was looking for. I had been studying many helpful approaches to psychotherapy, but I sorely needed some fundamental understandings of what made psychotherapy work that could tie all these methods

together. I knew from this first workshop that this approach would provide me with the cohesive element I was missing. (2005, p. 1)

So what is Focusing? Let's start with an example.

THE "LEFT BEHIND" FEELING

After a number of weeks, Brian has gotten to what feels to him like the central point of what brought him to therapy: a kind of holding back or inner aloofness that manifests in all his relationships. Sometimes the other person seems to be the one holding back; sometimes Brian finds the holding back in himself. It is a mystery to him. He doesn't know where this came from, and he would really like it to change.

The therapist invites Brian to pause and "get a fresh feel for this whole thing, a kind of holding back in all your relationships." Brian knows by now that he is being invited to let this "fresh feel" simply come, without words at first. He is willing. There is a silence. Then Brian's hand moves to his chest. "This in me feels left behind," he says.

"Left behind," repeats the therapist, slowly. This is new. There had not previously been a connection between the holding back in relationships and feeling left behind. Both Brian and the therapist resist the temptation to speculate about this, and Brian simply stays with what is there, open to more coming from it.

Memories come of times when he was left behind. These memories are not new, but they come now as instances, as if the left-behind feeling is showing them. There were many times when he was supposed to be picked up after a school event by his father, and his father would arrive hours late, leaving him standing there as darkness fell and all the other kids were picked up and went home. As Brian tells the story, he becomes aware of an aching in his chest, in the left-behind place. He says to it, "I sense how hard that was, to be left behind like that."

Supported by the therapist, Brian senses how it—the left-behind feeling—feels, from its point of view. "It wants me to know *that was wrong*, to be left behind like that. . . . I'm letting it know I hear it. . . .

I'm sensing that it thought IT was wrong. . . . If they left it behind, it must not have done what was needed to keep them around. . . . I'm saying to it, 'No wonder it's painful if that's what you believe.'"

The therapist invites Brian to sense what kind of contact this place wants. "What comes is: a long hug," Brian says. Then there is a deep full breath. "Ah! That's what would have been right . . . if my father had given me a long hug after I had waited in the dark for hours. He just drove up like nothing had happened. If I had gotten that long hug from him . . . like he knew what I had gone through, and he was sorry." There is a change in the way the body feels. The ache is gone. Brian takes time to sense how it feels now in his body.

Now another step comes: Brian senses that "it" no longer wants to wait. "It says, 'I don't have to wait!'" There is a quality of surprise and freshness that he can feel in his body. It is a complete change. He says it seems to change everything, all the way back into the past. Now he is sitting up, his eyes bright, shoulders back. "I don't have to wait!" In the days and weeks to come, Brian will discover how "I don't have to wait" plays out in his life. He will experience the difference in his relationships and his life choices. He doesn't know all this yet. But in the chair in the therapy office his organism has already changed, and both people can feel that.

You might be thinking that Brian is a sweetheart of a client, any therapist's dream come true. Yes, he is. He is self-aware, inwardly attentive, willing to stay open to new meanings. He is able to be strong and caring in relation to his more vulnerable parts. He can pause and wait at the edge of something felt but hard to articulate.

You would be right to wonder, at this point, how to help clients who have more trouble with self-attending than Brian did, who are analytical, caught up in stories, or overwhelmed by emotion. That is what the rest of this book is about. But first we need to know where we are headed, and why. So we'll look at Brian's session as a kind of ideal example—of course only one example—and draw out from it some characteristics of Focusing.

The change began with the left-behind feeling that formed in a deliberate pause. This was the key change, the forming of a felt sense. Before that, Brian could have talked on and on about his trouble with relationships—speculating, talking about examples, wondering. He might have felt and expressed a range of emotions, from sadness and longing to frustration and anger. But when he paused instead and allowed a felt sense to form, something quite new began to happen.

What a felt sense is, and why its forming is at the heart of change, is the key concept of this book, and I will say much more about it. For now, let's simply say that a felt sense is an experienced sense of a whole situation. Often a felt sense is unclear at first, hard to articulate, requiring fresh metaphors and possibly images or gestures to capture its quality. Clients will say, "I don't know how to say this," or "Uh-h-h-h-h . . ." Sometimes, as in Brian's case, a description comes nearly immediately.

Brian's hand moves to his chest. "This in me feels left behind," he says.

There is a bodily component—the client gestures toward his chest—but the felt sense is not in the musculature as such. This is not a muscle-held memory—though of course it relates to the past, since this body wasn't born in this moment. The felt sense has formed freshly, now. There is implicit meaning and coherence to it, from the start. It is "here," the gesture says: present, right now, in the experienced chest, in the lived-from body. "In me."

Supported by the therapist, Brian keeps his awareness with the felt sense with the same quality of open attentiveness that allowed the felt sense to come in the first place. He could have talked about it instead, guessing and speculating about what "left behind" meant. We will learn, later, how to help clients move back into inner contact if they leave it in this way. Brian's example shows what can happen when the client does not move away, but stays in an open, allowing, interested contact with what is felt. In the context of this open, allowing quality of attention, "more" emerges.

In this case, pertinent memories are part of what emerges. They are not new memories—this is typical—but the fact that they come from attending to the felt sense gives them a new context. "This is connected to that." It is as if the felt sense is showing what it is connected to, and its communication can be received in that same spirit. "I see what you are showing me."

A kind of inner relationship develops, in which Brian begins to describe his felt experience as an "it," as if it were communicating with him. Facilitated by the therapist, Brian stays in an empathic relationship with this "it," letting it know he hears it. What emerges is a kind of knowing of what was wrong and what would have been right in that childhood situation. A childhood experience is being processed, one that emerges naturally (without prompting) because of its relevance to the present.

In the context of this new kind of attention from both client and therapist, the client has new possibilities that were not available before. The left-behind boy had been waiting, waiting in his current life just as he waited as a child. Now, he no longer has to wait. What was longed for, and what was possible only in potential, can now happen. We don't have to know what that is, or what it will be—yet we can be confident it will be a positive outcome for Brian somehow.

Characteristics of a Focusing Process Within Psychotherapy

- A felt sense forms, and its forming is already a change in how one "has" the problem.
- There is an inner relationship, in which the client is "with" something that he feels.
- The client is able to hold qualities of compassion and curiosity toward her inner experience.
- The "knowing" of what was wrong and what would be right instead emerges, and the past is re-understood.
- The "body" is involved, but in a different sense from the merely physiological body.
- The therapist's relationship with the client mirrors and supports the client's inner relationship of openness, compassionate curiosity, and direct sensing.
- The change that emerges is in a particular kind of direction, one that we can call "the client's own change."

WHAT FOCUSING IS

Focusing, as defined in this book, is not a set of techniques or a therapeutic modality of its own. Rather, it is a way of understanding and facilitating what some human beings naturally do—and all have the capacity to do—when up against the need for change.

Focusing was found, not invented. It was discovered by listening to tapes of client sessions and comparing subtle differences between the clients' manner of experiencing in successful versus unsuccessful courses of treatment. The researchers found (Gendlin et al., 1968, Hendricks, 2001) that the client's experiential manner of process in the first or second session tended to be predictive of success in psychotherapy. "Focusing" as a facilitated process grew out of a desire to bring this manner of experiencing to clients who were not naturally doing it.

Many in psychotherapy today would agree that the relationship between client and therapist is an important factor in the client's successful change process, and that for the therapist to stay in close empathic connection with the client's experience—"experience-near," as Kohut put it—is a second key factor. However, the research done by Gendlin and his colleagues showed that close empathy in a context of mutual relatedness was not alone predictive of successful change. These two factors are crucial, yes—and a third factor is also crucial. The client also needs a certain manner of contact with his or her own experiencing. Clients who do not have that essential manner of contact in the first or second session of therapy do not come to have it later, and tend not to succeed in therapy, no matter how empathic and genuinely present the therapist is. Gendlin found this result so shocking that he became determined to find a way to facilitate this key manner of contact, and thus "Focusing" was born.

What is that key manner of client inner contact? Why is it so highly correlated with successful change?

In the research that led to the development of the Focusing process, clients who would later be successful in psychotherapy sounded—at some point in their early sessions—like this: "I don't know. . . . It's like . . . not exactly sadness . . . uh . . . [gesturing toward chest] . . . kind of like . . . like a little kid left out of the party. . . . Yeah, that's it. [Deeper breath.]"

When people do well in psychotherapy, this is how they usually sound, regardless of the orientation of their therapist. They pause and grope for words or images. They pay attention to an unclear, but bodily-sensed aspect of how they are in a situation. They don't just think about the situation and they don't drown in emotions. They attend to what we call a "bodily felt sense of" a situation or problem. Words or images arise directly from that sense. What comes is often a surprise. A new aspect of experience emerges, a small step of change that brings a body response, like a slight physical easing of tension, or tears, or a deeper breath. . . . This kind of process is one "motor of change" in psychotherapy. (Hendricks, 2001, p. 221)

Clients who pause in the midst of talking and allow a fresh "felt sense" to form about the life situation they are wrestling with, and then continue to pay attention to it, tend to do better in psychotherapy than clients who don't. This finding has been replicated in more than 50 studies (Hendricks, 2001).

The body was the key. Successful clients were in touch with something they could feel at the bodily level, something more than thoughts alone. But this body-felt experience was also more than mere emotion. And although it was experienced bodily, it was not what we would call merely physical or somatic. Gendlin redefined "body" as "interactional living process." Your body is your lived experience. This is a radical departure from understanding "body" as merely physiology.

Human beings, including you and me, *are* ongoing interaction. We don't exist separately from our environment and then start interacting with it. We *are* interaction between body and environment, so we (like all living things) are both body and environment. And for humans, the environment includes other people, language, and culture. (Parker, 2007, p. 40, italics in original)

Successful clients pause, and felt senses form. What is happening in this pause, what is actually going on when felt senses form, turns out to be the key—because it is not merely "getting in touch" with an emotion, image, memory, or thought, and it is not merely sensing in the physical body. There is an adaptive organismic process occurring when the felt sense forms that changes the whole constellation of the problem.

This is not the usual way of conceptualizing change, and to understand it, we will need to take on some mind-bending new concepts like "implying," "stopped process," and "carrying forward." Some of these concepts can be a bit hard to grasp at first. But bear with me, because the benefits of seeing change in this new way will be immediately evident in how we facilitate the conditions for change in our clients. Let's start with something called "manner of experiencing," or the way clients talk about their issues.

THE WAY CLIENTS TALK ABOUT THEIR ISSUES

It has frequently been observed—I am sure you yourself have noticed—that the way that clients talk about their problems and their lives has more bearing on whether they make progress in therapy than what they talk about (Gendlin, 1996; Purton, 2007). The observation connected to the development of Focusing was that this way of talking is not so much a matter of emotional or intellectual processing as a matter of contact with an emergent, not-yet-clear felt experience—in other words, with a felt sense.

> One way of expressing what it is that the more successful clients do would be to say that they make direct reference to their felt experiencing. The client who is simply externalizing, talking about the events of their week in an "external" way, gives most of their attention to the narrative of the story and does not give much attention to how they were feeling at the time or to how they are feeling as they tell the story. Similarly, the client who analyzes their situation may speak *about* their feelings but does not speak *from* the feelings. The client who simply emotes is different, but they are typically reliving old emotions without connecting to how it feels right now, freshly, today. In all three cases what seems to be missing is an ability to be in touch with one's immediate felt *experiencing* and especially with that *experiencing* as a whole. (Purton, 2007, p. 13, italics in original)

In order to measure and do research on this type of client process, an Experiencing Scale was developed by Gendlin and Zimring (1955), later elaborated (Klein et al., 1969) into what has been called "perhaps the most widely used and best-researched observer-rated measure of client involvement in the therapy process" (Lambert & Hill, 1994, cited in Hendricks, 2001).

In an earlier article, Hendricks gives examples of client excerpts at different experiencing levels:

LOW EXPeriencing LEVEL

One day he [the doctor] called me and said, "I'm afraid she won't last long. She's spreading like wildfire." They couldn't get all of it. It was too late. And so that's about the extent of it, you know. She went into a coma, she lasted for about three or four months. All together from the time she became ill, the entire time was about two years. After he performed the operation he said, "I'm surprised she lasted that long." We didn't know it had gone all the way back. There was no sign of it, nothing. But it was there all the time. Can you imagine that.

MIDDLE EXPeriencing LEVEL

A____ and I . . . spent about two hours talking over the luncheon about his problem. And I've never known him, until that time to be so low and despondent about his future in science. He said, "You won't believe this Dad, until I tell you, that it has been over six months since I had a test-tube in my hand" . . . and after listening *I was very much disturbed* by what he said because this was a very serious conversation, and it dealt with what I felt had to do with a decision he had to make regarding his work and his marriage, and they were both at stake. . . . I said, "But A____, don't you think if J____ were made to realize how desperate the situation is that she would elect to allow you to do more of your science . . ." And there was silence for a moment or two and he shook his head, and said, "She will never change." Now when he said that I felt he had already made a decision . . . to divorce rather than to continue. . . . *I felt absolutely consternated by that* because I knew they really loved each other, I knew they could have a harmonious relationship for many years to come if only she could understand.

HIGH EXPeriencing LEVEL

It's almost like . . . it kind of feels like . . . sitting here looking through a photo album. And, like each picture of me in there is one of my achievements. And, I think [inaudible] because I wasn't achieving for me. I was always achieving for . . . someone else so they'd think I was good enough. It's like it feels right to me to say . . . that . . . *I don't know quite how to say it. . . . It's like the feeling is there, but I can't quite put words on it. It feels right somehow to say it's like* I've chosen this man as my challenge . . . knowing that I'd be defeated. That this person wouldn't respond to me in the same way. So that I could kind of buy right back into the photo album being flipped through. I didn't have what it took (T: Uhhum) to get what I wanted. Which is kind of . . . (Hendricks, 1986, pp. 143–144, italics in original)

We notice that at the low EXP level, the client narrates events that we would expect to bring up emotions but without any reference to emotion, and without any sense that the material is being sensed into or processed. "Events are described as flat and self-evident. If emotions are acknowledged, they too are seen as obvious, self-evident, just what they are" (Hendricks, 1986, p. 144). It is a matter-of-fact sort of telling-about. At the middle EXP level, there are emotions in the narrative, but we don't hear the client sensing into them or exploring them. We are left wondering what it is about his son's marriage failing that brings up these feelings for him, or rather what it is about him that his son's divorce touches him so. And at the high EXP level we can see, even in the transcript, the unmistakable signs of a client in direct contact with something not only being felt but emerging freshly, unclear, hard to articulate, yet carrying the person's process further as it emerges.

Before we turn in the rest of the book toward how to facilitate this kind of process, we need to say more about what is really going on when the client is in the kind of inner contact in which a felt sense forms, and what it has to do with real, lasting change in the client's own direction.

THE CLIENT'S OWN CHANGE

Psychotherapy is a place of change. People come to therapy looking for change—or at least part of them does. But when we ask what the change is, the answer is not simple.

To start with, we can say that successful clients become stronger in a grounded way, more able to handle their own lives, less reactive to stressful triggers. Their relationships become more a source of support than burdens or torments. This much is noncontroversial. But when we get into the details, paradoxes emerge. The direction of positive change for one person might be a setback for another.

> One is the person one's living has made, and only by living differently does one become different. But the way one wants to change isn't just from one category to another, or from being like some people to being like other people. One wants to change precisely into oneself, into more of oneself than one has been able to be so far. (Gendlin, 1973, p. 342)

A person, withdrawn and emotionally closed most of his life, is able because of therapy to find a new ability to connect socially with others, and yet does so in a way that still honors his need for keeping himself company. Another person, dependent on having people around her, is able because of therapy to find a new ability to tolerate and even enjoy her "alone time," while still embracing her nurturing connections with others. What seem to be opposite outcomes are both movements in a positive direction and match the unique process of the particular person in a way that no generalized formula could get as precisely right.

People are missing different things, we can say, and therapy fills in what is missing. Gendlin (2011) says, "Therapy *is* going beyond your ways of being stuck." By this he means that in the process of therapy itself, there in the room with you, your client is (when therapy works) already developing in new ways. And those new ways of living are—need to be—the client's "own" change, change that emerges from that person and fits him, change that is what the client was missing.

The direction of change can surprise us. It should surprise us. Life can't be predicted or legislated in advance. But once it is happening, change in the direction of the client's own next steps has a characteristic "feel" to it. There is a rightness to it. It brings a bodily relief, a deeper breath, a feeling like fresh air—to therapist as well as to client.

This is a good reason to be somewhat humble as a clinician. You may know a fair amount about how to help. But you cannot know in advance this person's way forward. You may know a lot about typical patterns and common difficulties, but what will bring forward movement for this person is likely to be something unique, individual to her. Trying to be the one who knows can actually get in the way. Of course we don't want to forget what we know. We'll keep it on one side in case we need it—but we won't let it get in the way of tracking this person's meanings and feelings, and supporting this person's growth direction as it emerges.

So, not just any change. What clients gain from therapy is something we can call "the client's own change." And does this change come all at once? No, it seems to come, and be observable, in incremental steps, each one in the direction of growth.

FELT SHIFTS: STEPS OF CHANGE

We know that measurable changes in a client's life may take a while to show up. But if we pay attention, we can see small changes, what Gendlin (1990) calls "steps of change," in segments of single sessions. The client may not be aware, cognitively, that anything has happened—but her body process shows the change. In Focusing, these steps of change are also called felt shifts. They need to be protected when they come, and they can be facilitated. Over time, a number of felt shifts add up to large change. Many steps make up a whole journey.

There are observable indicators of these incremental steps of change. We see moments of relief and release, with physiological indicators such as deeper breathing (even a sigh of relief), shoulders dropping, pinkness in the cheeks. The client may say something like "Wow," or "That's new," or "I didn't know that," indicating that an insight has occurred. But not always—steps of change are not invariably accompanied by insight at the time they occur. (Conversely, insight can also come without real change.) New action, behavioral change, opening up of life possibilities—these can come later as well. An important learning from Focusing is that steps of change can be felt, and observed, before they manifest in insight and behavior. A client can say, "I feel more relaxed but I don't know why" and later realize that that session was the opening of new possibilities.

> The bodily felt sense of some problem or difficulty will move of its own accord. It will shift, and release. There will be an overall change in how the body feels, a release of energy. There

is a relief. Energy flows again as it had not for some time. Along with this there is often an involuntary exhaling of breath, a "wheewwww . . ." Simultaneously with such a release, there is a new emergence of words, or images, or aspects of the problem. These are a by-product. Usually the problem now looks different; often the problem is not even about what one thought it was about. Now one can connect backward to explain from here how one had been, how one had seen the problem, why it had seemed as it did. But there is no logic with which one could have come from there to here. The problem now posed in new terms may still not be solved; it may look worse (but it feels enormously better). . . . That is a step of experiential change.

It feels like one would feel, after having long sat in a cramped position, as one permits oneself to shift. It feels like the body doing what it needs and want to do. It feels like something happening that is exactly what the previous cramped constricted way of being was the lack of. (Gendlin, 1978, p. 328)

Whenever we look at what is alive, whether we are looking at a tree out the window or a laughing child running across the yard, we see life process moving forward. There is a natural process for moving from potential to actualization. What happens now was, a moment before, ready to happen, in potential. Yet what happens is not determined. There are possibilities, and while those possibilities are specific to that person, in that life situation, in that context, within that specificity, there is enormous creative potential.

We need a way to talk about the idea of change that occurs in a precisely ordered yet surprisingly open way, with a kind of order that is neither deterministic ("exactly this must happen") nor chaotic ("anything can happen"). To be able to talk and think about this kind of change, we need a new concept: "implying forward."

IMPLYING FORWARD

Something that is alive is always in process; always taking in, always responding, always changing in the direction of further life. Life doesn't stand still; there is always something *next*, and what is next emerges from what came before in a very particular way. Every breath you take changes your cells throughout your body, in the way that the cells were ready to be changed. Even in your sleep, the ongoing processes of your living do not stop. As process, something alive is fundamentally different from something manufactured like a chair—or anything that has an on-off switch. Something alive is already preparing for its next step in its very tissues.

Focusing has a term for this: *implying*. Gendlin (2007) says: "Living process always 'implies' forward." Because this is a new kind of concept, we don't have a familiar, easily understood word for it. We might be familiar with the word "implying" from the domain of logic, but it is new to use it to point to the deep structure of emergent change in living process. Some examples may help us take in this odd concept.

Consider the act of walking or running. When you are walking, and even more when you are running, your body leans into your next step. This is a metaphor for the process of life itself—we are always "leaning into" our next steps. When we inhale, our bodies are getting ready to exhale. The process of inhaling implies forward to exhaling. And of course the process of exhaling implies forward to inhaling.

What if we try to stop that process—what happens? As an experiment, try exhaling and then holding your breath rather than inhaling. The result is a feeling of discomfort—becoming stronger and stronger as time goes on. (Okay, you can inhale now!)

Another example of implying is the experience of hunger. Hunger is the implying of eating, taking in nourishment somehow. If we don't eat when we are hungry, hunger sharpens, food-seeking behavior intensifies, and eventually, if food is not found, there are body tissue changes. But if we do eat when we are hungry, the implying changes—we are no longer hungry—and there is a new implying: for digestion, we could say. (And perhaps a nap.)

The very fact that living process always implies forward tells us something about our client in her chair across from us. She too is implying forward. Our examples so far have been physiological: breathing, hunger and eating. But human beings imply forward in complex and subtle ways, at all levels. We imply meaningful connection with others, loving and being loved, being valued and respected, having joy and purpose in our lives. Babies are born implying a complex interactive sequence of attention from and with caregivers (Wallin, 2007).

When what is implied happens, we call this *carrying forward*. Carrying forward is the Focusing term for the satisfying experience that occurs when what is implied actually happens. What happens— what we do and what we encounter—takes its meaning from what was implied. If we are hungry, then eating is a carrying forward. If we are not hungry, eating is something else. We will also be using the term "life-forward direction," which refers to organismic implying in the direction of further life.

Implying can be felt, especially when it is not being satisfied, when it remains unfulfilled. If implying is not carried forward, there is, if you pause and sense in a subtle way, the feeling of something missing. In the feeling of something missing there is a "knowing" of what is missing, what would bring forward movement.

A "PROBLEM" IS THE MISSING
OF SOMETHING NEEDED

From a Focusing perspective, we see that a bad feeling implies its own change.

What is called a "problem" is actually the missing of something needed, something that would allow further process in the organism's life direction. What is missing may be something quite new that has never existed before, yet in a funny way the organism "knows" what is missing. There is a way forward that hasn't yet been found, and although the way forward can't yet be articulated, we can say that the experience of having a problem is a kind of knowing of what is missing. When you see a picture hanging crookedly on the wall, you get an uneasy feeling of wrongness that contains within it what would be right instead, and even knows the action—walking across the room and straightening the picture—that is needed.

Gendlin wrote in 1981, "Every bad feeling is potential energy for a more right way of being, if you give it space to move toward its rightness" (p. 76). That sentence, which sounds poetically optimistic and even a bit naive at first reading, is actually a statement of Gendlin's philosophical position on human change. By "right way of being" and "rightness," he is referring to the way that organismic process "knows" its next steps, just as your state of hunger "knows" that eating would be right. The oddly generic phrase "every bad feeling" points to a person's inner experience of something unpleasant, uneasy, painful—any contractive or difficult emotional or physical state. And when Gendlin says that every bad feeling *is* potential energy for a more right way of being, he is stating the tenet at the heart of his work: that nothing alive just "is." Life is always leaning toward—implying—its next steps, and life tends to move forward in a way that fits or emerges from what is implied, yet does so creatively, freshly, in a unique way.

The "problem" is the missing of something—and so is the "bad feeling" that points to or emerges from the problem. When you think of a certain colleague and your heart sinks, and you have a quick longing for the meeting with that person to be canceled today, there is something there. If you pause, take some time, explore, you could form that "something" into aware knowing. Perhaps you realize that the sarcastic way that colleague talks about people who are not present reminds you of your brother, and you recognize that you have some more inner work to do about your difficult relationship with your brother. Realizing this brings relief, clarity, a shift in how you feel toward your colleague and in your possibilities for action in the current situation.

Pausing and sensing and articulating took a bit of time, but it was all contained as potential in the first feeling. Your "bad feeling"— your heart sinking—had a "knowing," which even included a knowing (in potential) of what direction would be right.

This is already a radical notion, that an uneasy feeling contains— more precisely, it *is*—a "knowing" of both what is wrong and what would be right. We are, however, going to say something even more radical: When this uneasy feeling forms, in a context of awareness, the person is thereby already living beyond the problem, already living in and toward what would be right for her.

STOPPED PROCESS:
WHEN LIFE DOESN'T MOVE FORWARD

Clients in psychotherapy have issues more serious than a sarcastic colleague or a crooked picture on the wall. But even the most serious issues that bring a client to psychotherapy can be understood as stopped process, the stoppage of an implying forward (Suetake, 2010). When what is implied does not happen, the *implying* remains unchanged, and all the processes that would follow after this one cannot happen either, like when a big rig truck jackknifes across all the lanes of the freeway, and all other traffic stacks up behind it.

Stopped process does not mean the lack of behaving. There may be much behaving—as in addictions and other forms of acting out— that fails to carry forward the situation. Acting-out behavior is significantly not the implied behavior that would truly carry forward the person's process. Stopped process can be seen in every one of our clients—and doubtless in our own lives as well.

> A stopped process is not "good" or "bad," it is simply that our lives become blocked from time to time. Not all stoppages need help from a therapist. But there are times when we have lost touch with our experiencing, with the richness and intricacy of our situations. Then we respond to a situation in a very limited, stereotypical way. If this goes on for a longer period, it is as if our experiencing has become frozen into a particular form, a particular way of being, thinking, feeling, and our inner life circles around in fixed structures. (Geiser, 2010, p. 98)

As Geiser points out, when stopped process persists it results in the person losing touch with the intricacy of fresh experiencing, and with the possibility of carrying forward. Fixed (or frozen) structures are stereotypical ways of responding to partial aspects of a situation when stopped process has shut down our ability to respond to the richness of fresh detail in the current situation as it actually is.

> It is not only that I react poorly to authority. Rather, I react this way to *every* person whom I perceive as an authority. And, more important, I react *only* to his being an authority, not to him as a person, and to the very many present facets of him and our situation which are different from any other situation. (Gendlin, 1964, p. 121)

When you are inside the frozen structure, all the things you do— including all attempts to solve the problem—are just examples of the problem all over again. A person tries to solve her problem with loneliness by getting people to like her, when her very efforts to be likable are what put people off. Or a person works hard to arrange and organize himself out of his difficulties, when it turns out that those same difficulties essentially arise from a tendency to arrange and organize instead of allowing his own genuine motivation to emerge.

> We think in the terms and pieces of the problem as we have it cut up. And it is just these terms and pieces *that would change* if the problem moved toward resolution. Therefore, there is often no way to think about a problem except in a way that simply reinstates it in the very act of thinking it, and draws it, in heavy lines, all the harder. (Gendlin, 1978, p. 323)

The thoughts and beliefs that the client is conscious of, and can talk about, are only the tip of the iceberg. They emerge from and are instances of a deeply ingrained way of living that expresses itself in every situation the client finds herself in. No wonder our clients can feel frustrated, helpless, angry, as if they are going in endless circles or digging deeper in a hole they can't get out of. This is not just bad luck, and it is not being bad at something or defective in some way. It is an inevitable consequence of being "inside" the problem, stuck at a limited, stereotypical level of processing. The Focusing process is a way to shift levels, step outside the box of preset categories, and experience one's own change emerging from within, so that one is already living new possibilities that were exactly what the problem was missing. (See Parker, 2007, for a beautiful example of psychotherapy along these lines with a violence-prone adolescent in residential treatment.)

The forming of a felt sense makes experiencing available for the next steps of the client's own change, which takes the client beyond frozen structures.

FELT SENSING IS GOING BEYOND FROZEN STRUCTURES

So, having said all this, what can we say is happening when a felt sense forms? What makes Focusing the essence of change? When the felt sense forms, what was frozen is becoming free and available again. *When the felt sense forms, it is the person's next step of change already happening.*

Life situations (including relationships), and the way we live in them, can feel stuck, blocked, burdensome, impossible. If we can't find our way forward (however hard we try), we can get discouraged and depressed by what seems to be our inability to change. Yet human beings also have the capacity to shift levels, stepping outside the box of our narrow, frozen ways of thinking and feeling, living in new ways that are responsive to the current situation, which emerge naturally from the present living. This can happen because living process has the ability to form its next step. The next needed step can form as a felt sense before it can be planned or thought.

Hendricks-Gendlin (2003) describes a shift in levels that occurred when she did not simply respond to a challenging situation in an expected way. A few hours after her daughter was born, Hendricks-Gendlin was asked by a nurse to give permission for blood to be drawn from the baby again, a procedure that caused the baby visible distress. Instead of saying yes automatically, Hendricks-Gendlin said, "Wait, I need time." After considering and asking why the blood needed to be taken, she refused permission. There was a huge fuss, but she stood her ground. Later she found out that the blood drawing was not for the health of the baby but for the doctor's own research.

The felt senses that form with Focusing are not just the usual emotions, and are not just the bodily impact of familiar, repetitive thoughts. A felt sense is a very special kind of inner act or movement, which happens in a *pause*. Putting our usual ways of thinking and feeling "on pause," we stop and invite a whole sense of a situation. We wait for it—because we cannot command it to come. When it comes, it may be surprising, unexpected, difficult to put into words. We may need metaphorical language and gesture to describe it. We want to treat it with care, because something very important and precious is happening—a movement out of stopped process to a level where the rich detail of the current situation can function freshly, and thus new possibilities can come forward. All through this book there are examples of how Focusing allows a shift in levels from a narrow, fixed perspective to a wider, possibility-rich perspective.

In Brian's session recounted at the start of this chapter, there were many further steps after he got the left-behind feeling. All of this was important. But the key moment, what made all the rest possible, was his pausing and allowing that first felt sense of being left behind to form.

The Focusing Process

1. The precondition for Focusing is supportive relationship, externally (between client and therapist) and internally (within the client).

   The therapeutic relationship needs to be a safe (holding, supportive) space for new awareness to emerge. This means that the client's own perspective is respected. Being treated with respect, as a person in one's own right, and being safe from criticism, attack, dismissal, and abandonment, is a precondition for all kinds of learning and positive change, from schooling to relationships to therapy. There is more about this interpersonal space in Chapter 2 and Chapter 10.

   In addition to being empathic to the client, the therapist also supports the client's inner empathy to his own experiential process. A supportive inner relationship means that the client is able to be with his or her experiencing, rather than being merged with or taken over by the experience. There is more about this ability, and how to nurture it, in Chapter 5.

2. The first moment of Focusing is the coming of a felt sense. A felt sense is a freshly arising, immediately felt, more-than-words experience. There is much more about felt senses in Chapter 3. Felt senses can be (a) invited and (b) nurtured when they come.

3. The client stays with the felt sense, sensing it directly— instead of "thinking about," analyzing, internally arguing, evaluating, reacting to it with fear or impatience, and so on. This quality of aware contact can be facilitated and supported by the therapist. We will see how to support this in Chapter 6, and what to do if it's difficult in Chapter 7.

4. Describing the felt sense, often using odd combinations of

---

words and fresh metaphors, allows further contact without interpretation, and takes the process to the next stage.

5. From this nonjudging, nonanalyzing contact with the felt sense, new awareness emerges. There are shifts in the client's immediate experience ("The tight gripping in my stomach has relaxed completely now") and fresh perspectives are possible, along with new kinds of behavior. This takes many forms; we will see how to facilitate this phase in Chapter 6.

6. At the end of a Focusing process, there is an integration and completion-for-now that can help protect new awareness from old or critical voices and make space for new steps of behavior in the client's life.

This list of six stages makes it sound as if the Focusing process is always, or should be, complete in this way, with a beginning, middle, and end. On the contrary, Focusing can happen in moments, and one can move seamlessly in and out of other modes of processing. There is more about blending Focusing with other modalities in Chapter 9.

A FELT SENSE FORMS AND
CHANGE FOLLOWS: A VIGNETTE

Daniela came in for a session after several months away. She had been spending long days caring for her mother, who had a terminal illness. Her face looked drawn and weary, and she sat down with a deep sigh. The therapist's voice showed a tender concern as Daniela was invited to say how she was feeling right then.

"It's this overall feeling of exhaustion, just too much exhaustion. I can't deal with it. It's all through me, everywhere. I've got these dark thoughts, heavy emotions, my body is exhausted—all of it."

"And it's hard!" said the therapist, offering close empathic contact and letting her genuine warmth and caring show in her voice. "How the feeling of exhaustion is just all through you, everywhere."

Daniela sighed again, and sank a bit lower in the chair. "That's it," she said. There was already a slight change, just because what was experienced was allowed and accepted. But now the therapist will help the client to invite a felt sense, which is where the shift in levels becomes possible.

"See if it would be okay to acknowledge all that, and get a fresh sense of it, how it feels right now."

This was not the first time Daniela had heard this kind of invitation, and she trusted the relationship with the therapist, so she closed her eyes and took time—what might seem like a long time, if we didn't know what she was doing in the silence. This is a key moment: the client's willingness to pause and sense inwardly, to allow a felt sense to emerge. Let's see what happened next.

"It's like a giant squid," she said at last. "It has its arms wrapped around every part of me." This was not a guess, not a story, but a fresh sensing from inside. The giant squid was the exhaustion, but it was also two steps further: the whole feel of it, invited in the pause, and the metaphor that said what it was like. "It's loosening. As soon as I acknowledged it, it started to loosen. It's still there but not so tight." When a felt sense comes, along with a fresh metaphorical description that fits it exactly, there is often a relief of some kind. Forward movement is happening.

The therapist was closely following Daniela, responding to the precision of what came. "You're sensing it like a giant squid, with its arms wrapped around every part of you, and now it is starting to loosen." Another gentle invitation in the direction of inner sensing: "You might want to sense how *it* feels, from its point of view."

Another attentive silence. When Daniela spoke, the words come out of the inner sensing, not from some guess or speculation.

C: It's protecting . . . something precious. It's protecting something precious until it is ready.

T: You're sensing it is protecting something precious . . . until it is ready. . . .

C: Yes . . . [still sensing] it doesn't want something precious to be lost, blown away. . . . Something precious has been gained over a long time, a long process. It's not wanting all that to be lost.

T: You are sensing it is not wanting that to be lost, something precious gained over a long time. No wonder! You might want to say to it, inwardly, "No wonder it doesn't want something so precious to be lost."

C: Yes . . . I feel it responding . . . loosening even more. . . .

T: Maybe you could stay with that, allowing that feeling of loosening to be there. . . .

C: I'm sensing what it wants for me. It wants me to feel energy.

T: Ah, you're sensing it wants you to feel energy! Maybe you're sensing some of that energy in your body, right now.

C: Yes, I'm feeling it now, light energy coming up. It wants me to know that there is nothing to fear from death.

Daniela now looked deeply relaxed, as she took in what had come. The rest of the session included more: "Death comes before new life. . . . Sinking down is not depression. . . . Sinking down is necessary before new life. . . . It wants me to know that there are still important things to do in this life, and I will have time and energy to do them. It feels like a sweetness in the mouth . . . and a vast ocean . . . and so much more."

When Daniela smiled at the therapist as the session was ending, as the two of them celebrated the remarkable transformation that had happened and that Daniela would be taking back into her life, she looked like a totally different person from the one who had walked in the door.

Instead of the way it went, they could have spent the session discussing the exhaustion and its causes. Daniela might have gotten in touch with her emotions about her mother's impending death, and at the end of the session felt some relief. But the invitation for the felt sense to form, and attending to the surprising, unexpected, fresh knowing that came from there, was a different choice to make—and this vignette shows what can happen when life itself is given room to live forward.

KEY POINTS FROM THIS CHAPTER

- Living organisms imply their next steps of life process. What is implied is not one definite event, but a range of possibilities, many of which are novel and have never happened before.
- Implying is a readiness for and a kind of "knowing" of the next steps that would be the person's own change.

- When what is implied happens, this is called "carrying forward," and is correlated with immediate physiological changes such as relief and deeper breath, and affect and behavior changes.
- When what is implied cannot or does not happen, the organism experiences "stopped process." Stopped process that persists results in "frozen structures," which are stereotypical ways of responding to only partial aspects of a situation.
- The forming of a felt sense is already a change in how one "has" the problem, the life situation that the felt sense is about. Aspects of the situation that had been unavailable (frozen) are now available for processing.
- Held in a compassionate, curious awareness, the forming of a felt sense of the issue is the organism's life carrying forward, and this can be built on with further awareness.

The concepts from this chapter are new and may take some getting used to. Fortunately, there's no need to grasp them all before getting started. Putting the methods into practice may be just what is needed for the theory to make sense. In Chapter 2 we get ready to bring Focusing into client sessions by creating an environment that most cultivates Focusing.

Chapter 2

SETTING THE STAGE:
GETTING READY TO BRING
FOCUSING INTO CLIENT SESSIONS

Focusing is a natural process observed in many clients. It can be supported and facilitated in clients doing it already and invited in those not doing so. This is a powerful notion: Focusing is something clients do, or at least are capable of doing, and this natural process can be facilitated within a therapeutic relationship. As I hope to demonstrate in this book, if we can facilitate Focusing in our clients, they'll tend to experience embodied change that carries into their lives, change that carries them in their own positive, life-enhancing direction.

Because Focusing is not a therapeutic modality in itself, it is compatible and combinable with the other methodologies the clinician is already using. A Focusing orientation can be brought into any type of therapy and will enhance and strengthen the client's change process (more on this in Chapter 9). The research on psychotherapy effectiveness (Hendricks, 2001) suggests that a client who is benefiting from therapy may already be doing Focusing at some level, whether knowingly or not. Becoming conscious of the Focusing process can make any therapy modality even more effective and empowering.

In this chapter, I talk about setting the stage for bringing Focusing into psychotherapy sessions. I discuss whether and how to talk to your clients about Focusing, and what are the essential relational and attentional qualities that form the ideal environment for Focusing. These qualities are common to many forms of therapy, so it is likely you are already doing therapy in a way that is eminently compatible with Focusing. This is good news. I also offer suggestions for conducting a first session in a way that sets the stage for Focusing, and how to support clients with suggestions for Focusing-related self-care between sessions.

How you bring Focusing into your client sessions depends on many things, including your own personal style, your primary theoretical framework, and whether you are in private practice, or in an agency, or some other setting. Some ways of working with clients are already close to a Focusing style. If you are already interested in how your client experiences his world, if you already believe that connecting empathically with your client's felt experience is a good idea, Focusing will fit very well for you. If not, then bringing in Focusing will be a bit more of a stretch, but it can be done.

Bringing Focusing into client sessions will also depend on the clients. A new way of working will probably be easier to bring to your newer clients. If you've been working with someone for a long time, your way of working with that client is established. Doing anything differently may seem odd or upsetting to your long-term client. There are ways to handle this, but it isn't as easy as working in a certain way from the start. You may also have clients who are more comfortable trying something new or have an easier time being in a witnessing state with their own felt experience—or you may have clients who feel that therapy has fallen into the doldrums and are eager to try something that can get things moving again. All this can impact the way in which you bring Focusing into client sessions.

You may be wondering how to explain Focusing to your clients. The answer is simple: You don't have to. There's no need to explain Focusing to your clients. In fact, even mentioning Focusing can be counterproductive. The default mode of bringing Focusing to your client sessions is to not use the word "Focusing" at all. (We'll see some exceptions to this later.)

How could explaining Focusing to your client be counterproductive? Clients who hear that you are using some particular method may wonder if this is something they can fail at, or something they need to do well in order to please you. If you have been working with a client for a while, and you introduce a new method, the client may wonder why you felt the need to bring in something new. There may also be a sense of setting an expectation for a "right" way to be. Brenner (2012) said, "Clients pick up what we want from them, so we want to stay away from communicating expectations or judgments about the process."

One therapist said to me: "When I first learned about Focusing, I tried to tell my clients about it. I got a lot of mixed reactions. People wondered why I needed to try something different, what was wrong with what we had been doing. Some people got quite anxious at knowing there was a new method they might fail at. It felt like Focusing as a concept was getting in between me and my clients. What I do now is, I don't tell them. I just bring in a Focusing way of being. I think at first, when Focusing didn't feel natural to me, it was hard to bring it into client sessions naturally. It felt abrupt, really different. But now it's smooth. The Focusing way of being has become part of who I am, how I am with people. I couldn't even point to which part of my sessions are Focusing any more."

What I will show you in this book are ways of adding a Focusing dimension to what you already do. The interventions will probably integrate so smoothly that your client will not experience you as doing something different. Although I will be introducing you to some concepts that will underlie what you do, there is no need to explain those concepts to your clients. It is enough that *you* know them.

THE THERAPEUTIC ENVIRONMENT THAT SUPPORTS FOCUSING

Fortunately, the environment necessary to support Focusing processes is the very same environment most therapists already cultivate with their clients. A number of Focusing-oriented therapists have discussed cultivating the kind of relationship with a client that enhances Focusing (Friedman, 2007; Leijssen, 2007). Mia Leijssen describes how the working relationship she creates with a client has the qualities of both good mothering and good fathering:

> The welcoming space I offer right from the beginning has the quality of "good mothering." This means: being present in a

warm-hearted, friendly and affectionate way, and listening empathically to what the client tries to express. . . . Building a good working relationship also implies offering "good fathering," meaning that experiences get named, that structure emerges from chaos, that reality will be faced, and that there is authentic communication. (2007, pp. 25–26)

Bringing Focusing into clinical practice requires us to cultivate an environment where felt senses are more likely to happen. This includes safety, respect, trustworthiness, and openness to the other person's way of seeing things.

Creating a rapport with clients is the first therapeutic task, on which all the other tasks will be built. By tuning in to their experience, understanding how it is for them, not challenging them on how they see the world, you are building a safe environment in which clients can begin to trust you, and also begin to trust their own felt experience.

The analyst's own focus remains consistently on what the patient is experiencing. This encompasses not only the moment-to-moment experiences of the patient but also the continuous flow of these experiences over time. Kohut refers to the attunement to this continuous flow of moment-to-moment experiences as *prolonged immersion* or as long-term *empathic immersion* in the psychological field. (Rowe & MacIsaac, 1991, pp. 17–18, italics in original)

It has been shown in studies on attachment (Fonagy et al., 2002; Wallin, 2007) that the capacity to reflect on one's own experience develops within a relationship with a primary caregiver in which reflectiveness happens regularly. Vanaerschot (2004) discusses the importance of empathic attunement from therapist to client in relation to developmental deficits in the caretaker-infant relationship. DeYoung describes how infant studies have led to a more complex understanding of the intersubjective process of empathy in adult clients.

Infant studies support the claim that anyone's felt sense of self ("I know who I am, what I want, how I feel") comes into being only as there is response to a self's developing motivations, desires, and feelings. . . . Clients will begin to count on this respectful, open-ended curiosity, and then they will join in the shared process of "getting it." (2003, pp. 58–59)

Ultimately the deep process of a Focusing-oriented psychotherapy will be carried forward by the client's ability to be present with her own inner experience. The successful client will be able to bring qualities of empathy, compassion, and interested curiosity to her own felt experience. She will feel strong enough to stand steady in the presence of painful experiences, and she will trust that there is benefit in doing so, that on the other side of discomfort and pain something new and fresh opens and moves forward.

What will nurture and develop this inner relational connection between client and inner felt experience is a relational connection between therapist and client that has those same qualities of empathy, compassion, and interested curiosity. Those first steps of self-empathy will be nurtured in an environment of receiving empathy from a trusted other.

Early in therapy, we don't expect a client to already have the capacities for self-attending that will grow within the therapeutic context. The nurturing environment for the client's own ability to be self-aware, self-attending, and self-compassionate is the therapist's offering of those qualities to the client, from the very first moment of contact.

GENUINE EMBODIED PRESENCE: THE THERAPIST FOCUSING

Facilitating Focusing in our clients is an inherently relational process. This means that we are genuinely present, aware of our own thoughts and feelings even as we listen to and attune to the process of the client. A psychotherapy relationship is one in which both people may change, and we are open to that possibility. We understand that being in touch with our own feelings and our own embodied experience is going to be key to the success of the therapy process, even if we never explicitly say much about them.

There is more in Chapter 10 about "the therapist Focusing," but a strong stress on it also belongs here in the discussion of setting the stage for Focusing, because it is important to be genuinely present in an embodied way from the beginning. The client can feel your being present, which impacts her sense of safety, and you will receive vital information from your own experiential attunement.

Our clients really cannot be Focusing unless we are Focusing, ourselves. When you as a clinician are in touch, during a session, with your own implicit process, your own felt senses, and you are able to silently accompany yourself, you create an environment in which Focusing can happen naturally and smoothly for your clients—and you yourself have access to a wider field of intuition and presence. Psychotherapist Joan Lavender (personal communication, 2012) calls this the "experiential environment."

Let's talk about bringing a Focusing orientation to the very first meeting with a client.

AT THE FIRST CONSULTATION

Helene G. Brenner (2012), a psychologist who has been incorporating Focusing into her psychotherapy practice for more than 20 years, described in a recent training seminar how she establishes a Focusing-oriented relationship with her clients in the very first session:

> There are two vital components I am trying to get across in the first session. The first is a trusting relationship with me. The more relaxed and comfortable and met and welcomed the client feels, the more that they are going to feel relaxed and able to reveal more. Second, I really want to create a space for them to befriend their own experience—the inner relationship. I want for them to feel that they can be with their experience, that they are in their own experience internally, rather than externally thinking how does it look from the outside.

The first goal in the first session is that the client feel connected with by the therapist. This begins with the smallest details, such as whether you yourself go out to the waiting room to greet her, the warmth of your handshake and eye contact, whether she can feel your genuine interest in who she is as a person. Attunement to the needs of the client expresses itself in our not having one standard way of starting the interview. We can already tell that some people are ready to pour out their stories, and need no more than an invitation to begin, whereas others are clearly a bit held back and appreciate some structure and a series of questions to draw them out. As Brenner points out, there is every reason to follow the client's lead on this, because ultimately the client's sense of safety and comfort in the therapeutic relationship will determine what is possible in the therapy.

Brenner emphasizes the Kohutian notion of "experience-near" in the first session with a new client. She points to this quote:

> How do we go about sensing the inner life of another person? Perhaps the familiar phrase "to put one's self into the shoes of another" best describes this process, and most accurately captures what Kohut means by "experience-near." Simply stated, the analyst attempts to experience as closely as possible what the patient is experiencing (an approximation). (Rowe & Mac-Isaac, 1991)

In getting to know a client, Brenner listens for the edge, the spirit, the passion, the suffering, what really brought the person to her office. "What made you pick up the phone?" Brenner (2012) likes to ask. "Because then you're getting to the urge, the impulse, what was that present-moment experience of them wanting to come in to see you . . . rather than immediately talking about goals or what is wrong. There is something juicy, something immediate, about the behavior: *picking up the phone.*"

We may have the urge to correct clients. We may see how their beliefs or attitudes or behaviors are not serving them. But an atmosphere of argument is not a safe space. Change in beliefs, attitudes, and behaviors will optimally arise within an atmosphere of safety that begins with acceptance. Brenner (2012) said, "Especially at first, I always say 'Yes' to the client. I find a way to say 'Yes,' to understand why what they feel makes perfect sense from their point of view—and to reflect that back, and explore how it is for them."

She described a client who came in with the goal of getting rid of her painful rages.

> I knew that eventually we would get around to listening to the part of her that feels the rage. But I wouldn't bring that out in

a first session. I would start with empathy, get over there into her shoes. Because *she* wants to get rid of those feelings, and *she* is suffering, and it's causing her a lot of distress. I'll say, "Absolutely! This is really stressful for you! Tell me more about it! Sounds like that's really getting in the way of your life!" It's not just that I'm empathizing. I take seriously that that is their goal. I let them know I am aligned with them to work on that. They are no longer alone, I am an ally with them.

FOR NEW CLIENTS:
A FOCUSING-ORIENTED ASSESSMENT

No matter what our orientation, a first session always involves a kind of assessment, whether it is formal or informal. At first glance, an assessment that incorporates a Focusing orientation will be quite similar to what most therapists are already doing. The elements of attunement to the client's situation and intentions for coming into therapy are common to many modalities. The Focusing orientation can be seen in the attention to the client's *manner of process.*

Helene Brenner (2012) described eight elements or aspects that she assesses in a first session with a client. Because this is process-oriented work, these elements are not items to be noted on a checklist and analyzed later, but elements that are being oriented to immediately in the clinician's way of being with the client—as well as being noted and remembered for later sessions. These elements are not phrased as questions to ask clients, but as areas to be aware of, because it is preferable if they emerge in the natural conversation rather than being probed for. On the other hand, as Brenner pointed out, some clients prefer to be drawn out with questions, and in that case questions can be asked.

1. What is their concern, what they are really interested in getting? What brought them to therapy—and what *really* brought them there? Even during the initial interview, the presenting problem may be revealed to have layers and wider implications.

2. How are their meaningful relationships doing? Are they satis-

fied with, and receiving support from, their most important relationships: spouse or partner, children, parents, other important close people?

3. How is their work? Do they have a meaningful pursuit in life? Do they have something that brings them meaning? Passion? Are they happy with what they do in their work life from day to day, even if that is volunteer work, or unpaid work such as being a stay-at-home parent?

4. What are their goals? What do they want to get from this work? What will signify success?

The first four elements are about the content of the client's living and the issues that he is bringing to psychotherapy. There are four more elements, however, that are more process oriented, that are about the manner of the client's process rather than the content.

5. How readily are they able to be with their own experience? Are there any moments when they pause and check inwardly whether what they just said feels right? Or do they speak as if feelings are unchangeable facts, as in "I'll never forgive her for that betrayal"?

6. How do they talk about their problems? Is there an urgency? Is there a sense of an inner pressure of emotion? Are they very close to their experience? Is the volume way up? Or do they seem rather distant from their experience?

7. How do they speak about themselves? Is there space between them and their life? Is there a sense of an observing or reflective self? Do they have any humor, joy, passion? Is there a sense of excitement about being in the therapy office, or is it more a sense of anxiety?

8. Do they know themselves, or is there a sense they are unclear about or unready to express or embody who they are?

Noting these process elements during a first session will aid a clinician in being able to tailor the work of therapy to what a client is ready and able to do from a process perspective. Clients who are already pausing and checking inwardly while speaking will need very little prompting to bring a Focusing awareness to their inner experience. Clients at the edge of being overwhelmed will need immediate support in establishing a strong self (see Chapter 5) before Focusing is possible. Clients who are distant from their own experiencing and locked into fixed categories may need extra help to move toward a Focusing perspective (see Chapter 7).

If you work for an agency that requires you to do a specified intake, and collect information for a form, you can still do this in a way that enhances the client's experience of comfort and relaxation, and begins the process of preparing the client to be open to her own experiential process. The key would be to stay connected with the person across from you, to let the person sitting there be more important than the form on your desk. The form can always be picked up a bit later in the session. Obviously the form needs to be filled out, but the way in which it is filled out can be chosen so the client feels himself to be more important to you than the form.

As you ask for the information needed by the agency, you don't have to become "businesslike." You can have a slow and relaxed pace, a tone of voice that expresses true warmth, interest, empathy. For some people it helps to state the need for the information without asking a question, for example, "I'm wondering if you're on any medications right now. It would help us to know that."

In addition to intake for your agency, there may be other forms for the first visit, including forms for the primary care physician, consent forms for talking to other professionals working with the family, and so on. Working with forms can usually be done with empathy for the person across from you who is having to respond to these enquiries. It can help to extend that same empathy to yourself as someone who was trained to connect with people, and yet you have to deal with these forms in the first session. These first-session formalities may include making a diagnosis and filling in a treatment plan. It can be challenging yet important to stay with the relationship in the present moment despite these exigencies.

EXPECTATIONS AND
MUTUAL RESPONSIBILITIES

What are the ground rules of our relationship and our work together? What can the client expect, and what is expected of him? In a first session you already discuss items that probably include confidentiality, what to do in an emergency, what happens when either one of you needs to miss a session, and so on. There are also specific expectations and mutual responsibilities for a Focusing-oriented way of working.

What we hope for from our clients is that they will check what we say with their own internal sense of how things are, and correct us if what we say doesn't fit them. If clients know that they can correct us, this will advance the work of therapy in two important ways: (1) it makes the relationship safer because the client is respected as the authority on his or her own process, and (2) for the client to check inwardly is a key part of the Focusing process itself, as we will see. I say more in Chapter 3 about how to offer "experiential guesses" so that they are easier for the client to correct.

Psychotherapy is always to some extent an educational process. People arrive with ideas about how therapy works, and they bring methods that—more or less consciously—they have already been using to handle and manage emotional states, decisions, relationships, and so forth. The process of psychotherapy involves, among other things, a relational encounter between the client with these ideas and methods, and the therapist with his own ideas and methods.

For example, an assumption that a client may bring into therapy is that negative emotions need to be disrespected or pushed away. In a Focusing way of working, the client would neither push away "negative" emotions nor act on them, but rather turn toward them with interested curiosity to get to know what underlies them. A psychotherapist might explain that to a client in a first (or later) session.

> T: I'll be showing you how to turn toward difficult thoughts and emotions and get to know them better. I'll be helping you to find a strong, calm, compassionate way of being, so you can turn toward those difficult emotions without getting taken over by them.
> C: What happens then? How do I change?
> T: Well, in my experience, change happens *because* you are able to turn toward the negatives. They are aspects of yourself that have been trying to help you, but in an unhelpful way. If they are pushed away, they stay unchanged. But if you turn toward them and sense them freshly, there is an evolution that can happen. They themselves can change. That's what we'll be doing together.

IF YOU WANT TO TALK TO
YOUR CLIENTS ABOUT FOCUSING

As I mentioned at the beginning of this chapter, you don't have to explain Focusing to your clients. But you can. In some cases, it can actually be helpful. Clients who struggle with finding a relationship with emotional experience can be helped by knowing there is a method which has a name that they are learning to do. Having a process to study and read about between sessions may give some people a sense of support and control over what is happening for them in the psychotherapy. Brenner (2012) said, "I have some clients who need to know we are doing something that has a name: Focusing. If it has a label, it helps them feel more comfortable. They can read about it, and for some people that's a safer experience."

Focusing-oriented therapist Lauren Mari-Navarro told me in a personal communication that she prefers to tell her clients about Focusing. Here is how she does it:

> Most clients don't want to have a process or technique "applied" to them. I know I don't like that either. So when I speak of Focusing I use appropriate self-disclosure that I have found a process of listening to what is going on in my mind, or the big life issues I'm dealing with, by listening in a more internal kind of way. This might intrigue them, just to hear that I'm about to tell them something I myself have found useful, even life changing. So I invite them, if interested, to try a little bit of that kind of internal listening. We might just do this for the last 15 or 20 minutes of the session. Usually this is enough of a taste that they become intrigued and want to learn more. So I ask them if they might like to begin our next session listening in this kind of way. While some therapists may decide never to name this as "Focusing," I don't do that, because I love Focusing and I want to open up that avenue for my clients with all of the books and resources and the Focusing tips that are available. So, after one or two sessions perhaps, I mention the word Focusing, and let them know about Ann's book and other resources. I always stock up with multiple copies of *The Power of Focusing* (Cornell, 1996) to have on hand to lend to clients. I find that once they've had the actual experience of Focusing in

37

our sessions and have a feeling for what the felt sense is, that the book enhances their own process and understanding and our work together really blossoms using this process.

If clients are interested, if they ask, "What is this thing we're doing?" then it doesn't hurt to tell them. Some clients may be therapists or therapy students themselves, or otherwise interested in methods for change. The therapist might say,

> What we were doing today, when I invited you to pause and sense the whole body feel of your issue with your sister, and then stay with it—remember?—that is something called "Focusing." It's based on the idea that your body can "sum up" the whole way you feel about something you're going through, into a single felt sense. That felt sense actually contains both the problem and the way forward, but for it to reveal itself, it needs a bit of patience and acceptance. I appreciated how you were able to stay with how you were feeling today. What I'd suggest is that we might come back to that process next time, if you like.

Focusing-oriented therapist Carol Nickerson keeps a handout in her waiting room that explains some of the principles of Focusing and how to bring those principles into daily life for self-regulation (see the Appendix for the handout she uses). She finds that some people never notice it, while other clients bring it in and ask her about it. This is a natural way of discovering which clients want to know more about the kinds of processes you are using—and which do not.

HOW TO TALK TO OTHERS ABOUT FOCUSING

Whether or not you tell your clients about Focusing, there may be other people whom you want to tell about it. Depending on whom you are talking to and what their framework is, there are actually many ways to talk about Focusing. Here are some examples.

- "Focusing is a body-oriented, mindfulness-based practice that enables clients to have a more accepting relationship to their own emotional states, resulting in a greater ability to self-regulate in stressful situations."

- "Research at the University of Chicago, since replicated in more than 50 studies, showed that the way that clients pay attention to their own experiential process, even in the first session, is predictive of success or failure in therapy. Focusing is a way to bring that successful client process into any kind of psychotherapy."
- "Focusing is a way of working experientially by helping clients get felt senses. A felt sense is a fresh, bodily felt sense of a situation that contains its own forward momentum for change. When clients get felt senses and stay with them, therapy can often move more quickly and go deeper."
- "Focusing is a way of empowering clients to have a stronger sense of agency, to have better relationships with others, and to create positive coping cycles."

None of the statements offered here is a complete or exclusive definition of Focusing, but depending on the context, any of them may serve to orient people to what you are doing.

IN BETWEEN SESSIONS

If clients want a way to bring the self-regulating and empowering effects of Focusing into their daily lives between therapy sessions, we can give them some simple, practical, and effective ways to do this.

Lauren Mari-Navarro told me in a personal communication how she offers homework to her clients:

> I often let clients know that just saying "Hello" or acknowledging those feelings are there, and that you hear them, can create a huge shift. Just a little bit of space between the feeling and your self that can calm everything down, and bring some relief. I give them homework around this and love to hear how well this has worked for them. Not a big homework assignment really, but what a shift it can make. . . . Just as we find ourselves easily comforting the child who has just fallen on the playground and offer soothing support, so can we offer that kind of simple, supportive listening to our suffering parts. When we can be curious and caring, listening to our hurt

places is not hard, and those hurt places love nothing more than simply to be listened to.

I give clients "homework" if they ask me for it, often at the end of a session. "Is there something you can tell me to do at home?" If possible, I'll draw on the session we just had to point out processes they seemed to find helpful, and show how they can continue to use those processes if needed after they leave.

> Do you remember when you told me you felt a bit overwhelmed by how sad you were feeling, and I suggested you try saying, "Something in me is sad"? You told me that made a helpful difference in how easily you could keep company with those sad feelings. Well, that's something you can do any time you are concerned you might get overwhelmed by feelings. You can say "something in me" is feeling that. Here, I'll write down those words for you, to make it easier for you to have them with you when you need them.

Some clients actually learn Focusing as a self-help skill, because they want to have a supportive, empowering process outside of psychotherapy, and of course this enhances their psychotherapy. But learning Focusing as a self-help skill isn't the right step for everyone. Many clients in psychotherapy feel the need of the holding container of the therapy relationship, and don't want, or aren't ready for, what would be needed to do Focusing consciously and deliberately on their own.

When I felt a need to offer some of the most immediately useful self-regulating skills of Focusing without teaching the whole process, I created a five-stage e-course called Get Bigger Than What's Bugging You (Cornell, 2012). This is a free resource that a number of psychotherapists have started offering to their clients when the clients ask for something supportive to do between sessions.

Once you have set the stage for Focusing with the conversations and relational connections described in this chapter, the next recommended step is to begin to observe the felt senses that are naturally occurring for your clients, and support them when they occur. In Chapter 3 we'll talk about how to recognize felt senses and how to make sure clients get the most out of them when they come.

Chapter 3

RECOGNIZING AND NURTURING FELT SENSES

A client is sitting in your office with you. Perhaps her current issue is that she is not getting schoolwork done, or not paying her bills, or not speaking up to her boss. The two of you have been talking about it for a while, exploring what might be going on, and then she says this:

"I don't know what's wrong with me. I think I'm just lazy. I'm feeling . . . it's funny, I don't know what this is. . . . There's this little hard place in my chest, like a kid saying no. . . . Hm." There is bit of a silence. She looks down, as if into herself. And then she sort of shakes herself, looks up at you, and says, "Well anyway, I'm probably just resistant."

There was a doorway there. Did you sense it?

It opened for a moment, a flicker of possibility . . . and then she didn't go through. (Were you disappointed?) What might have happened if she had stayed longer with the "little hard place in my chest, like a kid saying no"? Very likely something new, fresh, unpredictable, and somehow carrying forward would have come from there. We can't say what it would be—but we can say that it would be her next step of change. That—the little hard place in the chest "like a kid saying no"—was a felt sense.

Bringing Focusing into clinical practice is really, in a way, quite simple: You invite your clients to have felt senses (or recognize the ones they're already having), and then help them to stay with the felt senses so that fresh new steps of change emerge. Having felt senses is a natural human process, and many people get felt senses spontaneously in the course of therapy sessions of all modalities. To consciously bring Focusing into our clinical practice, we want to listen for felt senses, notice them, encourage them. We also want to support people in working with the ways that trauma, dissociation, and inner conflict seem to prevent the kind of awareness that allows felt senses to emerge.

At the heart of it all is the felt sense.

WHAT IS A FELT SENSE?

"Felt sense" is a new term that emerges from a new way of looking at life and process, as we saw in Chapter 1. Although we have all had felt senses, the concept of a felt sense is new. We can't equate it with something we already know, however tempting it might be to do so. We need to see this odd bird, a felt sense, as something to encounter. Let's define it, and then go through the definition bit by bit.

A felt sense is a freshly forming, wholistic sense of a situation that has a "more than words can say" quality to it.

1. Felt senses *form freshly*. That means that a felt sense cannot be the chronic ache in the shoulder or the pain in the gut that has been there all week. For a felt sense to form, one needs an intention, a pause, an invitation—even if one doesn't know what a felt sense is. "Let me see. . . . How *am* I feeling about what happened?" One of Gendlin's key insights is that feelings are not simply "discovered" as if they were buried or stored, but they can also form freshly. The person may feel as if something "underneath" is being discovered, but actually something implicit is brought out explicitly, and can now function in a new way.

2. Felt senses are *wholistic senses*; they are of a whole situation. We know that we can have feeling reactions to parts or aspects of a situation. "I'm disappointed with Mom, and I'm angry with John for interfering." What is less well known is that we can get a sense of the whole situation. "When I think of the whole thing, I get this queasy uncomfortable feeling." Like the proverbial picture that is worth a thousand words, a felt sense is an intricate whole that sums up, captures, includes, contains, all the aspects of a situation at once. Those

aspects can then be unfolded or unpacked from the felt sense, and this process brings steps of change in a way that just having emotions or just talking about a problem does not.

3. Felt senses have a "more than words can say" quality. They are hard to describe. This is related to the previous point: Because a felt sense contains so much, is so intricate, it takes time to find a description that encompasses it. Often a single word is inadequate, and several words are needed instead, like "jumpy queasy" or "tight constricted." Metaphors and similes may be needed, for example: "Like a knotted rope," or "like a heavy boulder." Even after a description is found, there is typically a sense that there is more unspoken. It is for this reason that I call a felt sense a doorway to change. Attending to a felt sense is attending to the place of emergent process, where something new and fresh can occur—as opposed to a recycling of familiar thoughts and emotions.

Although the concept of "felt sense" may be new, it's quite likely that felt senses themselves are not new to you. Almost certainly you will recognize felt senses as having occurred in your clients and in yourself. But without a concept for what sets a felt sense apart, we don't know what we are seeing, or why it is so important. What we might have thought was merely an inability to articulate could be the place where fresh perspectives and new behavior possibilities are emerging.

We need to be able to recognize felt senses when they occur, and nurture them—because felt senses are doorways to the rest of Focusing, and to change itself.

SIGNS OF A FELT SENSE

Felt senses are:

- Experienced in the present, here and now
- Bodily experienced (in a special sense of the word "body")
- Hard to describe
- Often needing fresh, metaphorical language ("kind of like a wall inside," "like a kid saying no")
- About life situations, but containing more (implicitly) than has been previously known

Felt senses can form when we pause . . . when we are not feeling overwhelmed or identified with reactive emotional states . . . when we let go of familiar words or concepts for a while . . . when we sense at the body level of awareness . . . when we can stand it that what we feel is vague, unclear, hard to describe, impossible to explain.

A client says, "I think it must be a kind of denial. I'm feeling . . . it's hard to describe . . . kind of a wall inside. No, that's not quite it. It's . . . it's . . . I don't know. It's just very vague right now. I guess I'm just being resistant." What part of that client statement is the most interesting? (In contrast, what parts are probably just old dead-end concepts?) That's right—we're interested when clients start to grope for words, feeling something so freshly and so immediately that it's hard for them to describe. (And we're less interested when they start sentences with such phrases as "I think it must be . . ." or "I guess I'm just . . .")

> What one feels at any moment is always interactional, it is a living in an infinite universe and in situations, a context of other people, of words, and signs, of physical surroundings, of events past, present and future. Experiencing is not "subjective," but interactional, not intrapsychic, but interactional. It is not inside, but inside-outside. (Gendlin, 1973, p. 324)

WHAT IS NOT A FELT SENSE

Many important experiences happen for a client in therapy that are not felt senses. Clients may self-reflect, thinking about the possible sources of their difficulties. Clients may recount what happened, last week or 30 years ago, with more or less affect along with the telling. Clients may get in touch with emotions, not once but many times, and may learn to be more aware of and expressive of their emotions—and be met in that emotional experience by the therapist. And there are other possibilities as well.

So I need to be clear: I am not saying that only felt sensing is valuable. I do, however, want to draw some distinctions: For clients to self-analyze, to tell stories from their pasts, and to be emotionally expressive are all processes that could be accompanied by or lead to or from felt senses—but they are not in and of themselves felt sensing processes.

It is not felt sensing when a client makes guesses or speculates about the causes of her or his problems: "I'm probably just afraid of failure." "I think it's because I never had that when I was a child." The ability to self-reflect like this is significant; if people haven't been able to do it before, it is progress for them to begin. But there is a step beyond speculating, and that is direct contact with the felt sense itself. "I'm probably just afraid of failure" can become "It's . . . um . . . it's fear, yes, but not exactly of failure . . . uh. . . ."

It is not felt sensing when clients tell stories about what happened in the past, whether this is the past of last week or of longer ago. Again, telling what happened can be important for therapy. I am not saying it shouldn't be encouraged and welcomed. But there is a step beyond telling the story, and that is getting the felt sense of the whole situation that the story comes from. (In Chapter 4 I will show ways to help a client make this shift.)

When the client is emotionally expressive, allowing tears to come, or perhaps angry assertion, of course we welcome this. And again, there is a further step of felt sensing, beyond emotional expression. The client can get the whole underlying sense of it, the "place where the tears come from."

It is also not felt sensing to simply experience body sensations that do not have meaning or life connection—although a client who can't have body sensations easily will need some encouragement to practice having them. Felt sensing builds on the ability to feel in the body and is more than mere body feeling.

We can help a client go from any of these processes toward felt sensing. They are all good starting places. It is important to be aware, however, that emotional expression, self-speculating, storytelling, and physical sensations are not yet felt sensing.

FELT SENSE: DEFINING THE TERM

These days the term "felt sense" is being used more widely in the psychotherapy community. Unfortunately as the term spreads it is not carrying with it an understanding of how direct reference to experiencing forms the next steps of living. The way "felt sense" is spreading reminds me of the children's game we called Telephone, in which one person whispers a sentence to the next person, and then that person whispers what she heard to the next person, until when you get around the room the resulting message is unrecognizable.

Peter Levine wanted to include Gendlin's concept of "felt sense" in his own work. It's clear that he didn't just want to use the same words, he actually wanted to bring in Gendlin's concept. He cites Gendlin as coining the term "felt sense" and writes, "The felt sense is a difficult concept to define with words, as language is a linear process and the felt sense is a non-linear experience" (Levine, 1997, p. 67).

I assumed that "felt sense" was Gendlin's term, as Levine stated. Then, when reading Allan Schore, I seemed to find a different use of the term. He writes: "In recent psychoneurobiological models the felt sense is defined as 'the sum total of all sensations from all sense organs, both conscious and subliminal at any given moment' (Scaer, 2001)" (Schore, 2003, p. 81). So I looked up Scaer (2001), and I discovered that Scaer was attempting to follow Levine, who was attempting to follow Gendlin.

> Although Levine addresses the process of traumatic memory in the generation of symptoms, he emphasizes the role of procedural or implicit memory in the storage of traumatic energy, and incorporates explicit cognitive processes to a limited extent in his therapy. He uses the "felt sense" to pursue and access the trauma response. Levine describes this somatic state of being primarily by example rather than by specific definition. A working definition of the felt sense might be the sum total of all sensations from all sense organs, both conscious and subliminal, at any given moment. (Scaer, 2001, location 3877)

Assuming that Levine meant to follow Gendlin, and I think he did, Scaer's guess at what Levine intended is incorrect. It would be great to have a term for the "sum total of all sensations from all sense organs," but let's keep the term "felt sense" for what Gendlin meant by it, or we won't have any way to separate out the power of this unique concept.

46

A NEW CONCEPTION OF "BODY"

The innovative concept of the felt sense requires a redefinition of what we mean by "body." Felt senses form, we say, in the body. But what body?

As I said in the Introduction, some methods for bringing the body into psychotherapy today define body as "instinctual and nonconscious," and discuss processing from this level as "bottom up" (Ogden et al., 2006, p. 5). In contrast, in Focusing we understand "body" as the interactive process of being alive, experienced from the inside. Levine eloquently evokes this understanding of "body": "The way we *know* we're alive is rooted in our capacity *to feel*, to our depths, the physical reality of aliveness embedded within our bodily sensations—through direct experience. This, in short, is embodiment" (2010, pp. 286–287, italics in original). Images, emotions, moods, even many "thoughts," are experienced in and from this body. This "body" is not separate from mind, and is not "bottom-up" as opposed to "top-down." In this experienced body, we can touch directly what is preconceptual—not already divided into formed concepts.

Gendlin demonstrated that experiencing has an implicit dimension, an intricate structure of felt meaning that is richer and deeper than the formed explanations that people have for their own behavior. Seen through the lens of Focusing, what we mean by the word "body" alters, as we see a person in a living body in her or his life situations as one single life-interaction process.

> What is a living body such that it has the intricacy of our situations? . . . The body IS an interaction process with the environment, and therefore the body IS its situations. The body isn't just a sealed thing here, with an external situation over there, which it merely interprets. Rather, even before we think and speak, the living body is already one interaction process with its situation. (Gendlin, 2004b, p. 7)

To work with the body as defined by Focusing, we need to remember that we are not just talking about the body as seen by physiology or neuroscience, however grateful we may be for the insights from those fields. We can't understand what a felt sense is if we have already sliced up a person conceptually into a mere physical body that has nothing to do with meaning, versus a non-physical mind that has little to do with feelings. This is Descartes's error (Damasio, 1994), the mind-body split that has plagued our modern culture. There is no need to live out that split in the psychotherapy office. A whole person sits across from us, not a body-less mind perched on top of a mindless body. Body is in mind; mind is in body. Whatever a person is thinking or feeling becomes even more meaningful when it is experienced in the body, here and now. It becomes, not just meaningful, but available for fresh, forward steps of change.

DISTINGUISHING FELT SENSES FROM EMOTIONS

Because the healing power of emotion is coming even more to the foreground in clinical practice (Elliott et al., 2004; Fosha, 2000; Fosha, Siegel, & Solomon, 2009), it is especially important to delineate how emotions and felt senses do not function in the same way, even though they are profoundly related.

Felt senses and emotions are similar in three ways:

- They come of themselves; they are not in our control.
- They are essentially bodily experiences.
- They relate meaningfully to our lives, to events and life situations.

Emotions can take us over; they can come from behind and hit us over the head. Or we can invite emotions by remembering evocative situations, rereading old letters, watching certain movies—or simply by saying, "Okay, I am ready to feel it now." Either way, even when invited, emotions "come" of themselves—and do not always come. We don't control their coming. We can just invite them and be ready for them, or not. Felt senses work almost the same way. Felt senses can come when invited, and sometimes even when invited they don't come. But a felt sense will not knock you over the head. A felt sense comes because it is invited, and because you are at the level of awareness (I call it "Self-in-Presence; see Chapter 5) from which felt senses can be invited.

Like felt senses, emotions are rooted in the body. Damasio (1999) was one who pointed this out; Rothschild is another:

Emotions, though interpreted and named by the mind, are integrally an experience of the body. Each emotion looks different to the observer and has a different bodily expression. Every emotion is characterized by a discrete pattern of skeletal muscle contraction visible on the face and in body posture (somatic nervous system). Each emotion also feels different on the inside of the body. (2000, p. 56)

Rothschild goes on to name six emotions—anger, sadness, disgust, happiness, fear, shame—and describe the physical sensations and typical physical behaviors that go with each emotion. She doesn't state that there are only those six emotions, but surely, if each has its own pattern of muscle contraction, there couldn't be too many more. Fosha says:

Core emotions, such as anger, joy, sadness, fear, and disgust . . . are primary in the sense that they are universal, wired-in organismic responses, present if not actually from birth, from early in life. Core emotions are deep rooted, bodily responses with sensorimotor and visceral correlates. Many of these emotions have their own specific physiology and arousal patterns. (2000, p. 20)

Both emotions and felt senses are "about" something. They are bodily felt. Their coming and their being experienced is a transformative process. So how are they not the same?

Felt senses and emotions differ in at least three ways:

- Emotions are nameable and knowable; felt senses are hard to define.
- Emotions come in culturally expected places; felt senses are unique to the individual person's life situation.
- Emotions narrow our awareness; felt senses widen our awareness.

Emotions are named, and they come in culturally expected situations, as if the situation caused the emotion. What I hoped for did not happen, so I am disappointed. I got ridiculed, so I feel anger and shame. Wouldn't you? Wouldn't anyone? Felt senses don't work that way. There are not named felt senses; each felt sense, being an intricate mesh of meaning that goes beyond this situation and has resonances in many aspects of our lives, comes uniquely; it is how *this* feels, right now. No one else would ever feel, or ever has felt, quite the same way.

Emotions narrow our awareness. Evolutionarily, this is what they are supposed to do. When I am sad my attention narrows to the situation I am sad about; when I am angry, my attention narrows to what makes me angry. If I have to mobilize resources to fight or escape, this narrowing is extremely helpful; it lets me shut out what is irrelevant to this charged situation. But felt senses do the opposite. Felt senses widen our awareness to take in the whole situation and its many interconnections (Gendlin, 1991). Felt senses are not a response to immediate danger. To get a felt sense, we need to feel fairly safe. But when we do get a felt sense, we are in touch with a very wide field of knowing, more than we had realized we knew.

Even though emotions and felt senses differ, we cannot find a felt sense by turning away from our emotions. On the contrary: If an emotion is present, the road to the felt sense will be through bringing aware attention to the emotion. Gendlin explains it this way:

> A felt sense will have a certain body quality, such as jumpy, heavy, sticky, jittery, or tight. At times the body quality might best be described in words that are also the names of emotions, for example scared, shameful, or guilty. Even so it contains a whole intricacy of elements, not only what the emotion of the same name would contain. When a felt sense shifts and opens, emotions may emerge along with thoughts, perceptions, memories. . . . A felt sense often contains emotions. Thus one does not find a felt sense by avoiding or trying not to feel emotions. Rather, if there is already an emotion, one lets the wider felt sense form as something that can come with, under, or all around the emotion. (1996, p. 59)

Because both emotions and felt senses are bodily felt experiences, we may not know which one a client is having. A client who says, "It's sad, here" and puts her hand on her heart may be having a felt sense or an emotion. Luckily, being able to distinguish between the two at such a moment is unnecessary. We say, "You are sensing something in you is sad. Maybe you can be with that," and if it wasn't a felt sense before, it soon will be.

RECOGNIZING THE FELT SENSES THAT COME SPONTANEOUSLY

The most natural way to begin bringing Focusing into your clinical practice is to listen for the felt senses that are already coming in your client, and encourage them. If we listen for felt senses, and use attention and language to point to them, the results can be surprisingly facilitative. There is more than this to bringing Focusing into clinical practice, but this is a great way to begin, and can already in itself bring new steps of change.

The coming of a felt sense means that the client is in touch with his experiencing. This is a natural process. In the research that Gendlin and his colleagues did at the University of Chicago, a significant percentage of clients got felt senses naturally in therapy sessions—even in the first or second session. (And as we've seen, these tended to be the clients who ultimately benefited the most from therapy.)

With many of your clients, you won't need to do anything to encourage felt senses to come. Listening for the felt senses that come naturally is the best way to begin to tune your awareness to the Focusing process in therapy.

What are some of the indicators?

- Slowing speech, going quiet
- Looking down
- Groping for words, being suddenly inarticulate, saying "this is hard to put into words"
- Gesturing toward the middle of the body
- Using words like "kind of" or "something" or "here"

For example: "It's here . . ." (waving toward chest) "but I don't know how to say it. It's like . . . I don't know. . . ."

When this kind of inarticulacy is embedded in a longer sequence, it can be tempting to steer around it and respond only to the part of what the client said that is clear. You may even feel like you're helping the client by doing so. But once you realize the potential richness that felt senses hold, you'll want to help your clients stay with them. Steering someone away from the emerging, at-first-unclear felt sense isn't helping, it's avoiding.

Even without our "help," clients may steer themselves away from their own felt senses. We need to be ready to help them stay awhile.

THE TEMPTATION TO IGNORE FELT SENSES

Felt senses are subtle, and we're not used to paying attention to them. Many other things happen that are not felt senses, and if we only encourage those things, felt senses get lost. Clients may ruminate, analyze, speculate, tell stories repetitively—and it's very tempting to join them. A therapist who isn't aware of the importance of the implicit dimension can inadvertently direct the client away from these spontaneous felt senses.

> C: I don't know why I can't do it. I think it's my fear of failure. Actually . . . it's funny, but when I say that I get a bit choked up, like there's something tightening up in my throat. . . . It's hard to describe . . . um. . . .
> T: So you think it's your fear of failure.

Clunk. This therapist just led the client away from something, vague but potentially rich, toward the safe, known territory of fixed concepts. It's as if at some level the therapist was feeling, "The vague bodily unknown is unsafe. Let's go back to the nice safe analytical category." If we can't stand the uncertainty of clients staying a while with something they're feeling that's hard to describe, naturally we're going to pull them back to something more certain and clear.

What could this therapist have done instead? How about murmuring, "Something there in your throat . . . feels like tightening." And if needed: "Maybe stay a bit longer, just feeling that."

> C: I don't know why I can't do it. I think it's my fear of failure. Actually . . . it's funny, but when I say that I get a bit choked

up, like there's something tightening up in my throat. . . . It's hard to describe . . . um. . . .

T: [softly] Something there in your throat . . . feels like tightening. [Pause.] Maybe stay a bit longer, just feeling that.

C: Yes . . . it's like there's a hand there, cutting off my breathing. . . . No, not completely cutting it off, just constricting it. . . . Funny, it's almost like there's a leash around my neck!

T: That brings a note of surprise, when you feel it's like a leash around your neck.

C: Like there's a part of me saying, "Keep it in bounds. Don't go too far." Wow, I didn't know that was there!

In Chapter 6 we'll look at how a session like this might go further. But clearly there is already a further process, taking this client to a fresher place than just "I think it's my fear of failure."

Recognizing the implicit dimension is revolutionary; our usual assumptions are turned on their heads. Slow is good. Not being able to speak quickly means we're in touch with something profound and potentially transformational. Paradoxically, the more we slow down, the faster we get to the source of change. Slow is the new fast.

But our clients don't know this yet. Often a client will apologize for not being able to articulate something clearly. Growing up in our fast-paced culture that emphasizes speed and precision, we've all been taught that speaking slowly and being inarticulate, groping for words, is a bad thing, a sign of stupidity. "Slow" is used as a polite synonym for "stupid." Kids in school are encouraged to have the answer quickly, and the one with the hand up first is the winner.

It's up to us to reassure our clients that experiencing something that is hard to describe is actually a good thing. A client may say, "I'm sorry—I can't describe this thing I'm feeling," as if this means there is something wrong. We can say, "That's all right. Take your time. Not being able to describe something is actually a good sign. It can mean that you're at the edge of new integration emerging. Let's just take our time."

Your confidence that something valuable can emerge from an unclear, vague feeling supports your client in having the patience to stay with the unclear feeling long enough that something more clear can begin to emerge.

THE THERAPIST'S OWN FELT SENSING

Perhaps this is the moment to reiterate a crucial point from the previous chapter: In order to effectively bring Focusing into psychotherapy, therapists need to be Focusing, themselves. "In order to have a Focusing-oriented therapy, it is necessary for the therapist to know Focusing, not the client" (Preston, 2005, p. 4).

As I sit with a client, I have my own felt sensing with me, and it speaks to me of this client because we share one interaction. My own felt sensing, when I am with a client, becomes a grounded, genuine source for my responses and my interventions. If the client happens to ask me a direct question, I have my access to my self ready. I can, as Gendlin says, "go in there and see something" (1990, p. 205). Much more often, though, my felt sensing is simply a way to have "how I am," my presence with this person, without any need to give it primary attention.

I say a great deal more about this in Chapter 10, but it helps to keep it in mind all the way through the book.

THE POWER OF ATTENTIVE SILENCE
AND UNPRESSURED CONTACT

If you could peer through a one-way mirror into the session room of a clinician using Focusing and listen in, what would be different about it? What would let you know that Focusing was being incorporated? One big clue would be the times of silence. In silences, clients can take time to feel what is here for them now. Clients who look down or look away may be doing so in order to gather a sense of something not easy to put into words. Clinicians who are familiar with Focusing are comfortable allowing these silences, though of course there are other times when the client needs the contact of the therapist speaking.

A therapist I interviewed for this book told me:

When I was starting out, my timing for intervening with clients was completely the opposite of what it should have been. I got excited when I could tell the client was at the edge of something, and came in with my "helpful" ideas. Those were exactly the times when I should have been quiet! Now it's when nothing much is happening that I feel free to say things, to stir up something. But when the client gets close to an edge, I stay close too, but I don't say anything unless they start to move away from there.

Clients who grope for words, or who trail off at the end of a sentence, may be just about to get a felt sense, and may need our attentive, silent, contactful presence as an encouragement to stay there long enough to allow the felt sense to form.

We can do all sorts of things to help a felt sense come—as we will see in Chapter 4. But when the client is already in touch with a felt sense, the ideal move appears to be very little—perhaps being attentively silent, perhaps just a kind of saying back that points to the felt sense. The art is in doing just enough—because it's easy to overdo, and overdoing can lead to setbacks.

Felt senses are delicate. Think of the emergence of a new green shoot in a garden on the first day of spring. Something fresh and alive is surely growing there, but it is too early to know what it will become or whether it is worthwhile. The client can easily be distracted, taken away by his or her own thoughts, or can even stomp on that delicate fresh life with judgmental reactions. I talk about what to do if that happens in Chapter 7. But the kind of responding I am talking about will tend to prevent self-critical or dismissing thoughts from happening.

For Focusing to happen well, an inner contact needs to be supported, the contact of the client with his or her own felt experiencing. This inner contact happens within the context of the interpersonal contact, the relationship between therapist and client. If the relationship between therapist and client is not experienced by the client as safe, it will be unlikely that the client can have an empowering inner relationship.

All this may seem obvious, but what may not be so obvious is that the language forms we use with our clients have an impact on the perceived safety of the interpersonal space. We may have the highest respect for the client and the greatest wish for the client to exercise autonomy, but if we ask too many questions or give too many suggestions, the client's sense of safety and empowerment will be that much more compromised. The best of intentions can be undermined unintentionally by our way of speaking.

In the pages that follow, I demonstrate a kind of therapist state-ment that I call an "empathic prompt." Because it is a statement (not a question or a suggestion), and because it simply points to the cli-ent's experience without trying to change that experience, this em-pathic prompt is minimal. It's the least we can do.

If the minimal doesn't work, we can increase the strength of our intervention, next offering a "cushioned suggestion." It will be rec-ommended that questions not be used at all, except in very rare cases.

The empathic prompt implies an invitation, but does not make the invitation explicit:

C: There's this funny kind of squeezing in my chest as I talk about her. . . . I guess I miss her.

T: Right there in your chest . . . a funny kind of squeezing.

In this instance the therapist did not say, "Maybe you could stay with that." The invitation to stay longer and keep awareness with the "funny kind of squeezing" was implied. In general, this is preferable, because giving a suggestion to a client can bring up other issues. All of us are sensitive to being told what to do, and some clients are more so.

An explicit invitation may be needed. I discuss how to do that below. Valuing the minimal, we'll offer the empathic prompt first, and use a stronger mode only if necessary. The empathic prompt provides contact without pressure or expectation, and gently points to the felt sense. The gentleness of the empathic prompt translates into the client's own gentleness toward his or her own felt experi-ence.

C: It's vague but I'm sensing it right here in my throat, something kind of constricted, kind of scared.

T: You're sensing something there . . . kind of constricted . . . kind of scared.

Yes, we are saying back the client's words. It sounds a lot like em-pathic reflection or active listening, which has a long and honorable history within therapeutic settings—but it's not exactly the same. There is a key difference. The empathic prompt points specifically toward the felt sense and is intended as a supportive invitation to stay with what is presently felt. The purpose of the empathic prompt is not simply or primarily to show we understand, but to support the client in staying with the felt experience, and in checking whether the descriptions fit it well.

There is one particular word that we often use to form a powerful empathic prompt—"something," the most facilitative word I know.

"SOMETHING"—MY FAVORITE WORD

From my long study of *facilitative language*—the language that facilitates process—I am convinced that the most facilitative word in any language is "something." This word allows the client to have an experience without labeling it, keeping contact with a felt experience with an open quality of awareness—just what we need for Focusing.

"I feel something."

"Something is here."

In the following example, the client is shaking her head, as if she feels nothing. But of course she doesn't feel nothing, she feels something.

C: I don't know what I'm feeling in my throat.

Notice how the response with "something" shifts the possibilities for the client.

T: You're feeling *something* in your throat.

Compare a literal reflection: "You don't know what you're feeling in your throat." If you were that client, which response would be more likely to enable you to stay with the feeling in your throat?

The word "something" helps support the client in staying with an experience that is hard to describe—in other words, a felt sense.

C: In my belly, it's like it's . . . like it's empty, there.

T: There's *something* there in the belly, something you're feeling, like "empty."

Compare this therapist response to a more literal reflection: "In your belly, it's empty," or "You're feeling emptiness in your belly." Do you sense the difference? The word "something" holds the implication that the word "empty" might be just the beginning, there might be more coming from that place. This is just what Focusing is about. We want to encourage an inner contact with an experience that is more than its descriptions.

HOW DESCRIPTIONS FACILITATE CONTACT WITH "MORE"

When a client is in touch with a felt sense, descriptions naturally arise:

- "There's this little hard place in my chest, like a kid saying no."
- "I'm feeling . . . it's hard to describe . . . kind of a wall inside."
- "Like there's something tightening up in my throat . . ."
- "There's this funny kind of squeezing in my chest as I talk about her . . ."
- Something kind of constricted, kind of scared."
- "In my belly, it's like it's . . . like it's empty, there."

The descriptions that come are important. But what is also important is that these first descriptions are only the doorway. There is more. It is the nature of a felt sense that the person can feel there is more to it than the first descriptions. You can tell this from how often people use phrases like "kind of," "sort of," "funny," "odd"— and of course our favorite word, "something." There is often a quality of groping for words, with hesitations in the voice as the client reaches for a description that is elusive.

Using the empathic prompt, we offer back to the client the words and descriptions that have come. We use the word "something" even when the client doesn't, holding open the possibility that while this description is the starting place, there is more.

T: "There's *something* there in the belly, something you're feeling, like 'empty.'"

Notice how the empathic prompt has an invitational quality, as we've mentioned before; like holding a door open without pushing the person through it. In contrast, I would not recommend asking a question here. Asking a question such as, "What other word would describe it?" is pushy, abrupt, and takes people into the head and away from the body. It also doesn't welcome the description that did come, implying that the person has to come up with something else.

Let's appreciate how the empathic prompt, which is neither a question nor a suggestion—it's simply a statement—offers support and acceptance for the description that came, while holding open a door for the likelihood that there is more to come. Saying the client's descriptive words last is also helpful.

> C: There's this funny kind of squeezing in my chest as I talk about her. . . .
> T: There's something there in your chest as you talk about her . . . a funny kind of squeezing. . . .

THE CLIENT CHECKS HIS OR HER OWN WORDS INWARDLY

After the client has a felt sense, and we support the client with an empathic prompt to stay with that felt sense, next we want the client to check his or her words inwardly, to offer the descriptive words to the felt experience and sense if they fit. The second function of the empathic prompt is to encourage that checking.

> Recall that the Focusing approach works in a back-and-forth fashion. When a "content" such as a word or image emerges from the body you don't automatically accept this symbolization as an accurate fit with what the body knows. Rather the therapist invites the client to "pause" and check the words back with the body. . . . If there is not a "fit" then the therapist invites the client to try another word, gesture, or image. . . . When there is not this "fit," and the client continues to talk, the body process shuts down. (Grindler Katonah, in press)

The first words that came are not necessarily right, because the felt sense has more to it than any particular words, and because the felt sense is in process, not static. At first, clients may not understand that we are really asking them to check inwardly. We know we're doing well when the client tells us that his or her own words don't actually fit.

C: As I talk about her, I'm starting to get this constricted feeling in my throat.

T: You're sensing something there in your throat as you talk about her, something like constricted.

C: No, it's not exactly constricted. . . . Um . . . it feels like the word "tight" fits better.

Isn't that nice? Imagine what would be going on in that client, for him to say such a thing: "No, it's not exactly constricted." There has to be a direct, ongoing contact with that inner experience in the throat. The client has to be sensing the throat feeling, checking whether or how well the word "constricted" fits it. He finds that the word "tight" fits better. The therapist then supports this:

T: You're trying out the word "tight." . . . The word "tight" fits better.

This might be a good place to mention another important feature of the empathic prompt: When we repeat the client's descriptive words, we leave them unchanged. "Tight" is returned as "tight," not "tightness." "Heavy" is said back as "heavy," not "heaviness." I say more in Chapter 4 about why adjectives are significantly more facilitative than nouns, but for now the key point is not to change the word, even to another form of the same word.

> What do we assume the client will do with a listening response? We hope and assume that clients will check the response, not against what they said or thought, but against some inner being, place, datum . . . "the felt sense"; we have no ordinary word for that. An effect might then be felt, an inward loosening, a resonance. What seemed to be there was expressed and heard. It need not be said again. For some moments there is an easing inside. . . . Soon something further comes. What was there turns out to have more to it. We hope that clients will check not only what we say, but also what they say, against that inward one. (Gendlin, 1984, p. 82)

As we've seen in Chapter 1, a felt sense is a doorway into the implicit dimension, where the next steps of organismic life process are ready to come. The next life steps for the person are present implicitly, as potential, as a kind of "readiness." When the next life steps do come, we call this "carrying forward."

What is needed for the felt sense to carry forward is contact, a kind of steady, nonjudgmental awareness. Basically this is what Focusing is: finding felt senses, and then being with them with this nonpushing contact. Helping your clients do Focusing means helping your clients maintain this kind of inner contact. "What that [felt sense] needs to produce the steps is only some kind of unintrusive contact or company. If you will go there with your awareness and stay there or return there, that is all it needs; it will do all the rest for you" (Gendlin, 1990, p. 216).

The Empathic Prompt

The empathic prompt functions to:

- Identify the felt sense as something worth staying with
- Encourage the client to stay with the felt sense
- Stay close to the client's process; offer contact without intrusion
- Offer the client the felt sense description so he or she can check inside if it fits

The empathic prompt is formed by:

- Using the client's own words, the emotional or bodily sensed or metaphorical words; leaving descriptive words unchanged
- Adding the word "something" to point to the place where that experience is directly sensed
- Putting the client's descriptive words last
- No explicit suggestion or invitation

ON NOT TELLING YOUR CLIENTS ABOUT FELT SENSES

In the last chapter I suggested that we might or might not explain Focusing to clients. But even if you do introduce Focusing as a named process, it's probably not a good idea to talk about the concept of a felt sense. The concept of a felt sense as a freshly forming process of life already moving forward is an exciting one. It underlies the whole notion of facilitating Focusing in our clients. But it generally doesn't help to try to explain that to a client. From the client's point of view, the phrase "felt sense" is jargon, something strange to worry about, leading to self-questioning and worse. "Do I have a felt sense? Am I doing it right? Is this feeling a good-enough felt sense?" These are generally not helpful questions.

For this reason, I'd suggest never using the term "felt sense" with a client, saying instead, for example, "the whole feel of that," or "the whole way that sits in you now." We will see more in Chapter 4 about how to invite felt senses. When a felt sense is already present, as discussed in this chapter, we simply refer to it using the client's own descriptions.

In this chapter we've been dealing with how to nourish and encourage the felt senses that are already emerging in our clients. But not all clients get felt senses naturally. In fact, many clients need help to allow felt senses to form. We'll look at how to facilitate this in the next chapter.

Chapter 4

HELPING CLIENTS TO GET FELT SENSES

In Chapter 3 we showed how to notice the felt senses that arise spontaneously, to nourish and support them with our attentive presence and with empathic prompts. But many clients do not get felt senses spontaneously—and they are the ones most in need of some kind of intervention. Clients who get felt senses spontaneously are likely to do well in any kind of therapy, as the research showed (Gendlin et al., 1968; Hendricks 2001). One psychotherapist described a client's process, pre-Focusing, in this way: "I felt she was always circling around her issues but never really going in."

In this chapter I discuss how to invite, evoke, and otherwise support clients in getting felt senses. The moves that this will involve—slowing down, pausing, sensing inwardly—may be challenging for some clients, or at least quite new. But they can bring a significant shift in the client's whole manner of process and her ability to be present for her own experiencing, and thus for the forming of felt senses, which are themselves the forward movement that was previously there only in potential.

PAUSING, SLOWING DOWN

Sometimes you get the impression that your client is barreling along, speaking too quickly for there to be any space for feeling. I wouldn't call this speeding along "wrong"—sometimes it's exactly what the client needs to be doing, and for a sense of safety and rapport it wouldn't be good to give the impression that he shouldn't be doing it. Yet for a deeper process to happen he is going to need, at some point, to pause and slow down. The art is in the invitation—and the timing.

Facilitating a client to pause or slow down can be a powerful intervention when done with the right timing. *Pausing* is a gentle yet powerful interruption in the culturally set emotional and intellectual momentum that takes clients down repetitive pathways. *Slowing down* allows clients to become aware of experiences they may have been ignoring, while at the same time increasing clients' sense of safety so that previously ignored experiences are less likely to be frightening when they do emerge.

Psychotherapist Lauren Mari-Navarro told me how valuable she has found this aspect of Focusing:

> I notice that the "speedy" client, one who may be involved in telling the same repeating story, describing it quickly and with a worried or desperate tone, begins to shift in moments after being invited to a Focusing process. She becomes contemplative, her speech naturally slows, and she can listen from a reflective and curious place. Even her body looks completely different. A relaxed attentiveness comes, rather than a vigilant rigid body posture. This client doesn't seem to be the same person that walked through the door! The material that moments before appeared hopeless and chaotic is now taking on the quality of a deep and interesting conversation within the person. Fresh information is coming now, not the "same old same old" that the client has heard herself say far too many times without effecting meaningful change and a movement forward. This is exciting to the client to have newly emerging information about her situation for the first time, and it feels good to me as a therapist to have provided a container for something new and "life forwarding" to come. Pausing and slowing down are what got us there.

Pausing and turning toward one's own felt experiencing is key in the forming of felt senses. A client caught up in repetitive thoughts or emotions can be facilitated to slow down and make an inviting space for something new to come. But I wouldn't recommend saying, "Slow down." Let's look at four subtle interventions that have the effect of helping the client slow down and sense inwardly without implying that anything "wrong" is happening. They are: "I need a moment," inviting a moment of silence, the minimal empathic prompt, and inviting the felt sense directly.

"I Need a Moment . . ."

Perhaps the most genuine and effective way to support a client in slowing down is through our own slowing down. When we are in touch with our own bodily felt experience as we are sitting with the client, a slower way of speaking emerges naturally, not as a technique but simply as how we are. When we speak slowly, because of this Focusing type of inner awareness, this forms a natural invitation to the client to slow down as well.

When we are in this inner-body awareness and a client is speaking rapidly, out of a sense of inner pressure, we are likely to register that as a felt experience in ourselves—of pressure or tension, for example. Not immediately, but as this experience continues for a while, we might find ourselves saying, "Wait . . . I need a moment to take in what you are saying." Or: "Hold on. . . . What you are saying sounds important, I need to pause and digest it for a bit."

In saying this kind of thing, we are modeling and demonstrating slowing down and pausing. Furthermore, in speaking from our own need for a pause, we are less likely to be experienced by the client as saying he did something wrong. Of course we need to be telling the truth, and speak this way only if we do need a moment to take in what the client is saying. The genuineness helps the relationship. In the intersubjective field, if we are needing a pause, chances are the client is needing one, too.

There is more about the therapist's own inner sensing in the clinical setting in Chapter 10.

A Moment of Silence

If a client is speeding along, we could invite awareness to the speediness. But it could be an even better idea for the client herself to become aware of it.

A client came in one day carrying notes on her agenda for the session, speaking rapidly with her eye on the clock, saying, "I know we don't have much time to get all this taken care of." The therapist said to her, "Maybe this would be a good day to start with a moment of silence." It was a bit difficult for the client to make this shift, but her previously established relationship with the therapist allowed a trust in the invitation. They had had moments of silence in previous sessions. It was understood that the client would close her eyes and sense for a moment—but no special instructions were given otherwise.

After a moment of silence, with her eyes still closed, the client said slowly, "There is this speeding away from what I don't want to feel." The therapist responded, "Ah, you're sensing this speeding away. . . ." They were able to spend the rest of the session being with this "speeding away" and then touching safely on what the client was not wanting to feel, in a richly productive session.

Any clinician might have guessed or intuited that avoidance is what was happening, when the client started the session in such a rushing state. But how many other interventions would have taken the client so quickly to discovering that for herself?

The Minimal Empathic Prompt

Often the client is close to having a felt sense, but isn't quite there yet. There may be a gesture, a mood, a readiness to feel, that the clinician can sense, even if the client isn't quite aware of it yet. In these instances, we can use the empathic prompt described in Chapter 3 to point to what could form—and this facilitates the felt sense forming. The minimal quality of the empathic prompt allows the least interruption in the client's process, and the least likelihood that the client will be distracted by wondering what we are asking him or her to do.

C: Would you believe? He never even called me! After all of that agonizing over what I would say. Oh, boy.
T: There's a whole thing there, he never even called you. . . . Those words, "oh, boy," and your head shakes. Some whole way that feels right now.
C: Like all the air is let out of me. I feel like . . . yeah, like a punctured balloon. Huh. I didn't know that!

The therapist's phrase "Some whole way that feels right now" functions as an invitation. The fact that it is a statement—not a question or suggestion—enables it to enter the client's frame of reference with the least possible interruption. It is not "How does that feel right now?" or even "Notice how that feels right now." I recommend the statement formulation whenever possible, because for the client, it is as if you, the therapist, didn't do anything. You are close to him, and his process flows forward. The attention is on his inner felt experience emerging in the context of the supportive, interested attention that you offer.

That example shows this process working smoothly. The client takes the empathic prompt as an invitation to turn toward "some whole way that feels right now" and sense it. There is no guarantee—the client could have just gone on "talking about" instead of "sensing into." But at least the therapist hasn't caused any interruptions in the smooth flow of interpersonal contact.

Compare the intervention "How does that feel in your body?" used in a case like this. Yes, it works with some people, sometimes. But many others will be puzzled, confused, interrupted, thrown into a state of questioning (e.g., "What am I supposed to be doing? What does my therapist expect of me?"). The minimal empathic prompt is preferable—it works more often, and more smoothly, to invite the client into a fresh contact with what is emerging.

Inviting the Felt Sense Directly

In addition to modeling a need for pausing, suggesting a moment of silence, and using a minimal empathic prompt, we can also invite a felt sense directly. But we can't just say, "Now get a felt sense"— even with a client trained in Focusing, that does not work very well. There are subtly effective ways to invite felt senses that never mention the phrase "felt sense." Here are some examples:

- "Maybe there is a whole way that feels right now."
- "This might be a moment just to sense how all that sits in you now."
- "How about just pausing right now and sensing how the whole of that feels."

Timing is important, of course. The perfect phrase offered at the wrong time falls as flat as if it had been the wrong phrase. There is a rhythm to the client's process in the room with you, and with practice and attunement (including your own inner awareness), you will be able to sense the client's openness to an invitation from you. This may come after the client feels that her story and her feelings have been heard, or after one of the invitations to pause we looked at earlier. There may even be an explicit request from the client.

> C: I don't know—I feel like I'm going around in circles. What can I do differently?
> T: How about just pausing right now and sensing how the whole of it feels, all that you've been saying. There's a whole feel to all of it.
> C: Yes. . . . It's like there's this big cliff, and I keep scrambling and scrambling to climb it.
> T: Ah . . . like a big cliff . . . and you are scrambling to climb it.

INVITATIONS TO STAY LONGER AND TO CHECK INWARDLY

Fairly often, even after a felt sense appears, the client doesn't stay with it. This is understandable: Felt senses are odd and murky, and it seems unlikely that anything very promising will happen just from staying with them. This is where we come in. Our confidence that staying with a felt sense will lead somewhere conveys itself to the client. We can offer gentle verbal invitations, both explicitly and with tone of voice.

The empathic prompt, with "something," already implies an invitation to stay longer and sense further. This is supported by a lingering tone of voice, stretching out the word "something" and any descriptive words. We can add a few words of invitation to stay and sense, cushioned by a word like "maybe" so that this is nothing like a command.

- "You're sensing something there . . . something heavy and sad. . . . Maybe stay a bit longer there."
- "There's a place in your chest . . . like a kid saying no. . . . Maybe you can be with that for a while. . . ."

Encouraging the client to check his or her words inwardly also functions as an invitation to stay longer. In order to check, we have to stay longer. Checking whether a description fits brings the person into more immediate contact with the experience.

- "You're sensing something there . . . something heavy and sad. . . . Maybe check if those words fit the best how it feels in there . . . heavy . . . sad. . . ."

If clients don't check inwardly, just from hearing the empathic prompt, we can facilitate the checking. This might be needed with new clients fairly often. In most cases, they quickly learn to do it themselves.

- "I'm going to say those words back to you, so you can sense if they fit how that feels, or if other words fit even better."

RETURNING TO (NOT GOING PAST) SOMETHING IMMEDIATELY FELT

When a client seems to be turning away from or avoiding a felt sense or any kind of felt experience, the therapist can speak up for what is being passed over, as a kind of advocate for it. We are gently inviting a return to something that was felt or mentioned a moment before, rather than just following the momentum of the client's discourse.

C: There's a kind of dark, heavy sadness in my chest. . . . I can't describe it very well. . . . My boyfriend keeps telling me what I need is to just get my life together, just think in a different way. I don't know—I guess I should, but it's something I've tried before, and he keeps telling me to try again . . . [questioning look at therapist].

T: I'm kind of still with that dark heavy sadness you were mentioning. . . . That sounded important and very real. I'm wondering if that's still there, in your chest. . . .

In the example just given, the client moves away from what sounds like a felt sense after stating that she can't describe it very well. This

69

could just be a matter of not knowing that staying with a felt sense can be a rich experience. The therapist's encouragement to return to it and stay with it could be all that she needs.

But if the client is aware of wanting to move away from a certain emotional experience, this is another matter.

> C: There's a kind of dark, heavy sadness in my chest. . . . I don't want to go in there.

In this case, we would not ignore or take sides against the part of the client that doesn't want "to go in there."

> T: You're sensing something in your chest that feels sad . . . and you're sensing something not wanting to go in there. . . . Let's just sit here together, saying Hi to both, and not going in. . . .

"Not going in" doesn't mean not getting a felt sense. Actually, getting a felt sense is facilitated by not going right into the center of emotional content. So when a client expresses a concern or a reluctance about getting into something that could be "too much," we can totally respect that wish, and still do the key work that is needed. This is one of the reasons that working in a Focusing-oriented way is a powerful method for supporting recovery from trauma.

I'll say more in Chapter 7 about "resistance," and in Chapter 8 about trauma.

BEING A "PRESENT-EXPERIENCE DETECTIVE"

There is a way that people speak when they are talking about what they feel right now, and there is a similar way of speaking about what they feel habitually or usually—not necessarily right now. Though the two modes are similar, if you listen carefully, you can hear the difference. In listening to my clients, I try to be a "present-experience detective," using clues that include the form of language to give me an idea whether the client is describing a present experience or recounting a past one.

Sometimes people seem to be speaking from a presently felt experience, but are actually speaking in a general way, about something they "usually" or "always" feel in certain situations. There is a verb tense in English that indicates this kind of non–present time "habitual" experience. Paradoxically, this verb tense is called "simple present"—but it does not actually mean that something is happening in the present, rather that something is being done habitually.

In each of these pairs of sentences, notice that only the second sentence refers to something necessarily experienced in the present moment.

- "I get tired in the evenings."—"I am tired."
- "I get angry when I think about how little he cared about me."—"I am angry."
- "I worry."—"I am worried."

When you hear something that makes you suspect that a person is not having the feeling currently, you can invite the current feeling.

C: I get this burning in my stomach. I know it's about how angry I am at my parents.

T: And you might sense if you are feeling burning in your stomach right now.

C: [pausing] Actually right now my stomach is feeling more of an ache.

T: Ah . . . so see if it is okay to just be with the ache there, in your stomach right now.

BRINGING IN THE BODY

For many clients (not all), getting a felt sense is facilitated by adding body awareness to an issue that is being discussed. Once a client has been talking for a while about something of importance, he is likely to be able to get a felt sense of that issue, if invited. Bringing in the body can help.

C: My son has been through so many procedures, and some of them are painful. He's awfully brave about it, but it just kills me that he has to go through all this. I know it's not logical, but I keep thinking it's my fault somehow.

T: Yes, you see him going through all that, and you've got the feeling, somehow that's your own fault.

C: [sighs] Yeah.

T: I'm wondering . . . maybe take some time to sense how that's feeling in your body right now.

C: [pauses] It's like there's this heavy weight in my heart.

When Clients Have Trouble Feeling in the Body

A woman in one of my training programs told me that her therapist had often asked her, as they talked about some issue, "How does that feel in your body?" She didn't know—she didn't have any body feeling that she was aware of. When she asked her therapist to explain further, the therapist responded, "I'm not sure. I really need to learn more about Focusing myself."[1]

People who know a little bit about the Focusing process may have tried incorporating the following move into their clinical practice: "Notice how that feels in your body," or "How does that feel in your body?" But when clients respond, "I don't know," or "nothing"—or even more typically, continue on a familiar track of ruminating or storytelling—they haven't known what to do next.

Especially problematic is the question form—"How does that feel in your body?"—because it implies that the body feeling is already there, just waiting to have attention brought to it (see below for more about problems with questions). This may very well not be the case, since felt senses form, and also since the word "body" may point the client to a physiological experience rather than an emotional one (see next section).

You can help your clients come into body awareness (see Chapter 7), and you can also leave the word "body" out of your invitations to some people (see next section). You can use cushioned suggestions rather than questions. You can use your own self as an example: "For instance, right now, as we're sitting here, I'm aware of a slight tightness in my throat."

---

1. I applaud that therapist for her honesty and genuineness.

A Note on Using the Word "Body"

Let's be sensitive to the possibility that the word "body" may be distracting or confusing to our clients. Luckily, we do not have to use the word "body" in order to invite felt senses to form.

One problem with the word "body" is that people tend to think you mean the physiological body. You might hear: "Well, I don't feel anything in my body, but there is a little girl curled up in a ball . . ." Clearly, this person has a felt sense, but doesn't associate the "little girl curled up in a ball" with "the body." Or you may hear: "It's not in my body but there is kind of this uneasy jittery quality." In these instances we are lucky. The person has told us what she does experience. But quite often, after an invitation to feel in the body, we will just hear, "I'm not getting anything," or "I guess I don't know how to do this." This is usually because the invitation to feel in the body has come up against the assumption that "body" is physiology—muscles, organs, blood, and bones. What we mean by "body" in Focusing is not physiology, but the lived-from organism felt from the inside. We don't want to have to explain all this, so for some clients it may be easier just to not use the word "body."

Another big problem with the word "body" is that for some of our clients the word itself may bring up body image issues and negative feelings about the body. Instead of a felt sense, they may get reactive states of self-disgust or body image evaluations such as "my body just feels fat." Other clients may have trauma associated with the body. Focusing can be a powerful process for resolving trauma (see Chapter 8) partly because the client has choice about how much to feel in the body, and control over the pace of the inner sensing. We may find that avoiding using the word "body" with traumatized clients is indicated as a way to help them have the self-paced experience that will be most helpful.

Felt sense invitations without the word "body" include: "Notice how that feels for you now," "Notice what comes about that," "Take some time to sense the whole way that sits in you now," "Take some time to get the whole feel of that."

I am not suggesting that we drop the word "body." Just as some clients are not helped by the word "body," other clients need to hear it. See the discussion of "the intellectualizing client" in Chapter 7 for a good example of this kind of client. What is needed is to not fall into a routine of using the word "body" or saying "Notice how that feels in your body" with every client, but rather following a sensitive, moment-by-moment assessment of what this client needs and what will facilitate her process—or not.

HELPING FELT SENSES EMERGE FROM STORIES: "SOMETHING ABOUT"

Of course clients tell us their stories. They tell us the stories of what brought them to therapy, what happened to them long ago, and what happened in the past week. They may tell their stories eagerly, or reluctantly, or with a roll of the eyes as if something in them is saying, "Do I have to tell this again?" Stories connect us with our clients, and for clients, the way we receive their stories can greatly enhance their experience of safety in the therapeutic relationship.

Some clients seem compelled to tell stories, as if every real moment of contact in the present leads instead to a story, and the therapist may become frustrated in attempts to discover the point or the emotional meaning as every story seems to lead to another. A client telling a story, looking at you, speaking at normal speed, is probably not having a felt sense at that moment, even if there is emotion in the telling. (Remember, just because someone is feeling an emotion doesn't mean that person has a felt sense.)

For other clients, stories lead to tears, and there is so much emotion pouring forth that one wonders if the emotion is the point or if it is another way to avoid real contact.

Clients who tell stories about past events, with or without emotion, can be invited to get the felt sense of the story—and there is helpful language for doing this in a way that honors and includes the impulse behind telling the story. We don't need the client to shift away from the story and feel in the body "instead." Rather, we can invite the felt sense of the story with language so simple and transparent that the client moves smoothly into the felt sense of the story.

The key phrase is "something about . . ." with the words stretched out as an invitation to sense more, right there.

C: So by the end of the day, she still hadn't called me, and I was calling everybody else, all her friends. . . . I didn't get any of my work done. A wasted day, totally wasted.

T: Yeah, a whole day, wasted for you, calling everybody and waiting for her to call you. There was *something about* her not calling you that brought all that for you. Maybe wait a bit right there, feeling that . . . [In addition to the phrase "something about," the therapist offers a gentle invitation to pause and feel what is here now.]

C: [pauses] I felt so helpless. Like I was the baby instead of the mom. [The client's pause is an indicator that something fresh and immediate is happening in process, not just something the client has already formulated.]

T: And maybe some of that is there right now . . . [Since the client uses past tense in describing her feeling, the therapist gently invites attention to the here-and-now experience.]

C: [hand moves to chest, voice chokes up] It's here.

T: Yes . . . and your hand goes there. . . . Maybe you can stay with that a while. . . .

STARTING WITH EMOTIONS

When a client reports feeling an emotion, especially without a story or life issue connected to it, inviting a felt sense from there can bring forward movement. In the case of someone already feeling an emotion, inviting a sense of "where" it is felt usually works well.

C: I just feel terribly fearful today. I don't even know why.

T: You're aware of feeling terribly fearful today. That sounds hard to be going through. [Almost always, we connect empathically first, and wait to find out if there is an openness for a further invitation.]

C: And I don't know what this is about. It could be about lots of things, but I don't know.

It is probably not helpful to reflect "you don't know" to a client. One could say instead, "You'd like to know," or "you're wanting to know." In this case though, the therapist sensed that the client was implicitly asking for some help to feel into the "terribly fearful" experience, to feel it as a felt sense so it could open and change.

> T: You might want to take some time to sense where or how you have that "terribly fearful" feeling right now.
>
> C: [pausing] It's in my shoulders, my upper chest, my throat. Like this . . . clenching. Like something in me is gripping really tightly.

In the pause, with body awareness invited, this client has been able to turn toward her felt experience and begin to get a fresh feel for it. Having started with "terribly fearful—I don't know what it's about," we are now in an inner contact with "something in me is gripping really tightly." We can already sense how this client will be able to stay with "something gripping tightly" and feel what it is gripping in reaction to. (We'll see more about how to facilitate these next steps in Chapter 6.)

Sometimes the invitation to sense "where" brings back the answer, "all over" or "in my whole body." In these cases I have found it helpful to invite a sense of "where you are feeling it the most" or "where you feel the center of it."

The Problem with Nouns

Clients who describe their emotional experience with nouns (e.g., "I'm feeling a lot of fear," "There's a lot of anger here") can have a harder time getting a felt sense than if they used adjectives. This seems to be due to the reification imposed by nouns, the implication being that this emotion is an object or a thing that is something to manipulate rather than something that is itself a process. For example, "I'm feeling a lot of fear (anger)" is so easily followed by "I need to get rid of my fear (anger)." When we respond to the nouns that our clients use with adjectives instead, we support clients in forming a relationship of curiosity with felt experience, and we make it more likely that this emotional state will be experienced as a felt sense.

> C: I'm feeling a lot of fear.
>
> T: You're sensing something in you is afraid.
>
> C: Yes . . . something in me is afraid . . . and it's here [touches throat].

T: See if it's okay to just be with that. . . .

QUESTIONING QUESTIONS

Recently I was giving a seminar to a group of psychotherapists who had been studying my approach to working with the inner critic. One woman said, "I tried what you said in your article, to have my clients ask the inner critic what it is not wanting, and they just go into their heads. Or they don't know."

I asked her, "What are you actually saying? Can you quote yourself?"

She said, "I'm saying, 'What is that critical part of you not wanting?'"

"Ah," I said. "You're asking a question. Questions can take people into their heads. Next time, try saying this: 'Maybe there is something that it is not wanting.' Can you feel the difference?" She could. The difference between "What is that critical part of you not wanting?" and "Maybe there is something that the critical part of you is not wanting" can be significant in a client's process. The second sentence is not a question, but an empathic prompt. Most people who try this exercise report that the question brings a sort of frustrated thinking process, often ending in "I don't know," whereas the empathic prompt invites a sensing process.

One of my more controversial discoveries about facilitative language is that asking a question is generally not the most helpful way to facilitate a process of inner sensing for the other person. Questions have a powerful effect, primarily to draw the other person into interpersonal interaction. If what you want is for the other person to look at you and talk to you, by all means ask a question. But if what you want is for the person to take time to sense inwardly for something not quite formed yet, asking a question is probably at odds with your goal.

Many of us are used to asking questions to invite the other person to say more. But questions are not necessarily the most facilitative way to do this, and their use in some circumstances can block avenues that would otherwise open. Asking questions can be helpful, so we are not against all questions, but they need to be used consciously, with awareness of their impact.

A young therapist told me, "I ask questions because I'm curious. I become involved in my client's story, and I want to know more." Of course it's natural and good to be interested in your clients, and there is a therapeutic benefit for the client in someone being interested in what he or she has to say. But questions may not be the best way to invite more information. For every instance in which a question opens up a conversation, there are other instances in which a question shuts a conversation down.

I became interested in questions when I was studying the branch of linguistics known as pragmatics, which is the study of how people make use of language in actual situations. Research has shown (Schegloff, 1968) that questions have a "strong" effect in conversation—they highly determine what the next person can say. I found this result intriguing. Most people assume that asking questions gives the other person more choices, yet the truth is the opposite. Questions are strong, and in the subtle world of the implicit, a question can stop a process or throw it off the tracks.

I've discovered three disadvantages to asking questions as a way of facilitating process. (For other functions, such as making interpersonal contact and gathering information, questions are fine. It is specifically when the aim is to facilitate process that questions can be problematic.)

1. Questions control, shape, and limit what the person may say in response, as shown by Schegloff's research. Because of this, questions can be experienced by the "questionee" as intrusive, or as pressure to respond, often at a level below conscious awareness.

2. Questions draw the person questioned into interpersonal contact with the questioner. There is an "I-you" process. "I am asking you . . ." You might see a client with eyes closed or lowered, sensing quietly inside . . . but then a question is asked, and the client's eyes pop open and look at you to answer. This might be what you want. It's good to know that a question functions to bring more interpersonal connection. But if what you want is for a client to stay "in," to maintain that inner contact for a while, asking a question can tend to interfere. The choice of whether to use a question or not can be based on what we hope will happen for the client.

3. Questions tend to get a certain type of response: facts the person already knows and thoughts he or she has already had. Questions invite people to open the cabinet, so to speak, of already formed concepts. A question implies "you have this ready to tell me." Because of this, people who are asked a question go to what they already know, what they have already thought or planned—or they say, "I don't know."

At this point I need to say that many fine therapists use questions, and I have witnessed and heard of very facilitative processes using them. There are ways to counterbalance some of the difficulties of questions, with tone of voice and intention. The presence of the practitioner is a very powerful frame. I am in awe of those who make questions work. But then I ask, why start with a handicap? Those same modes of voice tone, intention, and presence will support whatever we do. And if we don't use questions, we don't start with an obstacle to get over.

Asking a question as a way to facilitate process can be counterproductive because the question form tends to draw the client's awareness outward into interpersonal contact and upward into thinking.

CUSHIONED SUGGESTIONS

There is an intervention that gets the same positive results as asking questions, but without the disadvantages in terms of facilitating process. I call it the "cushioned suggestion."

A simple suggestion, without a cushion, sounds like this: "Be with that."

With a cushion (or two), it would be: "Maybe you could take time to be with that."

Question: "How does that feel in your body?" or "Can you stay with that?"

Cushioned suggestion: "Take some time to gently stay with that, keep it company, right there."

To illustrate the difference in effect between a question and a cushioned suggestion, imagine that you are speaking to your therapist about a recent incident that troubled you. You've been talking for a while, exploring the implications, and you feel you are being understood. Now the therapist says: "How are you feeling about it now?" Notice what happens. Now go back and compare instead what happens if the therapist says: "You might sense how you're feeling about it now. . . ."

Most people find a question draws them out and toward the therapist (which could be good), but it also draws them into the known and already thought-about. You'll hear a person who is asked a question say, "I think it's . . ." or "It's probably that . . ." When people are given a cushioned suggestion, they typically stay "in"—in an inner contact with something they may not have articulated before. They take a bit more time to answer, and may even be surprised by what they find. "Actually, that's funny—I'm not so bothered by it now. Huh! Who knew?"

Even with all the invitations in this chapter, some clients are still far from felt sensing. The trouble is that they are identified with a narrow, partial-self state, and they need help to shift out of that state before they can get a felt sense.

In fact the subtle dimension of the implicit cannot be contacted unless the client is disidentified from reactive states such as anger, fear, and self-criticism. A client who is caught up in (merged with) a reactive state does not have the inner spaciousness to allow a felt sense to form.

In Chapter 5 we take a look at the kinds of supportive interventions that make it more likely that a client can get felt senses instead of being caught up and merged with reactive emotional states.

Chapter 5

FOSTERING THE CLIENT'S STRONG SELF: THE ESSENTIAL ENVIRONMENT FOR FELT SENSES

People don't typically seek therapy because they're feeling calm, collected, and steady. They often arrive flooded by the very emotions that drove them to seek help in the first place. The experience of being inwardly fragile, easily knocked over by other people's emotions and flooded by one's own, can be painful and distressing. When the client is in the state of emotional overwhelm, therapy goals can be hard to achieve. She feels small, easily tossed about by life's vicissitudes, at the mercy of powerful forces much larger than herself. Or his self-worth suffers, and he becomes even more convinced that he is out of control of his own life.

People struggle for emotional regulation. "I don't want to cry" may alternate with floods of tears. "I hate my anger!" sounds like the anger is being turned on itself. A person who says, "This sadness is too much for me," or "I'm afraid my hopelessness is going to take me over" has at least some self-awareness of the struggle; others may be identified with one side or the other of these "emotion wars"—overwhelmed or shut down—without even being aware that an inner war over emotional regulation is at the heart of what they are going through.

For the work of therapy to move forward, clients need a measure of emotional regulation, and there a number of ways to accomplish this. The Focusing approach is to support the client in being identified with a stronger sense of self that we call "Self-in-Presence." In this chapter I explain what this means and show practical ways to help it happen.

There are two reasons we want our clients to be stronger in their sense of self. First, experiencing a stronger sense of self is a primary goal of therapy. Clients who have a strong sense of self have increasing ability to self-regulate emotional states, give themselves soothing in times of distress, and make wise behavioral choices instead of impulsive ones.

The second reason is that being the strong self allows the work of therapy to happen. When the client is able to *be with* his or her emotional experience and reflect on it, the causes of these emotional struggles can begin to change. If a client experiences his "self" as being small, fragile, easily breakable or broken, or even nonexistent, the work of therapy, in general, is harder to do.

For these and other reasons, effective therapy involves facilitating the client's development of a strong self. Many approaches recognize the value of supporting clients in finding this state, which is variously described as witnessing, observing, large, compassionate, spacious, content-free, and so on.

Ogden et al. connect this state with what is called "mindfulness":

> Through mindfulness of present-moment organization of experience, the client shifts from being caught up in the story and upset about her reactions to becoming curious about them (Siegel, 2007). . . . Rather than reliving the experience . . . she is learning to step back, observe, and report it. She is discovering the difference between "having" an experience and exploring the organization of that experience here and now. (2006, p. 169)

In Internal Family Systems Therapy (IFS), a highly elaborated process for working with parts or aspects of a person developed by Richard Schwartz, the core concept is "Self," which is a state of mind that has qualities of compassion, clarity, curiosity, and calm. Schwartz emphasizes that in his view this Self is not a passive, nonjudgmental observer or witness, but rather an "active, compassionate leader" (1995, p. 37).

The Self is relaxed, open, and accepting of yourself and others. When you are in Self, you are grounded, centered, and non-reactive. You don't get triggered by what people do. You remain calm and unruffled, even in difficult circumstances. The Self is so much larger and more spacious than our parts and is not frightened by events that would scare them. The Self has the strength and clarity to function well in the world and connect with other people. When you are in Self, you come from a depth of compassion, enabling you to be loving and caring toward others as well as yourself and your parts. (Earley, 2012, p. 26)

In Acceptance and Commitment Therapy (ACT), a similar concept is known as "self-as-context":

Self-as-context is not a thought or a feeling but a "viewpoint" from which we can observe thoughts and feelings, and a "space" in which those thoughts and feelings can move. We access this "psychological space" through noticing that we are noticing, or becoming conscious of our own consciousness. It is a "place" from which we can observe our experience without being caught up in it. "Pure awareness" is a good alternative term because that's all it is: awareness of our own awareness. (Harris, 2009, p. 173)

In Dialectical Behavioral Therapy (DBT) there is the concept of "wise mind." "'Wise mind' is the integration of 'emotion mind' and 'reasonable mind.' It also goes beyond them. . . . It is the calm that follows the storm. It is that experience of suddenly getting to the heart of a matter, seeing or knowing something directly and clearly. Sometimes it may be experienced as grasping the whole picture instead of only parts" (Linehan, 1993, pp. 214–15).

Diana Fosha, in her work known as Accelerated Experiential-Dynamic Psychotherapy (AEDP), says that fostering an internal secure attachment through self-to-self relatedness is a key aspect of her work, and calls a similar kind of state "the core state":

The core state is the self's internal affective holding environment. . . . The core state is marked by effortless focus and concentration, ease and relaxation, a subjective sense of clar-

ity, purity, even truth, and often, remarkable eloquence. . . .
The core state is one of deep openness, self-attunement, and
other-receptivity in which deep therapeutic work can take
place. (2000, p. 142)

Although there may be distinctions among these various approaches to the strong self in both theory and methodology, they are
all rooted in the conviction that strengthening the client's larger self
is an important therapeutic goal. Helene Brenner (2012) says:

My first goal in therapy is to bring a stronger self, a stronger "I,"
a stronger sense of self-efficacy, of self-autonomy, that there's a
strong "I" there. A self that is coming from a place of "I" and
their own experience, rather than what everybody else tells
them they should feel, rather than what they think they should
feel or an externalized self.

With regard to bringing Focusing into clinical practice, fostering a
strong, witnessing self is key. The experience of a strong self is more
than just a goal of therapy—it is a key "environment" that makes
therapeutic change possible. From the viewpoint of Focusing, felt
senses form when the person can pause and allow the fresh, present
feel of "something" to be there. The quality of "I" or "self" that is
needed for this pausing and sensing is one of not being merged, at
that moment, with an emotional reactive state. When clients are
able to pause and sense their feelings without being merged with
them, they typically experience this as being "larger" than their
emotional states. Facilitating this "larger I" state, even with clients in
great distress, is not difficult, in most cases—and it brings immediate
benefits.

By the end of therapy, we hope our clients will be living their
lives in this strong self state much of the time. Yet therapy will work
best if our clients can be in this state at least some of the time from
the very first session—able to turn with compassionate inquiry toward their own emotional experience instead of being frightened of
it or embattled with it. But this seems paradoxical—for therapy to
work well, clients need to be in a state which, if they could have it,
would mean they didn't need therapy anymore. How's that going to
work?

Luckily, as I will show, fostering the client's strong, witnessing self is possible from the first session and at the same time that a therapeutic alliance is being formed and other therapeutic goals are being pursued.

INTRODUCING SELF-IN-PRESENCE

My colleague Barbara McGavin and I have developed the term "Self-in-Presence" to refer to a state of self that is witnessing and compassionate toward one's own inner aspects and processes (Cornell & McGavin, 2008). Self-in-Presence is the experience of being larger than one's problems and emotions, able to explore with curiosity the emotions and thoughts that are there. As usual, language is important. We say that a person is (or would like to be) Self-in-Presence (in contrast to "having" or "accessing" Self-in-Presence), in order to support identification with this witnessing state.

Being Self-in-Presence is the alternative to being in a reactive state. By definition, Self-in-Presence is a state of calm, curious, accepting, warm attention. Turning with this kind of attention toward an emotional state results in significant relief in itself, and at the same time opens up a state in which a felt sense can form, creating new possibilities of thought, feeling, and behavior. Self-in-Presence is a key environment for the felt sense.

In our view, presence is the natural state of the self: calm, curious, interested, and able to act in mature and balanced ways. We assume that the client is capable of being Self-in-Presence, even when that is not his experience of himself. The practitioner speaks to the client from this assumption, and may also offer suggestions that strengthen and support the client's experience of Self-in-Presence.

Within the inner relational space thus created, felt experiences appear that are in need of the client's support, compassion, and empathic listening from Self-in-Presence. The role of the practitioner is to support the client in offering these qualities to the partial-self experience that is in need of them. The relationship between the practitioner and the client supports this inner relationship.

Embeddedness, Mentalizing, Mindfulness—and Self-in-Presence

How is the relationship of Self-in-Presence similar to and different from the concept known in attachment theory as "mentalizing" (Fonagy et al., 2002) and the ability known as "mindfulness"? Attachment theorist and psychotherapist David J. Wallin (2007), in a chapter called "The Stance of Self Toward Experience," discusses a three-way distinction among embeddedness, mentalizing, and mindfulness.

Wallin's embeddedness sounds like our identification with emotional reactive states.

> When we are embedded in experience, it's as if we *are* the experience as long as the experience lasts. . . . Within such an unreflective frame of mind, somatic sensations, feelings, and mental representations that might provide *information* about reality are instead felt to *be* reality. (2007, p. 135, italics in original)

The next state is mentalization. Mentalization is the ability to grasp and reflect on our own underlying mental states, as well as to imagine that others may have mental states different from our own. It is this ability that has been shown to correlate with secure attachment (Fonagy et al., 2002).

In Wallin's view, the first work of psychotherapy is to strengthen the reflective self, going from embeddedness to mentalization. "We must be able not only to respond emotionally to the patient but also to reflect on emotion—our own and the patient's—so that rather than simply being gripped by feelings we can try to make sense of them" (2007, p. 146).

Wallin goes on to describe "mindfulness" as a third "stance of self toward experience," a way of being that is not the same as mentalizing. "Rather than making sense of the *contents* of our experience, mindfulness directs our receptive awareness to the moment-by-moment *process* of experiencing" (2007, p. 159). He quotes Germer et al. (2005) on mindful awareness being nonconceptual, present-centered, nonjudgmental, intentional, participating, nonverbal, exploratory, and liberating. For Wallin, the state of mindfulness is highly desirable. "In addition, experiences of mindfulness foster a growing identification with awareness itself, rather than the shifting self-states (positive or negative) that we become aware of. The more strongly we feel identified with awareness, the greater our sense of internal freedom and security" (2007, p. 161).

The question that naturally comes to mind is whether mindfulness as Wallin describes it is equivalent to our Self-in-Presence. I would say that it is very close. The process of moving into mindfulness is understood in a way very similar to our Self-in-Presence, as a disidentification from emotional states. Further, there is an equivalent emphasis on this state as one that can be used for processing emotional states rather than ignoring or reacting to them.

> Repeatedly noting and naming our thoughts, feelings, and sensations—and in meditation, returning attention to the breath and to awareness—can strengthen our ability to "disidentify" from troubling emotional states. Such disidentification enlarges the mental space within which patients and their therapists can attempt to understand these emotional states rather than resist or be dominated by them. (Wallin, 2007, p. 163)

From a Focusing viewpoint, one thing missing from Wallin's view is the same thing missing from discussions of mindfulness in general, and that is the felt sense. The idea that a new kind of felt experience of the problem can form only in this spacious state, and that this new kind of experience is itself the organism living beyond the problem, is an idea brought in by Focusing. Another difference is that Self-in-Presence feels more like a good parent, with a warm acceptance rather than a neutral observational tone. From Self-in-Presence we are not just observers of our emotional states; we are compassionate, empathic, and interested. This itself is a healing and remediative stance.

THE HOLDING ENVIRONMENT OF THERAPY

When our clients come to us in emotionally fragile states and struggling with emotions that threaten dysregulation, we need to be present to them as our own strong self, be Self-in-Presence ourselves, because our own ability to hold a container for strong emotional states will be what enables our clients to learn to be that container for their own process. As Diana Fosha writes: "Affective experiences between self and other eventually become internalized and reflected in the individual's psychic structure, in the form of something akin to an internal affective holding environment" (2000, p. 22).

The clinician's Self-in-Presence is an environment that enables the client's own Self-in-Presence to grow stronger over time. The

87

clinician is that holding environment for his or her clients, and facilitates them to be that holding environment for themselves. Clients experience being in a steady, strong, holding relationship of contact and acceptance, a relationship that offers them emotional regulation in a way very similar to the attachment environment that babies ideally receive from their caregivers.

Carol Ivan, a psychologist who began bringing Focusing into client sessions several years ago, told me in an interview how much the process of being Self-in-Presence helps her as a therapist: "Being open to all of my own internal reactions, being with them in a more neutral compassionate curious way, making room for all of them, not having to push any of them away . . . that allows me to be with my clients just the way they are, and not have to need for them to be different from how they are, either."

We can picture the inner relationship of the client's "I" to the client's felt experience as nested within the parallel relationship of psychotherapist to client. Frans Depestele (2004) writes of consecutive "spaces" within psychotherapy, where the client and therapist first create a *relationship space*, then within that space a *reflection space* becomes possible in which the client turns his attention toward his own experiencing, and then within that space a *Focusing space* occurs when the client's reflection opens to freshly forming experience.

As we will see, being Self-in-Presence is not some kind of ideal state requiring a saintly degree of non-attachment. It is simply a grounded, present state where we acknowledge what we are feeling, thereby experiencing acceptance of feelings and reactions because we are not getting caught up in them. With practice, this state isn't hard to access, even when there is a lot going on. We can do it before a session, while preparing for a client, and during a session, as reactions come up.

Being Self-in-Presence as a clinician allows you to have empathic contact with the client without riding the same roller-coaster. Focusing-oriented therapist Carol Sutherland Nickerson remembers a client asking, at the end of a therapy session marked by deeply emotional process, "Do you get tired of sitting with people when they're doing this?" Nickerson did not feel at all tired, but rather touched and energized—and said so. Being Self-in-Presence, and being able to facilitate the client to be Self-in-Presence insofar as possible, enables psychotherapy to be a place where deep emotional work can go forward without it being energetically draining—for either person.

I will say more about the clinician's ability to be Self-in-Presence in Chapter 10.

FACILITATING SELF-IN-PRESENCE

Being Self-in-Presence means *being with* how we feel rather than *being* how we feel. My emotions are felt just as fully, and are still owned as "mine," but I can also feel myself as being "more than that." Neither dissociation nor distraction, neither repressing nor acting out, Self-in-Presence is a state of contact and presence with what is felt, the optimal stance from which to explore one's emotional states with interest and curiosity. (In fact, curiosity is one of the primary markers of being Self-in-Presence.)

The clinician can offer interventions that support the client in shifting into Self-in-Presence with even the most intense emotional states, even when the tendency would otherwise be to control the emotions, distract from them, or repress them. The client can be helped to acknowledge, be with, and keep company with emotional states. This enables felt senses to form and thus allows access to the dimension of change that felt senses make possible. It also gives clients the self-worth-enhancing experience of being able to regulate their own affect.

Clients—even the most overwhelmed and reactive clients—can generally access Self-in-Presence, even in a first session. They may not experience that state as being as stable or as solid as it could be, but they can usually access it—at least a little bit. Each experience of accessing the strong self—Self-in-Presence—adds to the client's resourcefulness and resiliency. A little bit of Self-in-Presence generates more of itself. The ability to take one deeper grounding breath, for example, becomes a resource that makes it more possible to feel one's feet on the ground and seat on the chair, which in turn makes it more possible to feel "I am here." Self-in-Presence is not an "on-off" state, but an ability that can be developed from a small beginning.

Example: Fostering the Strong Self
in a First Session

A client arrived at her first session reporting feelings of "sick terror, dread, and doom." Like so many survivors of trauma, she was caught up in an inner war between the strong emotions of the younger self who went through the trauma and the need to manage and contain those emotions. Long ago, at the time of the trauma, the feelings of terror, abandonment, and betrayal had truly been too much for her, and the result was a process in which a "part" of her functioned to contain those feelings as far removed from awareness as possible. Now the long-held emotions were threatening to flood out.

> C: I don't want to have these feelings. I know I need to go into them and go through them, but I feel like I'm going to die if I do.
> T: So let's see if I can show you a way to make contact with the feelings in a respectful way that also honors the need to go slowly and be safe while you do that. Would that be okay?

Rothschild (2000) talks about the importance of showing the client how to "put on the brakes" in a process with trauma. Warner (2000) talks about the importance of responding to clients in a way that supports their own ability to be connected with emotional experience without being overwhelmed. Facilitating Self-in-Presence offers a way to do both of these.

> C: [nods yes].
> T: So just take some time to bring your awareness into your body, and invite a sense of how all this feels there right now.

As we saw in Chapter 5, this is the invitation for a felt sense to form. Sometimes a client is able to do this at the first invitation, and sometimes more help is needed.

> C: [pausing, sensing] A tension in my chest. And something in my stomach.
> T: So you might acknowledge each of those two places, as though you're saying to each one, "Yes, I know you're there."

Acknowledging is a key move in facilitating Self-in-Presence. When the client acknowledges something that he feels, he has a clear experience that he's not identified with the feeling and not pushing it away.

> T: And you might notice if your awareness is especially drawn to one of those places right now.
> C: It's my stomach.
> T: So you might take some time to describe what that's like, there, in your stomach.

Describing, which is a key move in Focusing (see Chapter 3), also supports a client in being Self-in-Presence, because the attentive quality needed for describing is not pulling away, evaluating, or trying to make the feeling change.

> C: [sensing] It feels heavy, dull, and black.
> T: You're sensing . . . something there in your stomach . . . feeling heavy . . . dull . . . and black. . . .
> C: Yes, that's exactly right!

The therapist invites her to acknowledge this feeling now.

> C: [gasps, hand moves to chest] When I do that, I get this overwhelming sensation here!

It's not surprising that acknowledging one place or aspect has brought up something else. This is a natural movement of the process. The therapist will continue to support this client in being Self-in-Presence with what comes up.

> T: So you might move your awareness to something strong you're feeling in your chest, and acknowledge it as well. Maybe sensing how you'd describe it.
> C: I'm feeling really, really afraid.

Notice that the client has moved from describing her experience to identifying with it. The clue is that she says, "I'm feeling" instead of "it's feeling." The therapist will reflect with presence language ("you're sensing . . .") to invite her back into Self-in-Presence.

> T: You're sensing something in you that is feeling really, really afraid.
> C: Yes, and it's also sad . . . and lonely. . . .

The client shifts back from "I" to "it" to describe the feeling place. This indicates that she is coming back to being Self-in-Presence. The therapist will support and reinforce this move by offering another key kind of invitation: an invitation to hear or listen to the inner "something" that the client is being with.

> T: Maybe you could let it know you hear how afraid it is . . . how sad it is . . . how lonely it is. . . .
>
> C: Wow! I'm doing that, and it says that's right and it has a lot more to tell me!

The client's face is alive with amazement. She is sitting up straighter, and her voice sounds bright and excited for the first time. She almost looks like a totally different person from the one who first sat down at the start of the session.

Notice what a special moment this is. An inner experience that started out as something physically described and frightening in itself has come alive with its own point of view, its own meaning. ("It says it has a lot more to tell me!") By being in relationship with her inner experience, the process has carried forward. Imagine how much harder this would have been, coming from the stance of "I'm feeling afraid."

Identification and Disidentification

Let's look further at what is happening when a client is able to be with emotional experience. The key concepts for understanding Self-in-Presence are identification and disidentification.

Being identified with a feeling state is equivalent to being merged with or taken over by that feeling. A person who says "I am angry" is likely to be identified with the feeling of anger. "I = angry." "Angry" is what the person identifies with.

In contrast, if the person is disidentified from the feeling of anger, he or she would be able to feel the anger, and have the anger, but would not be the anger.

Disidentified is not the same as dissociated, which would mean being cut off from awareness of the emotion. There are other familiar indicators of dissociation, such as spaciness and emotional numbness. Ideally we would be not identified, and not dissociated: not merged, yet aware.

Because language alone is not definitive, we cannot be sure that a person who says "I am angry" is identified with the feeling of anger. Such a person might be illustrating or expressing the feeling but at the same time able to sense into it and accompany it. If you listen alertly, you can usually tell the difference between a person saying "I am angry" and a person saying (quoting an inner aspect) "'I am angry.'"

"Something in Me"

When I work with groups of clinicians, I have a simple exercise to help them experience the difference between being identified and being disidentified. I ask people to think of an emotion that they are feeling now, or have felt recently, and say it like this: "I am——," or "I feel——." For example: "I am angry," "I am upset," or "I feel bored." (For reasons we don't need to go into right now, I ask for difficult emotions, not enjoyable ones.)

Then I ask them to shift the language of their sentence by changing the words "I am——" to "Something in me is——." "I am angry" becomes "Something in me is angry." "I am upset" becomes "Something in me is upset." I invite them to take the words into body awareness and feel the difference. (Perhaps the reader could try this now.)

Here are some of the things people say after trying this exercise: "It's like I became a caring observer of my own feelings." "I feel I'm no longer defined by my emotions." "My nervous system just calmed down immediately." "I feel distance from the emotion, like a spaciousness in me." "With the first sentence I felt there was no solution, and with the second sentence I began to relax." This isn't an intellectual exercise—doing it actually changes the felt experience in a discernible way.

If changing words with intention can make this kind of difference—and it can—we owe it to our clients to offer it to them.

"Something in You"

We saw what a difference it can make to shift our language about our own emotional state from "I am upset" to "something in me is upset." This is when we are speaking of ourselves. When we are speaking to a client, the phrase becomes "something in you."

C: I am feeling full of dread.

T: Something in you is feeling full of dread.

Speaking this way is not always recommended or appropriate—see below—and when we do it, we should consider it an offer to the client. The client may or may not take the offer. Our attitude is that it is okay either way.

A client who is "taking the offer" will shift his language from "I" to "it" and will often start talking about a body experience—without even having been invited.

C: I am feeling full of dread.

T: Something in you is feeling full of dread.

C: Yes—it is in my stomach—heavy like a stone.

A client who is not "taking the offer" will continue to speak in an identified way.

C: I am feeling full of dread.

T: Something in you is feeling full of dread.

C: I am so afraid I'm going to come apart.

This response seems to indicate that the client did not take in or feel supported by the therapist's use of the phrase "something in you." There are many possibilities for what to offer next. One of them is to invite the client himself to change his language, as an experiment. First, we might engage the client's agreement to try the experiment.

T: This sounds really hard, what you're going through. I'm wondering if you'd like my help to be able to feel yourself stronger, in relation to all that.

C: Yes, I really need help with this.

T: Let's just take a moment to have you feel your feet on the ground . . . your seat on the chair. . . . That's right, it looks like your breath is getting deeper as you do that. . . .

C: It's a little better but I'm still so scared [tears]. . . .

T: We want to make sure that that scared place in you gets the company it needs. Let me invite you to say, "Something in me is so scared."

C: Something in me is so scared.

T: And notice what happens when you do that.

C: I feel a bit better. The scared place is here [touches stomach].

T: Great, let's have you just *be with* the scared place there, in your stomach. . . .

We'll see more of how this session might go forward in Chapter 6.

"A Part of You"

Just a note about the difference between "something in you" and "a part of you." These two phrases are not the same; they have different effects and consequences, and of the two I prefer "something in you" unless the client is already talking about parts.

I used to say "a part of you." For example, "A part of you is feeling dread." Often the client would refuse this phrasing: "It isn't a part— it's me!" Naturally I would hasten to match the client's words: "Right, it's you feeling dread." But then we would miss the helpful disidentification that would have happened if the client had accepted my rephrasing.

Something remarkable happened when I began to use the phrase "something in you" instead of "a part of you." I noticed that the incidence of overt refusal dropped to nearly zero. Clients don't always take the offer, as I pointed out above. They may continue to say "I feel" instead of "something in me feels." But they almost never say, "It isn't something in me—it's me!"

The two phrases, "something in you" and "a part of you," are experienced differently, and in general I would recommend saying "something in you"—unless of course the client has introduced the word "part," as in: "It seems like there is a part of me that has never accepted my father's death."

When Not to Say "Something in You"

This powerful phrase for supporting disidentification—"something in you"—is not a move to be used automatically or in all circumstances. The very fact that it is so powerful means we should use it judiciously, only when needed. Quite often when a client first talks about her feelings in a session, it is usually supportive to meet that communication empathically, without changing it in any way.

C: I am having a hard time just holding things together.

T: [in a warm tone] Yeah, so that's hard for you, you're having a hard time just holding things together.

In most cases we would lose some rapport with the client if we were immediately changing her language, as in, "You are sensing something in you having a hard time. . . ."

I take the attitude that there is plenty of time to empathize first and then offer interventions later. Interventions are more likely to be accepted by the client once he feels accepted and understood as he is.

"You Are Sensing . . ."

In addition to the phrase "something in you," a second powerful, simple phrase that you can use to support clients in being Self-in-Presence with their emotional states is "you are sensing. . . ."

"You are sensing . . ." evokes Self-in-Presence by speaking to the "you" in the client who is sensing. We could also say, "You are noticing . . . ," "You are aware of . . . ," or "You are realizing. . . ." The alternatives are nice for variety's sake, but I far prefer "you are sensing," because it both evokes and invites the inner sensing that we are encouraging.

The word "you" refers to Self-in-Presence in the client. Typically it will come at the beginning of the sentence in all of the interventions that support Self-in-Presence. If you remember this, you will not find yourself saying this awkward and not-as-helpful phrase: "Something in you is sensing. . . ." The recommended phrase is: "You are sensing something in you that . . ."

"You are sensing" can be combined with "something in you" as we have seen, and it can also be used on its own.

One function of a phrase such as "you are sensing" is that it makes a space for the client's experience without our needing to agree or disagree. When the client makes a statement of belief as a fact, we may feel as though the only ways to respond will either validate the belief or contend with it. But the important thing here is to let the client have the experience, as a place to go forward from. "You are sensing" makes that possible.

C: It's a hard life.
T: You are sensing it's a hard life.

Alternative phrases: "What comes is . . ." "The words that come are . . ." As in: "The words that come are, it's a hard life."

An example of the two phrases used together, with a client who says, "I am so frustrated with her," would be: "You are sensing something in you that is so frustrated with her." Our term for either or both of these powerful phrases is "presence language." The use of presence language contains an implicit invitation to experience the emotional state as a felt sense—as a "this"—which can be sensed into further. This language may seem simple but it is surprisingly effective and empowering for the client.

"It" in the Inner Relationship

As we discussed in Chapter 1, in Focusing an inner relationship naturally develops, where the client is able to be with his or her inner emotional state. When the client is Self-in-Presence, then the inner emotional state is "something," or "it," or "this." When people are Focusing, even without prompting, they speak this way naturally, as we saw in Chapter 3. "It's here," indicating the chest, "and it is feeling tight."

To some, this might seem like an odd way of speaking. We may be used to encouraging clients to own their experience. A client who says quietly, "Yes, the funeral was last week, and it was sad," might be encouraged to say, and feel, "Actually, I am sad!" If people have never owned and felt their own feelings, of course it is a positive, life-forward step for them to do so. The sentence "it was sad," referring to a funeral, is a displacement of an emotional state, externalizing and projecting outward what is more accurately one's own feeling. Similar phrases are: "It was disgusting," "It was overwhelming," "It was scary."

But the "it" of "it is feeling tight," pointing for example to the chest, is something quite different. There is a direct experience, being pointed to—sometimes literally with a hand as well as with the word "it." This is a concretely felt experience that is not being displaced or disowned. It is here.

Is this "it" a felt sense? This is a tricky point. As we saw in Chapter 3, felt senses form—they are not already there. So the "it" that is felt in the body may or may not be, technically, a felt sense. Crucially, however, acceptance of what is there is required as an essential environment for a felt sense to form. The client's experience of being Self-in-Presence will involve turning with acceptance toward what he does feel, not with evaluation as in "Is this a felt sense? Is this what I should be feeling?" but with awareness and direct sensing.

The order of process is as follows:

1. The client is merged with an emotional experience that is probably not a felt sense.
2. By acknowledging and turning toward that experience, the client is able to be Self-in-Presence.
3. The Self-in-Presence environment enables a felt sense to form, very possibly growing out of or developing from the emotional experience.

By accepting the client's experience at each stage—and supporting the client in accepting it as well—we create a smooth path for the client's natural process of attention to the immediate felt experience, and for the forming of felt senses.

Using the words "it" or "something" for the felt experience allows us to bypass the concern about whether this is a felt sense or not. We are talking about process here, after all, so the subtle shadings of when an emotional, felt experience "is" a felt sense are not as important as the environment of attention the client is able to bring to his own felt experience.

"You" in the Inner Relationship

When I am asked what word I use when I am speaking to a client, to refer to Self-in-Presence, the answer is surprising but makes sense when you think about it. I use the word "you."

"Maybe *you* can be with that sad place inside you." I put a slight emphasis on the word "you" when it is used in this way, to show that it has content; it refers to something important. I want to encourage the client to identify with Self-in-Presence, and the word "I" (or, in speaking to another, "you") is used for that with which we identify.

C: [in a teary voice] This place in me, it's feeling really sad. It's a wounded place.
T: Ah. You're sensing how sad and wounded it is. And maybe *you* can be with it.

The slight emphasis on the word "you" carries my intention to point to the whole person, the whole self.

In an interview with Germain Lietaer, Gendlin described this "new I":

> Gendlin: "And the other thing that I would like to mention . . . is that in attending inwardly in a Focusing way, there is always a difference between the self and whatever is there. Because a small distance . . . is made as the body forms the whole sense of the problem. . . . And a new 'I' comes there."
>
> Lietaer: "Do you mean by that: it is ego-strengthening somehow?"
>
> Gendlin: "Yes, but it is not the same ego. It's a self that has no content, because every content is *there*. . . . Now, that 'I' becomes very much stronger, and becomes very much more able to be in a sense the owner of this whole, it becomes strong in relation to whatever is there." (Gendlin & Lietaer, 1983, p. 90)

SELF-IN-PRESENCE INVITATIONS

There is a series of invitations that facilitate and support the client's being the large "I" (Self-in-Presence) in empathic contact with an "it" or "something there." They are: acknowledging, keeping company, attending to contact, and hearing/receiving.

Acknowledging

The next intervention after using presence language might be to invite the client to acknowledge or say hello to the "something." For example: "You're sensing something in you is worried. . . . Maybe you could say hello to it." When a client can acknowledge or say hello to a felt sense or inner emotional state, he or she experiences being that stronger self which is separate from and yet connected to the emotion.

> "So you might acknowledge that place, like you're saying to it, 'Yes, I know you're there.'"

Clients typically say about this, "I feel that I *have* the fear, but not that I *am* the fear. It doesn't have *me*."

Keeping Company

Maintaining an inner relationship of empathy can be an empowering and deeply facilitative move, especially for clients who tend to get overwhelmed by emotional states.

C: It's just very sad in there.
T: Maybe *you* could just be with that sad place.

or:

C: It's very scared.
T: See if it's okay to keep it company, something that is scared.

A helpful move, especially in cases of agitation, anxiety, distress or upset, is to invite the client to "let a gentle hand go there." Notice this carefully chosen language, different from "put your hand on it."

C: It's really agitated—my heart is almost jumping out of my chest.
T: So maybe it would be okay to let a gentle hand go there, to your heart, like you're saying to it, with your hand, "Yes, I am with you."

This is a form of self-soothing that many clients find helpful to take home with them.

Attending to Contact

We can invite the client to attend directly to the quality of contact that he has with his felt experience. This is especially helpful if there is any indication that what the client refers to as "it" is feeling shy, wary, suspicious, or untrusting, or if there is any possible question about that inner contact being solidly there.

C: I'm not so sure it trusts me.
T: You might sense what kind of contact it would like from you right now.

C: It seems to just want me to back up a little and give it some space.

In the following example, we see a client who seems to have become a bit identified with the need to make something happen. Inviting attention to contact is a way to bring the client back to identification with Self-in-Presence.

C: It's very elusive. I can't seem to get ahold of it. It keeps backing up.
T: Ah! Maybe you could just sit down there, and let *it* come to *you* when it's ready.

Hearing/Receiving

One of the key qualities of Self-in-Presence is empathy. As Self-in-Presence, the client is empathic toward the felt emotional experience that she is having. We have already noted the key function of empathy from therapist to client. In addition, the therapist can facilitate the inner quality of empathy between the client and his felt experience with an invitation such as, "You might let it know you hear it."

C: It feels like it has to be the one who takes care of everyone.
T: You might let it know you really hear, it feels like it has to be the one who takes care of everyone.

A slightly different version of this invitation helps strong emotional states receive empathy without identification.

C: It's really really scared!
T: Maybe you could let it know you hear how scared it is.

Notice that, even though what is explicitly happening is an invitation for the client to be inwardly empathic, the therapist's own empathy is also being conveyed. The warmth and energy in the therapist's voice says, "I too understand that it is scared." This kind of invitation serves double duty and is therefore richly valuable.

The next invitation, building on this one, might be, "You might check if it feels understood by you."

Using Presence Language to Shift Emotional States

Spoken by the Client

"I am sensing . . ."
"Something in me . . ."
"It, this"

Spoken by the Clinician

"You are sensing . . ."
"Something in you . . ."
"You"
"You might acknowledge it."
"See if it's okay to just be with it."
"You might sense what kind of contact it would like from you right now."
"Let it know you hear it."

ENJOYABLE FEELINGS AS A RESOURCE FOR SELF-IN-PRESENCE

It is a good idea to be alert for those moments when the client begins to feel something enjoyable, whether this is the tiniest feeling of relief ("it's not quite as heavy as it was") or an unmistakable shift in the quality of what is felt ("wow, the whole thing feels so much lighter now"). We want to recognize these moments when they come, because they are a clear signal from the process itself that life is moving forward in the direction of the client's own change (see Chapter 1). We will also want to support and encourage the client to have and experience these enjoyable feelings as fully as possible, and enable this life-moving-forward to fill out and go further. We will see more about how to do this in Chapter 6.

In addition, all enjoyable feelings are a resource for the client's ability to be Self-in-Presence. This includes feelings that are expansive, warm, open, alive, relaxed, peaceful, and so on. Just being able to have and experience these enjoyable feelings adds to the client's ability to be a self that is a compassionate, gentle, and strong container for more challenging feelings.

There may be aspects of self that find it difficult to tolerate enjoyable feelings, or it may be that a client simply doesn't see that enjoying his feelings is part of the work of therapy. We can encourage the client to stay longer with enjoyable feelings, allowing them to be there, and feeling them more fully in the body.

C: It's starting to feel more relaxed in my stomach.

T: Maybe you can take your time to allow that "relaxed" feeling to be there.

C: It's like there is this warmth starting in my stomach and spreading out.

T: Ah! So really having that feeling, that warmth in your stomach spreading out. Letting it be there as fully as it wants to be.

Enjoyable feelings that are experienced as Self-in-Presence do not push away more challenging feelings, but instead form a welcoming environment for any aspects of self that are in need of attention.

C: I still have that warmth in my belly but now there is this constriction in my throat.

T: So maybe you can still *be* the warmth in your belly and from there, send some gentle attention to the constriction in your throat.

THE FEELING ABOUT THE FEELING

Disidentification from an emotion that they are experiencing (e.g., "something in me is angry") is usually not too difficult for most clients. More challenging, and potentially much more important, is disidentification from the reaction to the emotion, a reactive state that we call "the feeling about the feeling." "I don't like my anger" is an example of this. The client has anger (the feeling) and not-liking-the-anger (the feeling about the feeling). We would want to help the client disidentify from both of these states. Another example: "It's scary to be so vulnerable." There is a vulnerable feeling *and* there is a feeling about being vulnerable, a scared feeling.

As Self-in-Presence, the client feels accepting and curious about his or her own feeling states, creating the optimal environment for those feeling states to change in their own life-forward direction. But often clients are not Self-in-Presence, not accepting, not curious, but instead are identified with their reactions to their feeling states. Unless the client can turn toward these reactions, these "feelings about the feeling," and be with them as well, these reactions tend to strongly interfere with being Self-in-Presence.

For example, clients may speak of needing their feeling states to change, longing to feel something different, or being frightened of being overwhelmed by strong emotional states. Another possibility is that the client may be so identified with a reactive state that he doesn't speak of it, he just behaves from it.

Much of what troubles our clients are the holdovers in their current lives of their attempts as children to solve the problem of overwhelming emotion. It's as if something in them decided, long ago (for example), "If I don't allow the scared feeling to come up at all, then I won't have to feel unbearably fragile and threatened." Obviously this wasn't a formed, articulated thought, but a process in which defenses of emotional avoidance were mobilized. Other examples: "If I just don't have needs, I won't make anyone angry," or "If I'm never scared or sad, I won't get hit." These early strategies are often what appear as the "feeling about the feeling" in an experiential process.

If we sense the client is ready for an intervention, we can treat the feeling about the feeling as a second "something in you" to be acknowledged and turned toward. Quite often this is what needs attention next.

> C: [hand moves to chest, voice chokes up] The sadness is here. I am so tired of feeling this way!
> T: Yes, you're sensing it there, in your chest. And you're sensing something in you that is so tired of feeling that way.
> C: Yes, it's both.
> T: Maybe you could spend some time just being with that tired-of-feeling-that-way feeling.
> C: It's like this cape of tiredness spreading over my shoulders. . . .
> T: You're sensing it there in your shoulders . . . like a cape of tiredness. . . . Maybe you could let it know you know it's there.

C: Now it's relaxing. . . . Funny. . . . Like it says it's okay to be with the sadness now.

T: Okay, so moving awareness back to the sadness. . . .

Some sessions go like this, with the feeling about the feeling relaxing or "stepping back" spontaneously after being acknowledged. In other sessions, what started out as the feeling about the feeling becomes the feeling, the focus of awareness. We are open to either way the process goes.

TALKING TO A CLIENT
ABOUT SELF-IN-PRESENCE

It can be very helpful at times for a client to have a concept of this compassionate, witnessing self that we call Self-in-Presence. In general my tendency is to give minimal explanations of the theory behind the work I do, not wanting to take away from the present-moment experience. There is a delicate balance to be walked here, and I find that if a client is thinking too much about a concept I have presented, it can take him into unproductive questioning of his experience, rather than attending to it. For example, I tend to stay away from any discussion of the term "felt sense" (see Chapter 2). But familiarity with the concept of Self-in-Presence can be supportive for a client doing deep experiential work.

I would not actually use the term "Self-in-Presence" unless people already have acquaintance with it. Instead I use phrases like "all of you" or "the larger you" or "you in the chair." I might say something like: "And maybe *you* can be with that sad feeling, the larger you, you sitting in the chair, just being with the sad feeling." (For a client who is sensitive about his or her physical size, we can say "the whole you" or "all of you" rather than "the larger you.") If a client asks for more clarification, I will give it.

C: I don't know what that means, "the larger me."

T: It's just the idea that the whole "you" is here, not just your different emotions and thoughts that come and go, but you, all of you, how you can feel your whole body sitting in the chair.

Here's a sample of a little talk I might give to a client:

Most people have no idea how transformative it is to sense exactly the feelings and experiences that are here, without changing or judging them. We think we're feeling how we feel . . . but we're probably not. Usually we're feeling the state of reactivity to our feelings, feeling scared or rejecting of how we feel. In a reactive state, we're sure we already know what we feel. What helps is if we're curious, interested, and wanting to get to know how we feel. That starts with direct sensing, no assumptions, just sensing how it feels in the body right now. Getting curious, letting go of assumptions, sensing how it is right now. . . . It can be startling how quickly this can bring change.

SELF-IN-PRESENCE: A WAY OF BEING, NOT SOMETHING TO FIND

I don't recommend saying to a client, "Look for a compassionate part of you" or "See if you can find Self-in-Presence," because it's not a good idea to use metaphors of "looking for" or "finding" in regard to Self-in-Presence. We want the client to *be* the strong self. The instruction to "look for" a compassionate part carries the assumption that the client is not the compassionate one already. (Also, we don't want to give the idea that Self-in-Presence is a "part.")

What if the client doesn't feel compassionate toward an aspect of her experience? Rather than saying, "Maybe you can find a part of you that can be compassionate," I would invite the client to turn toward "something in you" that is having a hard time feeling compassionate right now. "Turning toward" is an action taken by Self-in-Presence. By taking that action, the client is being Self-in-Presence.

One client of mine learned about Self-in-Presence and thought it meant she had to feel compassionate and kind in order to be disidentified from her painful emotions, and do Focusing. I said, "No, it's the other way around! Once you are disidentified from painful emotions, and able to be with them instead of being caught up in them, I predict you'll find compassion and kindness arising naturally. Start by just doing something to disidentify, like saying hello to the sadness."

One doesn't have to feel compassionate in order to say hello. The action of saying hello can come first. The resulting disidentification leads to the ability to sense into and listen to what is there, which in turn leads to a naturally arising experience of compassion.

We cannot change how we feel. To some extent we can choose whether to know or express our feelings, but we certainly cannot make ourselves feel compassionate. If feeling compassionate were a prerequisite for being Self-in-Presence, this state would be quite rare. Luckily, feeling compassionate is not a prerequisite—it's a result.

Another common misunderstanding about Self-in-Presence is that it is a state of bliss or the absence of painful feeling. Not at all. One can have a lot of painful feeling and still be Self-in-Presence, by being with the feeling instead of being merged with it, or struggling with it. Perhaps this is what is meant by the Buddhist proverb: "Pain is inevitable; suffering is optional."

WORKING WITH PARTS IN FOCUSING

The concept of Self-in-Presence, and the language of "something in me," seems to imply the existence of "parts" or aspects of self, sometimes called "ego states." Clients say things such as, "This place in my chest is sad. *It* is sad." We will typically hear clients using "parts" language spontaneously: "Part of me wants to tell her off, but another part of me doesn't want to make her mad." For many clients, using parts language helps them have their emotional experience while remaining Self-in-Presence.

Actually, the Focusing process is neutral with regard to working with parts; it is possible to bring Focusing into psychotherapy even if your therapeutic modality does not have a model of ego states. However, in our development of Inner Relationship Focusing, Barbara McGavin and I have found that speaking of parts—which we prefer to call "partial selves"—is a way to accurately express and effectively work with the dynamics of dysfunctional process. Here are a few of our main points.

- An aspect of self ("partial self") may be out of awareness and yet function in dysfunctional patterns. We can make a guess, based on behavior, about the existence of such a part, for example: The part that wants to drink, the part that wants to die, the part that doesn't want to write.

- This "missing" part can be invited into awareness, and sensed into, using Focusing.
- If there is one part out of awareness, there is another, its counterpart, that the person has been identified with, that is implicated in pushing the other one out of awareness. ("I know I need to get back to work. I don't know why I'm not.")
- As partial selves struggle with each other, a person is most likely to be identified with one side of the struggle or the other. ("This need to eat sugar is a primitive side of me.")
- Being Self-in-Presence means being identified not with any partial self, but with a larger, nonpartial Self that is not biased toward one part or the other. This allows a Focusing process to happen for each part. (See Chapter 8 for a discussion of how listening to the felt sense of the part that wants to drink or eat addictively can be an effective adjunct to treatment for addictions.)

We appreciate the Internal Family Systems parts work of Richard Schwartz (1995), developed as a way to reach therapeutic goals with clients who have a wide variety of serious issues, notably eating disorders and other addictions, and also dissociative states. We have been helped by Schwartz's formulation although we differ somewhat from him, both in our way of working with parts and in our understanding of what parts are. A discussion of how IFS can combine with Focusing is found in Chapter 9.

One of our primary differences with Schwartz is that we do not believe that parts are permanent. A "part" is a metaphorical—and useful—way of referring to stopped process (discussed in Chapter 1). A process that is implied but has been unable to carry forward, over time, begins to look like and feel like an entity, a "someone" in there. When carrying forward does happen and the stopped process resumes, parts disappear without a fuss because they were never really there in the first place. To facilitate this fluidity, we prefer to work with parts without naming or labeling them. Rather than "the inner child" or "the inner critic" or "the Pusher," we would say: "Something in you that feels like a child right now," and so on. (To be fair,

Schwartz also recommends not labeling parts, because for him, although the part itself is permanent, its dysfunctional role is not.)

> Partial-selves are repetitive reaction states that need empathic company from the Focuser as Self-in-Presence. This in turn, over time, allows a felt sense to form. Self-in-Presence is both a process of sensitive and compassionate relating to partial-selves that need attention, and it is the space that allows felt senses to form. (Cornell & McGavin, 2008, p. 22)

"Parts" are not the same as felt senses. The stopped process that results in the experience of parts can persist over many years, resulting in the experience that these inner states are nameable entities. A felt sense, however, is always freshly formed, arising in this moment and therefore not a nameable entity. One can, however, get a felt sense *of* a part.

Neither therapist nor client may know whether an inner experience that is contacted and referred to as "something" is a felt sense or a persistent reactive state called a "part." Luckily, for most purposes, this doesn't really matter. In Focusing, we treat the experiences equivalently, in almost all situations. McGavin and I believe that when it is difficult for a person to find or feel a felt sense, this is because there is identification with one or more parts. Being with parts as Self-in-Presence may be a prerequisite step to being able to get a felt sense. It follows that, when a client feels "something in me," what is being felt is either a felt sense or on the way to being one.

SELF-IN-PRESENCE SKILLS AS HOMEWORK

Self-in-Presence skills are also something that the client can learn to use, even outside sessions, to maintain a calm, accepting relationship with emotional states.

Clients can be taught:

- To use the phrase "something in me" for emotional states
- To acknowledge or say hello to those "somethings"
- To let a gentle hand go to the body feeling place, especially if it is strong or intense
- To use the phrase "I am sensing" for emotional states

"I don't like my anger," said a client. "It takes me over and I feel like there's nothing I can do." Could she say more about when and how her anger feels most like a problem?

"It's with my sister. I have to see her because of family get-togethers. But every time I see her, I feel my throat choking up and I want to strangle her. I feel like she has dismissed me so much, she's rejected everything I've ever offered her. When she's so-called 'nice' to me I know she's mocking me. I'm afraid I'm going to lose it next time I see her."

The therapist asked if this client would like to learn some skills that she could take with her into those interactions with her sister. The client replied that she didn't know if anything would help but she was willing to try.

T: When you are anticipating that you will see your sister, that's a good time to already start being aware of your reactions. Like right now—we can try it together. Notice how you are feeling about her at this moment.

C: Mad, I'm furious with her.

T: Okay. And now try saying it this way: "Something in me is mad and furious with her."

C: Something in me is mad and furious with her.

T: And notice if there's a difference.

C: Yeah . . . it's not so big. I am bigger than the feeling now. And I can tell I'm not only mad. I'm also sad that it has come to this.

T: Great, and also say, "Something in me is sad."

C: "Something in me is sad." Right. I feel that in my chest.

T: So maybe you can let a gentle hand go to the place in your chest, let it know you are with it.

C: "I am with you." Wow, that feels a lot different.

T: Do you sense you might be able to do this yourself? Even this weekend around your sister? I'll write down the two phrases we just practiced on this card, and you can take it with you.

C: I can try!

The client came back the following week and had this to report: "I did use the skills you showed me when I was with my family this weekend. I was amazed—it really worked well. I was bigger than the feelings that I had. I had a really nice time. I was reactive, but I was able to tone things down."

Once clients themselves have some training in Focusing skills, which include being able to be Self-in-Presence, they are often able to bring those skills into situations where they feel the need for more self-regulation, both outside of the therapy hour and in it.

A therapist had been working for several years with a client who had a history of complex trauma, symptoms of PTSD, and some dissociation. This woman had a strong motivation to change, so in addition to being in therapy she took a self-help course in Focusing for herself. In a recent therapy session, the client was spending time with a part of herself that she described as terrified and sad. She spoke tearfully about how difficult this experience was to stay with, and was sobbing intensely, to the point that the therapist, with one eye on the clock, was wondering how she might begin to help the client pull herself together for the end of the session.

Suddenly the client said, "Oh, wait," and opened her pocketbook, pulled out the cue card from her Focusing course, and read the steps, including, "I'm letting it know I hear it." That one fit. The client took a deep breath and smiled at the therapist. "I had forgotten to do that! Now it feels so much better." As the end of the hour arrived, the client walked out calm and collected.[1]

When clients consciously learn and practice the Focusing skills of emotional self-regulation, also known as being Self-in-Presence, this can enhance the work of therapy and it can also immediately improve their lives outside of therapy.

The felt sense is the doorway to fresh possibilities. After the client has a felt sense and is able to stay with it, there is more to Focusing. Chapter 6 is about how to facilitate the client who needs support going beyond the felt sense to deeper levels of process.

---

1. This cue card can be found in the Appendix to this book, as well as a one-pager to give a client for support using presence language at home.

Chapter 6

GOING DEEPER: FACILITATING
THE FELT SHIFT

Change in Focusing comes in three stages. The first stage is the forming of the felt sense, which, as we have seen, opens the possibility of
new experiencing, and often brings a somatic experience of relief—
even though more change is still implied. The second stage is what is
called a "felt shift," often accompanied by insights and a fresh sense
of possibility. The third stage occurs in the new ways of living and
interacting that the client finds as a result of the felt shift.

Chapter 1 introduced the concept of "carrying forward." I spoke
of "steps of change" that occur when a client has an insight that is
simultaneously felt at the body level, and how new understanding is
accompanied by relief and release, with physiological indicators such
as deeper breathing (even a sigh of relief), shoulders dropping, pinkness in the cheeks. The felt shift is another way to talk about the felt
experience of change and movement in the direction of more life.
Although a felt shift cannot be made to happen, there are ways to
support it and make it more likely.

In some cases, once we invite a client into contact with a felt
sense, this is all the process needs. There is an "unfolding" that occurs naturally, with images, associations, memories, new connections emerging.

But what if that natural unfolding doesn't happen? In Chapter 5
I discussed the most common difficulty: when the client is identified

with or merged with an emotional reactive state and needs help to be Self-in-Presence. The processes described in Chapter 5 show how to help with this. Once the client is in Self-in-Presence, there is often a natural flowing forward of the process.

But not always. Even when the client is being Self-in-Presence and is in contact with a felt sense, the Focusing process may need support to go further. That further support may take the form of invitations to do something inwardly, such as ask a question or offer empathy. Often not much is needed; it's as if we give little nudges in the direction of further process. There is an art to giving the invitation and then stepping back to see whether it got in the way or was helpful.

Perhaps even more crucially than what we help the client to do, we may need to support our client in *not* doing something that would interfere with the process. For example, left to his own devices, a client might try to talk himself out of his feelings instead of giving company to those feelings. The invitations described in this chapter are designed to support a client in staying in a Focusing type of contact with inner experience rather than trying to evaluate, figure out, suppress, deny, or otherwise try to change that inner experience.

I will discuss four moves that can help a client go toward a felt shift once a felt sense is there:

- Supporting the client in being with a felt sense, also known as "keeping company" with what is felt
- Facilitating the client in offering inner empathy, by "sensing from its point of view" and "letting it know it is heard"
- Offering support for open-ended inquiries such as "what it is not wanting" and "what it is wanting"
- Listening for and supporting process movement in the direction of fuller life ("life-forward direction")

BEING WITH, STAYING WITH, KEEPING COMPANY

Contact is everything. This is contact that doesn't try to make anything change, contact that doesn't evaluate or judge, contact that sensitively notices whether it is welcome to come closer or needs to pull back. It's the kind of contact that, even done imperfectly, brings secure attachment between mother and child. It is the kind of contact that a psychotherapist intends to offer a client. And it is also the kind of contact that facilitates change when the client can offer it to his or her own inner process.

Gendlin writes about this kind of contact in a beautiful passage describing how the therapist and the client together provide what the inner process needs:

> The client and I, we are going to keep [the felt sense], in there, company. As you would keep a scared child company. You would not push on it, or argue with it, or pick it up, because it is too sore, too scared or tense. You would just sit there, quietly. . . . What that edge needs to produce the steps is only some kind of unintrusive contact or company. If you will go there with your awareness and stay there or return there, that is all it needs; it will do all the rest for you. (Gendlin, 1990, p. 216)

After a felt sense forms for a client, it is a further process for the client to be able to stay with it, to keep it company, giving it attention without moving into a reactive state of trying to change it. When the client can be with his or her felt experience spaciously, neither pulling away from it nor pushing beyond it, this is the optimal environment for the client's own change process. We can recognize this quality of contact and company as being the state of Self-in-Presence (see Chapter 5).

One invitation for this kind of inner contact is: "Maybe *you* could just be with that." Note the slight emphasis on the word "you" that reinforces and supports the client's identification with the larger self. Here is an alternate version that serves the same purpose: "See if it's okay to just keep that company awhile."

The therapist can include herself in the invitation, for a greater sense of support if needed: "Let's you and I just *be with* that sad place in there." "Let's you and I keep that company."

The invitation to "be with" one's felt experience is something for the client to do instead of nonfacilitative moves such as reacting to the feeling ("it's scary"), evaluating it ("this is not a helpful way to feel"), or manipulating it ("I need to just set this aside").

OFFERING INNER EMPATHY
FOR ITS POINT OF VIEW

What comes after "being with it, keeping it company"? Often the client spontaneously begins to speak empathically of the emotions and point of view of this inner felt experience. For example, after being with a tight feeling in the chest, a client reported, "It feels smothered. Something in me wants to get free." Another client, spending time with a sense of heaviness in the shoulders, then said, "It's like something in me feels I have to carry the whole world on my shoulders." There is a deepening, an elaboration of meaning, that emerges from the inner contact. Notice these clients are not saying "I think" or "it's probably about. . . ." This elaboration is coming from the contact with what is felt. There is a distinct quality to how this sounds and feels.

If this kind of deepening into elaboration of meaning doesn't happen spontaneously, it can be supported with an invitation. In Chapter 1 we had the story of Daniela, whose exhaustion felt like a giant squid wrapping its tendrils around her body. The therapist said, "You might want to sense how *it* feels, from its point of view." After an attentive inner silence, Daniela said: "It's protecting . . . something precious. It's protecting something precious until it is ready." If you had been listening to Daniela, you would have known, as the therapist did, that this did not come "from the head" but was emergent from her direct contact with what she was sensing.

In my experience this move of "inner empathy" is more effective if the client is first in a "being with" type of contact with the felt experience.

In Chapter 5 I discussed this segment and said we would see how one might go further with it:

> T: And notice what happens when you do that.
> C: I feel a bit better. The scared place is here [touches stomach].
> T: Great. Let's have you just *be with* the scared place there, in your stomach. . . .

At this point the client is in touch with a "scared place," in the stomach, and the therapist invites her to just be with it. This is an invitation which, as we have seen, serves two interrelated purposes: to support the client in being Self-in-Presence and to create the environment for the next step of change. If the therapist had given an inner-empathy kind of invitation at this early point, without first supporting inner contact, there is a greater likelihood of the client losing contact with felt experience and answering with a guess, saying what he thinks the therapist wants to hear, or going blank.

C: I feel a bit better. The scared place is here [touches stomach].
T: Ask that place what it is scared about. [Not recommended.]

The client might say, guessing: "It's probably scared I can't get past this block." But once the client is in inner contact, helpful invitations can be made, and the further movement is more likely to come from inside the process.

C: I feel a bit better. The scared place is here [touches stomach].
T: Great. Let's have you just *be with* the scared place there, in your stomach. . . .
C: Yes, okay [silence]. It's still there.
T: And maybe you could sense how it's doing in there, how it is feeling, itself.
C: [takes a bit of time to sense] I feel it kind of pulled back in, like it doesn't feel safe right now.
T: Ah! You're sensing it's like *it* doesn't feel safe. You might sense what kind of contact it needs from *you* right now.
C: [first a pause to sense] It needs me to give it time.

The Leash Example

In Chapter 3 I gave you this segment from a session in which a client got in touch with a felt sense, and a further process started to happen:

C: I don't know why I can't do it. I think it's my fear of failure. Actually . . . it's funny, but when I say that I get a bit choked up, like there's something tightening up in my throat. . . . It's hard to describe . . . um. . . .
T: [softly] Something there in your throat . . . feels like tightening . . . [Pause]. Maybe stay a bit longer, just feeling that. . . .
C: Yes . . . it's like there's a hand there, cutting off my breathing. . . . No, not completely cutting it off, just constricting it. . . . Funny, it's almost like there's a leash around my neck!

T: That brings a note of surprise, when you feel it's like a leash around your neck.

C: Like there's a part of me saying, "Keep it in bounds. Don't go too far." Wow, I didn't know that was there!

Just that much from the session offers an illustration of how a freshly emerging felt sense, with its metaphorical imagery, can bring a surprising insight that goes beyond the usual ways the client had been thinking about and experiencing the problem. But where might the session go next? What is a Focusing way of continuing?

It is important to be aware—always—that nothing is fixed; everything is in process. So just because there is something in the client now that is like a leash around the neck, saying "keep it in bounds," doesn't mean it will be like that always. It has a next step it has been implying, waiting to take. Empathic aware attention is what it has been needing, in order to take that step.

Therefore what we would not want to do is anything that treats this living process as some kind of fixed entity. For example, we would not want to say, "Can you take the leash off your neck?" This treats the "leash" as an object rather than as a process that has its own implying forward (see Chapter 1). Another thing we would not want to do: "Can you explain to it that you are now able to be safe without its help?" Although this type of move at least treats the "leash" part as something alive, it stops the living process by not allowing the forward steps to come from inside the process. Instead, with a cutting-off move like this, we assume we know the answer and impose it from without. There is not actually a problem with this—if it works. But, in my experience, moves like this often lead to dead ends.

What I would recommend is supporting the client in a quality of attention (to the "something") that could be described as "inner empathy." Inner empathy is contact plus an intention to get to know it. For this, my favorite invitation is simply to say, "You might let it know you hear that."

Here's how the "leash session" continued:

C: Like there's a part of me saying, "Keep it in bounds. Don't go too far." Wow, I didn't know that was there!

T: Ah, it's letting you know it wants you to keep it in bounds, and not go too far. You might let it know you hear that.

117

C: Yes. It says I need to be careful—it's worried about me.

T: You might let it know you hear that it wants you to be careful; it's worried about you.

We will come back to this session.

When a Client Interferes With Her Own Process

Sometimes supporting the way forward means gently intervening when a client does something with a felt experience—arguing with it, explaining to it, or manipulating it—anything other than keeping company with it with inner empathy. While not making wrong what the client did, we can offer an alternative—once it has become clear that the first move didn't bring a shift.

A professional speaker came to me for a Focusing session because for the past few months she had had a persistent constriction in her throat. She experienced it as a physically felt block that could actually be heard in her voice when she spoke—at least, she could hear it. She said she knew that a part of her was afraid of self-expression, but she had already done a lot of work on this and was ready for it to change. Invited to get a fresh sense of it, as if she had never felt it before, she said it felt like a lump. I invited her to stay with the experience and check if the word "lump" fit well. Yes, it did.

T: See if it's okay to stay with it, to get to know it better. Maybe sensing its emotion, from its point of view.

C: It feels very determined.

T: Ah, you're sensing that it feels very determined. And you might just ask it gently, what it feels determined about.

C: It's telling me that it has saved me many times, by not letting me say something that would have gotten me in trouble.

I suggested to her, "Let it know you hear that," and a silence followed. After a minute or two, I started to get curious and perhaps a little worried about what was going on. The silence was going on longer than I expected, and I had a feeling she was doing something other than what I had suggested. That would be her privilege, of course, but . . .

I said, "I'm just wondering how that's going for you now."

She reported, "I did let it know I heard it, and now I'm telling it that

I really appreciate what it's been doing for me, but now it's time for me to take back the power to protect myself, and give it a different job."

This sounds like a very empowering move on the part of the client, telling this lumpish constriction in the throat that she appreciated what it had been doing for her but now she was ready to take back the power to protect herself. The problem is that, as with any human interaction, the one being spoken to rarely feels truly understood by a sentence with a "but" in the middle. "I appreciate what you are saying *but* my point of view is blah blah blah."

I've learned through hard experience that when a client speaks like this to a part of herself, there's a very good chance that nothing will move. But I also know that every person is different, and I am constantly being surprised. The way to find out whether this client-initiated move was helpful is to check with the process itself.

T: And you might notice how that place in your throat feels when you say that to it.
C: It's still the same, no change.

This was a clear sign that the client's process did not find what the client did to be helpful. Now I felt okay about offering an alternative move.

T: Well, you know, I really appreciate that you were able to tell it your feelings. But I'm thinking that if I were that lump, I wouldn't be feeling very heard right now. See if you'd be willing to try something a little different, just as an experiment.
C: Sure!
T: See if you'd be willing to just tell it that you hear what it's saying, and then stop. No "but." Tell it that you hear it, and then just keep sensing.

The client followed this suggestion, and there was another long silence. This time, though, the silence felt different to me. I was sensing through my own felt awareness that the client was probably in a deep contact with her process.

After a long time—nearly 3 minutes—the client let me know what had been happening.

C: Wow. . . . It showed me so many scenes! It's been showing me chapter and verse all the times it saved my bacon by not letting me speak. And I did what you said—I just kept letting it know I heard it. And then, oh my gosh, it melted! It just melted down the sides of my throat! There's a clear channel there now. My throat hasn't felt this good in years! This is amazing!

T: So really take time to feel and let in the good way it feels now. [A version of this session is found in Cornell, 2005a, pp. 98–99.]

WHAT "IT" IS NOT WANTING TO HAPPEN

Once the client is in contact with "something" inside, able to be with it, able to sense its point of view or its emotion, a further step can be the invitation to sense "what it is not wanting to happen to you."

Barbara McGavin and I have determined that inner aspects of self tend to push and pull, driven by motives to protect or hide vulnerable aspects of self, to avoid painful feeling states, and to solve what they see as life problems. These deeper motives tend to be covered over by layers of belief and explanation that are displaced from what is really going on (McGavin & Cornell, 2008).

Especially with feeling states such as anger, sadness, fear, and versions of fear (e.g., worry and anxiety), there is a deeper layer of "not wanting something to happen" that can open up further process when it is contacted.

As an example, let's return to what we were calling the leash session. The client discovers the vivid experience of a metaphorical leash around his neck, like a part of him is saying, "Keep it in bounds—don't go too far." The therapist invites inner empathy to that part—"Let it know you hear it"—and this is what happens next:

C: Yes. It says I need to be careful—it's worried about me.
T: You might let it know you hear that it wants you to be careful; it's worried about you.
C: Right, I can feel how worried it is, how tight the leash is around my neck.

Rather than inviting the client to sense what it is worried about, we are going to invite him to sense what it is *not wanting to happen*.

This slight shift in language can have a powerful difference in results:

> T: You might invite it to let you know what it is not wanting to happen.[1]
> C: [silent while sensing] It's not wanting me to make a mistake, a terrible mistake. I can sense that it feels I could make a mistake that would ruin everything forever.
> T: [first empathizing, then inviting inner empathy] Ah, you're sensing it feels you could make a terrible mistake that could ruin everything forever. You might let it know you really hear how much it is not wanting you to make a terrible mistake that could ruin everything forever!
> C: Yes . . . it's relaxing. . . . That was right.

We often find a felt experience of relaxing and releasing following the client's empathy to the not-wanting-to-happen of a part. If not, if there is not an experience of relief, what may be called for is an iteration of the not-wanting invitation, at a deeper level.

> C: I let it know I heard it, but it's as tight as ever.
> T: Okay. You might invite it to let you know what it's not wanting to happen to you if you make a terrible mistake that could ruin everything forever.
> C: [pausing] It's not wanting me to be crushed. I have this pain in my chest, feeling crushed.
> T: So really acknowledge that pain in the chest, feeling crushed—that's what this is not wanting you to have to feel.

As we go deeper into what is not wanted, it becomes increasingly likely that the client will contact a not-wanted feeling or body experience. If we go slowly, and support the client in being Self-in-Presence (see Chapter 5), it becomes possible for a "stopped" experience that had been guarded against, and had never previously formed, to be

---

1. A note on language: This long phrase "you might invite it to let you know" is used in preference to the shorter "you might ask it," because problems arise with "asking" inside. Often, when invited to "ask it," a client reports, "It doesn't know" or "It doesn't talk." Questions asked inwardly seem to have the same issues as questions asked interpersonally. (See Chapter Four.) If you find "you might invite it to let you know" too cumbersome, however, try, "You might sense . . ." as in "You might sense what it is not wanting to happen."

held in awareness in present time. This allows a movement into forward steps, past the place of stopped process. We recommend going slowly when a not-wanted feeling is contacted, being sure to let the client's own process set the pace.

WHAT IT WANTS: THE WANTED FEELING

The other side of the coin of "not wanting" is "wanting." When a client is in contact with "something" in her inner experience (a felt sense, a partial self), and when she has been spending time with it for a while, she often begins to be able to sense what it is wanting for her. Ultimately, all parts of self want some experience for the person, and this wanting is connected to what is implied and what is still missing (see Chapter 1).

Often, wanting emerges naturally, spontaneously. If we listen for it, we can hear it. Wanting is often expressed as "can't" or "not able to." It's very facilitative to pick up the wanting in "not able to" statements, and say it back:

C: I can't seem to find a way to feel a sense of peace about what happened with her.

T: Yes . . . you're really *wanting* to find a way to feel a sense of peace . . . about what happened with her.

C: I guess that's right.

T: Maybe you could let your body feel that wanting, the wanting for a sense of peace.

C: Yes . . . that feels good . . . like a more settled feeling in my chest. That feels better.

We can work with experiences of wanting, longing, and desiring by inviting the client to feel what it would be like if the longed-for state actually happened. "When clients . . . vividly feel what is needed, I can provide the suggestion that they can let *their bodies* feel the longed for thing as *actually happening*. Then what is needed fills itself in." (Gendlin, 1996, p. 279, italics in original).

Sometimes clients need some support to let go of the need to know "how" something is going to happen before they can feel it as a possible outcome.

T: So maybe you could take some time, to let the feeling come, how it would feel if you did have the kind of relationship you are wanting, if it was here already.

C: I have no way to meet people. Everyone I meet is already married or at least paired up.

T: And that's discouraging, it sounds like. I wonder, though. . . . I was suggesting something a little different. Just as an experiment, maybe we can find out how it would *feel* to be in the kind of relationship you're longing for, even without knowing how you're going to get there. Okay?

The experience of wanting often leads to a powerful experience that we call the "life-forward direction." I talked about life-forward direction in Chapter 1, when I discussed the philosophical view behind the transformational potential of Focusing. Now let's see how to bring this perspective into the process of psychotherapy directly.

THE LIFE-FORWARD DIRECTION

A client may see his or her life as being hopelessly stuck and mired in painful feelings, but even in the most despairing emotional states there is what Gendlin calls "life-forward direction." Many of us have observed this in our clients—and we haven't always had a concept to give us confidence that it is always there. Fosha has a similar concept she calls "transformance": "*Transformance* is my term for the overarching motivational force, operating both in development and in therapy, that strives toward maximal vitality, authenticity, and genuine contact. A felt sense of vitality and energy characterizes transformance-based emergent phenomena" (2008, p. 3).

In Focusing, our confidence in the life-forward direction rests on the view of life as always implying its next steps. The living organism knows its way forward. The very pain that the client is experiencing can be seen as "knowing" that something is wrong—and contain a knowing of what would be more right.

Clients are more than mere bundles of problems—even if that is how they see themselves. Even if clients believe themselves to be completely stuck, with no way forward, they are alive, and their life process is always generating new possibilities. Part of one's job as a therapist is to listen for the clues to those new possibilities that may show up in a shift in posture, a stronger tone of voice, or an image that has life energy in it.

> What might it be that points "toward more life"? It might be to let oneself have feelings (if they have been blocked), or to assert one's own perceptions (if one has long discounted them). It might be to say something one has long felt but not said. It might be to permit oneself to feel a little bit of hope. . . . When a therapist senses a life-forward process beginning, the first shy bits need response and confirmation. (Gendlin, 1996, p. 259)

In phrases such as, "This week for the first time I didn't hate my life" or "I'm not quite as scared as I was," we can hear the life-forward direction, and it is important that we can hear and point to the life energy there, which the client may be passing over without really noticing. At a minimum, I would repeat those words back slowly, thus inviting the client to feel more fully what is in them.

> T: Wait, before you go on. . . . You said something that is staying with me. . . . This week . . . for the first time! . . . You didn't *hate* your life!

Listening for and supporting life-forward direction is one of the major ways we can help our clients. One place to be alert for life-forward direction is whenever a client speaks about "wanting," especially when there is a wanted feeling, such as "I want to be able to feel confident" or "There is a desire to be relaxed with it all." A client may also speak of deeply held values, as in, "What matters to me more than happiness is a sense of meaning in my life."

From a Focusing perspective, what matters is not the statements themselves but the fact that these felt experiences are arising in the client right now, as fresh new steps of self-understanding and embodiment that have never happened before in this way. If we notice these glimmers of fresh life, and don't let them pass by but invite the client to "have" them, the process of life moving forward is strengthened and supported.

> C: I just wish I could wake up some morning and not hate my life.
> T: There is a wishing there . . . that some morning you could wake up . . . and not hate your life.

C: [sighing] Yeah.

T: And you've spent a lot of time, haven't you, feeling how bad that feels, hating your life. And right now I heard something, I don't know, maybe a bit new. That you *wished* you could wake up and *not* hate your life.

C: [a bit more energy] I do!

T: Maybe there is a bit more energy there . . . ?

C: [sensing] Yes . . . maybe a little. . . . I do wish that.

Life-Forward Energy Emerges as a Resource

In a surprising number of instances with Focusing, the client's process shows what the client needs and begins to move toward it at the same time. This is the essence of change in action.

In this complete session that was done in a training class, the client discovers that her body already knows what she needs to do to heal her relationship with her husband, and that this in fact is already happening.

C: A part of me is feeling stuck with my relationship with my husband. And I've been . . . I've had this image of seeing this target, and arrows were all over, but no arrows had hit the target. They were fallen all over the ground. And it was from both of us, not just from me. And I just got in touch with the fact that there were a lot of things that happened between my father and myself around when I was 19 to 22. . . . This is the age that my daughter is. . . . I'm seeing behaviors in my husband toward her, that my Dad did to me when I was her age, and it's keeping me from connecting . . . from even wanting to connect with him.

T: Yeah, so this is what you've got, sort of, so far, is the image of nothing hitting the target, not from either one of you. And there's something about you and your dad, about what felt so not right, with him.

C: [tears] Yeah.

T: That might be a place just to pause and let something come. . . . Maybe it's already here as you talk about this.

C: It's something big. It's in my belly and it's also in my chest. . . . It's so interesting because I had eating disorders around that

125

age. I was bulimic, and now I can feel there is something in me that just wants to throw it all up!

T: So how about staying with that right now, really sensing the *something* that wants to throw it all up.

C: [sigh] Yeah.

T: It shows you the memory of having eating disorders back then, but here it is right now too.

C: Yeah. And it's not food. I don't want to throw up food anymore. It's like throwing up . . . my dad or the whole lack of respect he had for me. . . . Just wanting to get rid of that.

T: Yeah, you're sensing what it is that wants to be thrown up. It's something like your dad, or the lack of respect he had for you.

C: Yeah, and as you say that, there's something in my throat. It's like I had no voice—I had no power! [The client checked inside what I said, which was what she said, and because of that inward checking, more came.]

T: Uh-huh! And you're remembering in your throat now, how you had *no voice* then, *no power*. [Past and present are linked; the relevant past is also in the present. My response embodies that when I say, "you're remembering . . . in your throat now . . . how you had no voice then.]

C: So just hearing that . . . I get a breath in my belly. . . . [A breath of relief means something inside has been heard.]

T: That brings a breath, yeah.

C: Being heard. . . .

T: Yeah, let's take that in. "Being heard" now is here too. Mm-hm. [This is a bit of a pause, just being with what has happened. From the pausing, more will come.]

C: [pauses] The tears are still here a little bit, and the whole chest area and stomach. . . . There's definitely . . . it's almost as if there was fire there. And now it's just kind of calming. Not as hot and fiery.

T: You're sensing it's like there *was* fire there, and now . . . it's calming. So being with how it feels now. As it's calming.

C: [deep breath] Yeah. And I'm noticing still this place in my throat. It just feels a little . . . like something's caught there. [This is a person experienced with Focusing, who brings her own attention back to her throat. If she hadn't done that herself, I could have invited, "Maybe sensing how it is now in your throat," but not until after the experience of calming had some space.]

T: There in the throat . . . like something's caught there. . . .

C: It's like um. . . . It's way back in my throat, it's as if something a long time ago got caught in between . . . something. There's something about, it got caught in between being . . . eaten and throwing it up, something like that. Like something just got stuck there. [We can tell from the way the client is speaking that she is in immediate contact with an emerging experience. Descriptions are coming freshly, and she uses the word "something" to hold the places where no other word fits yet.]

T: Yeah, you're sensing it way back in your throat. Like the process of eating, going down the throat got interrupted, stopped. Something got stuck there.

C: Yeah, like some . . . some ability to process something at some point. So it just, it latched onto the back of my throat. Yeah, it's just a stoppage, a stopping of something. . . . [Her hand moves to her throat.]

T: Yeah, your hand is going there. You're sensing it just as it is right now.

C: [tears] Yes, so some tears are coming back. . . . Something about . . . an inability to be seen.

T: Yeah . . . something about an inability to be seen. "I can't be seen."

C: Yeah! So it just hid back here.

T: Ah! Now you're sensing it's something that's been hiding.

C: [sigh] Yeah.

T: And the breath gets deeper when you say that, it looks like.

C: Yeah.

T: It's been hiding.

C: Like in a deep cave, in a cave in the back of my throat. Like it carved a cave for itself. . . .

T: What comes now is, it's been in this cave, and it carved that cave for itself. [I feel the important thing here is the client's contact with "this" that has been hiding at the back of her throat, "this" that she feels present, now. Each thing that either of us says and does is oriented toward maintaining that contact. She is sensing it, and I am supporting her inner sensing.]

C: Yeah, it's been very resourceful! It got a sleeping bag, it got . . . like camped out there, or something. There's something about that. . . . Oh, actually, because it wanted to be—even if it knew it was going to hide out, it wanted to have some comfort. [chuckle] [Here is the place where I am hearing life-forward energy, and that informs what I say next. When aspects of self have been resourceful, when they have known what was needed, this points to a powerful life energy that the client may not have been acknowledging.]

T: You're starting to take in how resourceful it's been. And how . . .

C: [sigh] Yeah.

T: Yeah, that brings a deeper breath too!

C: Yeah, I'm quite impressed with it. With its ability to be—it's definitely my 22-, 23-year-old.

T: Right. This is a 22-, 23-year-old you, not just somebody suppressed and not allowed to speak, but with some resources. [Again, pointing to the other side of the pain, this was not just a victim; this had a resource in it.]

C: Yeah. Because when I was that age I did a lot of camping. Just being outdoors hiking. That's where I felt so happy.

T: And so the memory of that comes now. . . . You felt happy when you were outdoors camping, hiking. Maybe your body is giving you some of that now. [I could have asked the client earlier for memories of times when she felt strong and happy, and that might have been helpful—but it might just as well have been met with resistance, "never felt that way," or felt in a way that was disconnected from the painful experience. In the way shown in this session, it is the painful experience that has the resources, and points to the enjoyable experiences, which can then be felt. The life process already has the resource integrated with the trauma, if we give it time and open attention.]

C: Yeah.

T: How nice!

C: Yeah, so I'm smiling. Just—oh, just her ability to know what she needed to do to take care of herself, amidst just not feeling like she had a voice. She had feet! She could walk, she could go out and be in nature.

T: Mm-hm!

C: There's something about . . . oh, just like this willpower, like dammit, if I'm not going to be seen by my own father or understood, I'm going to—I'm just going to get out there and—I don't know. I know the sun will see me. I know the mountains will see me.

T: You know the sun will see you. You know the mountains will see you.

C: There's something about that, that feels, um—it's just like this beautiful life force, there.

T: Yeah, wonderful to take your time to feel, to let your body have that right now, the beautiful life force, how much you're appreciating and living it. Inviting it in now. [Now comes my invitation to "let your body have that," to support the process that is already happening and ensure that it is happening in the body tissues.]

C: Yeah, it's like my whole body is filled with, just memories of hiking and . . . seeing mountain views, sitting on rocks, and just filled with that. . . .

T: Yeah!

C: How healing it was. . . .

T: How healing it was. . . . Now you're really having all that . . . in your body now, both the memory of it in the past, and it's here now too. [Memories are not just past—in fact, they never are. Memories are what come now, from the past, and can be bodily felt.]

C: Yeah, and I'm also just reminded that one thing that my husband and I are doing, is that we're hiking the whole Appalachian Trail, taking it by chunks. We're starting in Virginia . . . and that. . . . Oh my goodness! It just dawned on me! I'm doing this with him, to find some wellness. [tears]

T: Yes, that touches something.

C: My body already knows what it needs to do with him! [tears]

T: Wow. So really taking time to let that in. Your body already knows what brings healing and wellness. Wow.

C: Yeah, it's like something in my chest just got . . . Like it can feel it just got soft. . . . Yeah, so my whole . . . you know . . . I'm already doing what I need to do, without even realizing. . . . [This experienced Focuser felt for herself the impact of this

129

shift in her chest. With another person I might have invited, "Maybe sense how that is in your body now."]

T: Yeah . . . so feeling that place in your chest that got soft, and taking in that knowing that you're already doing what you need to do—it's already been set in motion.

C: Yeah! Because we have a lot of time on the trail just to be together and talk and . . . [Deep breath].

T: Yeah, deeper breath. Let's take 3 minutes or so more, and let's just invite you to keep having what's coming now, this inner knowing, this body feeling of what brings healing. It's already here.

C: I'm just seeing this picture of him and I on the trail, holding hands in the sunshine . . . our backpacks on, like no worries. . . . I'm just grateful. . . .

Life-Forward Direction in Action

In this second example of life-forward direction happening in a session, we can see how the emergence of "wanting" from an experience of frustration and upset can provide a pathway to accessing resourceful experiences, yet without turning away from presently felt experience.

This client, who had been job seeking for quite a while, arrived for her session feeling frustrated and angry. She had three job interviews set up for the next day.

C: I asked a person from a past job for a reference and she said no to me. I can't believe it! How could she do that? Sure, I have other references, but getting rejected like that really set me back. Now I'm going to go to those interviews tomorrow feeling not as confident as I want to feel.

It was clear that the client could have talked for her whole time about how frustrated and angry she felt at the woman who refused the reference. This could have included feeling and expressing emotions, especially the anger. Let's look at how the session actually went. The client was invited to get a fresh sense of how all this felt, right now.

C: I'm aware of this sensation in my chest, and it feels . . . achy there. I feel hurt.

T: You're sensing that place in your chest. It feels achy. And the words that come are, "I feel hurt."

C: And I'm sensing that's not the only thing that's there. I'm feeling angry also. I'm frustrated because prior to that phone call I was feeling very confident. And that "No" just—aargh! I hate it when something comes up like that and it sticks. It feels like it stuck to me.

T: So what it feels like is that *it stuck to you.* [The therapist chooses the vivid metaphor "it stuck to me" to offer back to the client, rather than the generic emotion words "angry" and "frustrated."]

C: It brings that, um . . . that sense. . . . I feel with that particular job that I had, I felt as though it wasn't really. . . . It didn't really let me do my best work, and . . . so that rejection about "No" to the reference feels like it brought that whole feeling of how unhappy I was at that particular job.

T: You're sensing how that "No" brings this whole thing about *that job,* and what was missing for you there.

C: Mm-hm.

T: How it wasn't right. You couldn't do your best work there. Something like that.

C: Yeah . . . there's a deeper breath that comes now. . . . Yeah, I'm still aware of a kind of pressure inside. And . . . um . . . and I don't want it to be there. [The client's "I don't want it to be there" is a feeling about the feeling (see Chapter 5) and the therapist will offer a nonintrusive invitation to disidentification simply by reflecting with "something in you . . . and something in you . . . and both are there. . . ."]

T: Yeah . . . so you are sensing something like a pressure . . . and you're sensing something in you not wanting it to be there . . . and both are there. . . . And then sensing if one or the other of those needs your company first.

C: Yeah, I think what wants my company first is the part that doesn't want that feeling to be there.

T: Yeah! So turning toward the one that doesn't want the other one.

C: It really wants me to be feeling confident tomorrow, and sail from one interview into the other.

T: Yeah, it's showing you what it *wants* for you tomorrow, that you'll *feel* confident, that you'll *sail* from one interview to another. Maybe you're feeling a bit of that in your body right now, as you can taste what it wants for you. Feeling a bit of that sailing, confident feeling. . . . ["Sail from one interview to another" is a vivid metaphor, already nearly a body feeling, that the therapist is careful to pick up and say back, followed by inviting the client to notice if she is feeling that in the body now.]

C: I actually usually interview very well.

T: Uh-huh! So now memories come, of times when you have been confident just the way you're wanting to be tomorrow. And letting that be there in your body, the feeling that comes when you remember interviewing well. [Memories of past success, and especially the body feelings that come with those memories, can become a resource for the client.]

C: That feels good. That feels good to remember that.

T: Taking your time to feel the enjoyable feeling, the good feeling that comes.

C: And I think there's something else in here and it's wanting me to . . . um . . . let's see if I can get this. . . . It wants me to remember and to recognize what I have to offer.

T: Ah!

C: And it also doesn't want me to think that I have to be perfect. That I had to have had only wholly positive experiences in every job I've ever had.

T: So there might be a part of you that's been thinking that you had to be perfect, and you had to have only positive experiences in every job.

C: Ah.

T: And if there's something like that you could say hello to that too.

C: I have other references—that's the other thing. I'm not doing without references. It's just that that whole job is one I could take a big eraser to, and just pretend I didn't work there and I didn't have that job. It wasn't fun. It wasn't a fun job.

T: Yeah! So you're really in touch with something in you that wants to take a big eraser to that whole job. How it feels in you right now to remember it, is just not fun. And letting it know you hear that.

C: I really like that. I took my hand, and I even made the gesture, erasing the board. . . .

T: Ah! So the hand makes the erasing gesture, and you can feel the *liking* for that.

C: Yeah! I like that, looking at the clean slate there.

T: So take some time to feel in your body the feeling that comes with looking at the clean slate there.

C: Yeah, I like that. It likes that. Smiling.

T: That might be worth staying with awhile, the feeling of smiling, the feeling of liking that. Yeah.

C: Yeah, that feels really good. It feels like something really let go. It's a good place. It feels like it's . . . uh . . . it's been erased!

T: Oh, so you're really feeling the "let go"—it *has* been erased! Your body is showing you a letting go of that.

C: Yeah, it's showing me, and really feeling that in my body.

T: Mm-hm! Taking time to feel that.

C: I'm letting myself feel the lightening that's happening in the center of my chest. The smile has come back.

The client reported later that all three interviews the next day went well, and she had the feeling of confidence and flow in the interviews that she had been wanting to feel.

When we make Focusing invitations, and clients don't find them easy to follow, there are further ways we can help with these difficulties. In Chapter 7, I discuss some typical challenges that clients face when invited to the inner moves of Focusing, and some possible ways of helping with those challenges.

Chapter 7

WORKING WITH MORE CHALLENGING TYPES OF CLIENTS

If you've tried the interventions and processes suggested in the previous chapters, you've probably encountered clients who don't take to them readily. They keep on doing what they're doing as if you had said nothing, or they go a little way into a Focusing process and then pop back out to a more at-the-surface way of talking, or they question what you are asking them to do and why you are asking them to do it.

The clients who are potentially most helped by Focusing are often the ones who don't take to it easily. Instead, they seem stuck in repetitive processes that don't carry them forward, such as telling the same stories, repeating the same intellectual concepts, experiencing the same emotions over and over. Or they seem unable to access an affective level of inner awareness, apparently having little contact with emotion or body sensation. Or they may be identified with an aspect of self that seems determined to keep them "safe" by not allowing a contactful, affective process to happen.

In this chapter we look at five types of challenging client process, classified as intellectualizing, low-affect, "resistant," evaluating, and self-criticizing. What might be called a sixth type of challenging client process, when the client feels easily overwhelmed and fragile in the face of emotional experience, was covered in Chapter 5. Naturally, all these types of process are interconnected and can even be understood as occurring for similar reasons. But the types of client process can seem quite different when first encountered, and that is why I discuss them separately here.

THE INTELLECTUALIZING CLIENT

A client says, "I think this is my self-hatred. I know my mother hated herself, and I learned that from her. I just always seem to sabotage myself."

This sounds like a fairly self-aware client, and certainly this level of willingness to turn toward inner causes is preferable to chatting about what other people did and said last week (Klein et al., 1969). But from a Focusing perspective, this person is far away from getting a felt sense. She is thinking, analyzing, guessing, speculating, and doing so in terms and concepts (e.g., "self-hatred," "sabotage") that are already set and fixed.

Many responses might be appropriate. But assuming we wanted to support Focusing next, how might we offer an opening toward Focusing for such a client? We would start, as always, by meeting her empathically and accepting where she is. We're listening not just for what she is saying but for what she is trying to say, what she is "up against" as Gendlin would put it. We might say, "There is something going on here that you are seeing as 'self-hatred,' like how your mother hated herself. You're trying to understand what seems to be you always sabotaging yourself." "Trying to understand" isn't what the client said, but what we hear her doing. We could be wrong, and if we are, we hope she will correct us. But either way, right or wrong, we are inviting a pathway to sensing what is under or behind what is being said.

Especially if we are successful in empathizing and communicating our empathy, the client may keep on talking, elaborating but probably not going in. "Yes, I had a chance at work to do a presentation. A lot was riding on it, and that was the day I got sick." We'll keep on empathizing, showing that we hear not only what is being said but also why: "There's an example of it, that time you had a chance to give a presentation but you got sick. Looking back, that seems like you sabotaged yourself."

At some point there will be a readiness in the client's process for a felt sense invitation. When people feel heard they typically relax a little, and there is an openness for an input coming in from another person. If that input comes too soon, before there is a readiness, the person usually keeps repeating what didn't get heard. This is one way that people can appear resistant when they are actually following a natural course.

C: I think this is my self-hatred. I know my mother hated herself, and I learned that from her. I just always seem to sabotage myself.

T: [giving an intervention before giving empathy] Let's just pause and invite you to feel that self-sabotaging place. [Not recommended.]

C: [sounds resistant but is actually just persisting in what hasn't been heard] I just feel that I learned it from my mother. She was always putting herself down in these little ways. . . .

There is an art to sensing for the right timing, when there is an opening for an invitation. Having our awareness in our own body (see Chapter 10) helps a great deal, because it will be easier to sense the signal of an opening, rather than thinking our way toward it. One common signal is the client saying there is something he or she doesn't know, or wants to know. We can offer a Focusing move as a way to help the client's direct knowing to come.

C: Yes, the presentation was an example of me sabotaging myself. I remember the night before, when I started feeling sick, there was this little moment of—"Oh, good! I don't have to do it."

T: You're really getting that there must be *something in you* that is sabotaging you. Like that night, the feeling of "Oh, good!"

C: I felt so mad at myself for blowing my chance again. I don't know. I just don't get it.

T: I'm wondering if this might be a time to make an invitation to that *something*, so you can get to know it better.

C: How would I do that?

T: Maybe just feeling your body as you're sitting there in the chair. . . . Being aware of your breath. . . . That's it. . . . And remembering that whole thing about doing that presentation—you got sick. Something in you got you sick. And you might invite that right now, the feel of that right now. Take your time.

Whenever you say something like this to a client, especially when you sense it might be a stretch, a bit outside her comfort zone, remember that this is an offer that the client might or might not take. If the client doesn't take the offer, no need to be offended or hurt. This is not a power game. You and the client are both engaged in the same enterprise, which is helping the person live more fully. She just didn't take your offer, that's all. So you meet the client again, where she is, and later make the offer again, in different words.

C: [not taking the offer] It's probably just that I can't stand to be judged. I've never been able to do contests or competitions.

T: [back to empathic mode] That feels like part of it, that there is *something about* being judged . . . that you just can't stand. . . .

Thinking Is Welcome

I don't recommend telling clients to stop thinking, or to drop their thoughts, or to get out of their heads. We won't get far by judging or fighting with the client's preferred mode. Some clients are comfortable in the thinking realm, and where they feel comfortable, they also feel safe. The experience of safety, as we saw in Chapter 2, helps any therapeutic process work more effectively, and Focusing is no exception.

In addition to the safety of the preferred mode is the fact that thinking is not the enemy of process. In the old days, when we thought that "body" was opposed to "mind," we used to ask people to set aside thinking in order to get into their bodies. Now we understand that body and mind are interwoven, and you don't get to body by excluding mind—or vice versa.

So we don't ask people who think to set aside their thinking. Instead we'll say something like, "Let's have that idea here with us, as you also take time to sense the whole thing freshly. . . . Maybe there's something you're aware of that you haven't quite put into words yet."

Coming Into Body Awareness: The Lead-In

Even though we don't ask people to drop their thoughts, we may well ask them to expand their awareness to include their bodies. People who approach their problems by thinking can be helped into a Focusing mode by including body awareness.

When I first encountered Focusing, I was a fast-talking graduate student at the University of Chicago. Intellectual argument and verbal sparring were the way to connect with friends, as well as the way to get ahead with teachers. The realm of emotion and the body was a dangerous and unknown territory. When Gene Gendlin invited me to "go to the place in your body where you feel things," I didn't have a clue what he was talking about. If I had dared, I would have said, "Body? Feel things? Huh?"

Before I could learn to do Focusing, I needed help just to feel my body at all. I needed someone to talk me through my body, encouraging me to slow down and wait for how my feet felt if I wiggled my toes a bit . . . how my weight felt in the chair . . . how my throat felt, tight or open. . . .

Luckily, there were people who helped me do that, or I would not be writing this book today. Later, when I began facilitating others in Focusing, I developed a way of helping people into body awareness as a preliminary to being able to do Focusing and invite felt senses. I call it the "lead-in." In form and effect it is quite similar to what others call "mindfulness practice" (Linehan, 1993; Wallin, 2007).

Clients who favor a thinking mode often appreciate a bit of explanation. Here's how one might introduce the lead-in with a new client:

> T: [after a discussion of the presenting issues, during which the client reveals a thinking mode] It's been shown that these patterns of feeling and behavior are easiest to change through direct bodily experience in present time. We can try to think our way through our issues, and that's fine as far as it goes, but to really get life change, we need to include mind and body both, in the present moment. Does that make sense?
>
> C: That makes sense but I don't know how.
>
> T: Don't worry—I'm going to show you. So if it's okay with you, and if you're ready to get started, I'd like to take you through a brief exercise in body awareness. Okay? We can always stop

any time you want to. And for this you may want to close your eyes, although it's also okay to leave them open. . . .

So take your time . . . to let your awareness come to your body. Maybe sensing your hands, what your hands are touching and how they feel . . . and sensing also your legs, and your feet. . . .Sensing your body's contact on what you're sitting on . . . being aware of the support that's there, and letting yourself rest into that support. . . .

And then bringing your awareness inward, so you're sensing in your throat . . . your chest . . . your stomach and belly area . . . just resting your awareness in that whole inner area. . . .

And remembering that issue you spoke of, you called it [repeat client's words]. Taking your time, inviting a whole fresh sense of what comes right now, as you sense all that. . . .

And when you're aware of *something*, you might let me know.

The lead-in can be longer, and it can also be quite brief, especially once people have experienced this way of working. With an ongoing client, the therapist may ask at the start of the session, after preliminaries depending on the methodology, "Would you like a lead-in?" The client may reply, "Yes, a short one." A short lead-in might sound like this:

T: So take your time to bring your awareness to your body, sensing your whole body in the room around you . . . being aware of your body's contact on what you're sitting on . . . being aware of your breathing . . . and letting your awareness come inward, into that whole inner area, that includes your throat, your chest, your stomach, your belly . . . and remember what you spoke of, that whole thing about [client's words], take your time to invite a sense of that to come in your body now.

There are two more important points about offering a lead-in. It needs to be done in a slow tone of voice, with pauses added to give time for the invitations to be followed. And the therapist or facilitator would ideally be following along in his own body. For example, when saying, "Sensing your body's contact with what you're sitting on," the therapist would be sensing her own body's contact with what she is sitting on. The second point will help the first one. If you are following these moves yourself, your voice will be slower, and you will be putting in natural pauses.

THE LOW-AFFECT CLIENT

What if you invite your client to pause and allow the "whole body feel" of some situation or issue, and the client looks at you as if you started speaking a foreign language? You can offer a guided lead-in into the body, as we've seen. But for some clients the result is still: "I feel nothing," or "There is nothing there."

No one actually feels nothing. People who report feeling "nothing" are feeling something and not counting it. What they may be feeling is a numbness or a blankness or a sense of an absence of something expected. Numbness isn't nothing. It is something, a starting place. In fact, it may be an important place to spend some time. Clients who have low affect or have difficulty accessing emotions can often be helped to feel *something*, even when what is felt is subtle and hard to describe.

A client came to therapy wanting to be able to know what he was feeling. He was being "pressured" by his wife to be more expressive about feelings, and he didn't know what to say to her when she asked. The therapist assured him that he had feelings—everyone does—and it probably wouldn't be too hard to learn how to feel and describe them.

T: Let's start with having you sense how you feel right now.

C: I don't know. That's always the problem. I don't think I feel anything.

T: Okay. That's a starting place. Now, how about your body? Maybe you could take a little time to feel your body in the chair, just getting the sensation of touching, resting on the chair. Maybe rolling your shoulders. . . . That's it. You can feel the chair?

C: I can feel the chair.

T: Great! Let's move now to having you sense the inner area of your body. Like your throat. Feeling your throat is no harder than waking up on the morning after you had a sore throat, and you're just checking if you still have one. You know?

C: Okay, I guess I feel my throat.

T: And now, your chest . . . and now your stomach. . . .

C: I can feel them, but I don't feel anything in there. It just feels like usual.

T: I'm just wondering if "usual" feels the same way in your throat compared to your chest . . . or in your chest compared to your stomach. . . .

C: [in a surprised tone] My stomach is tight!

It developed that his stomach had been tight for years, but he had become so accustomed to it that he did not recognize this as a body feeling.

Another thing to offer to a client who feels "nothing" in the body is an invitation to notice if there is an enjoyable feeling there, such as "relaxed" or "peaceful." A client has a different kind of experience when checking whether her stomach feels relaxed than when asking, "How does my body feel?" If her stomach does feel relaxed, this is not an experience of nothing. If it doesn't feel relaxed, this too is something to describe and explore.

It's true that these experiences are probably not yet felt senses, but in order to get felt senses, a client needs access to the dimension of body feeling. These and other ways of supporting clients in experiencing what inner feeling is like definitely prepare the way for felt senses and Focusing.

However, there may be other reasons, in addition to lack of familiarity with a body feeling process, that clients are not feeling or finding felt senses. We'll have a look at some of them in the next section.

THE "RESISTANT" CLIENT

I'm not fond of the word "resistant" (thus the quotation marks) but it is a convenient way to point to a group of similar client processes:

- The client doesn't go into an emotionally connected process when invited. We spoke of this—and the possible reasons for it—in the section above, The Intellectualizing Client. When a client doesn't feel that what she is saying has been heard, she tends to keep saying it.

- The client pops out of an emotionally connected process into chatting, storytelling, or intellectualizing.
- The client says "I don't want to go there" about the body, about emotional content, or about a particular issue.
- The client experiences sleepiness or blankness when the process starts to "go deep."

None of these "resistances" are contraindications for Focusing. All of them can be seen as "process communications" that, when respected, are not obstacles but doorways. Let's discuss each one in turn.

Popping Out of Emotionally Connected Process

In Alice's first session, the therapist's impression of her was of a highly intelligent woman who spoke quickly. Alice said she had come for help with an issue about flaring up with anger, reacting with irritation without thinking first. This had become a problem in both her close relationships and her work setting. In discussing the issue, the therapist framed it this way: "We're going to get curious together about *something in you* that flares up with anger, without thinking first." Alice agreed that was a good way to say it.

Guessing that Alice was a person who needed some extra help to feel her body, the therapist invited her into a long lead-in, ending with "you might invite that part of you that flares up with anger to come into your awareness now . . . and sensing how that feels in your body."

But it was as if the lead-in had never been given. As soon as Alice could tell the therapist was done with the lead-in, she opened her eyes and started talking again about her issue. The therapist understood from this that Alice had not had enough time before the lead-in to really feel heard about her issue. This time the therapist was careful to stay in an empathic mode and really grasp each point that Alice needed to have understood.

C: It was that way with my whole family. Everyone would go off the handle, all the time. When I moved away and went to college, it was a big shock to find out not everyone was like that.

T: You came by it honestly. . . . Everyone in your family was doing it, going off the handle, getting angry. It came as a shock to discover that not everyone did that.

C: Right! But it's really a problem. It's why I lost my last job. I just can't help it.

T: Sounds like it's worrying you a lot, if it's why you lost your last job but you don't feel like you can help it.

C: That's right. My daughter has been trying to help me with my anger. She says I need to count to 10, think first and be diplomatic. I'm trying to do that.

T: That's what you've been trying, what your daughter suggests, to think first and be diplomatic.

C: My daughter is the best person in my life. She really has her head on straight. She is amazing.

T: I'm noticing that your voice changes when you talk about your daughter, and your face gets softer. Maybe this is a moment to pause and feel in your body again.

C: Okay.

T: Just sensing in that middle area of your body, throat, chest, stomach. . . . How it feels in there as you remember your daughter, how it feels to have a daughter like that.

C: [closing eyes again] My body feels really warm, especially in my heart.

T: See if it's okay to stay with that feeling . . . in your heart . . . really warm. . . .

C: It's like there's a nest in my heart with a bird in it, warming her eggs. [This is an exciting moment, when the sensing of a rich metaphorical image indicates that a felt sense has come.]

T: Wow, you're sensing like a nest there, and a bird, like she's warming her eggs. See if it's okay to stay with that.

C: [speaking slowly] It feels wonderful. . . . It's such a new feeling. . . . My arms and legs are getting relaxed. . . . It's really an odd feeling.

T: You might let that wonderful feeling be there as fully as it wants to be. [The therapist is encouraging the enjoyable feeling to get stronger and be felt even more, a move we discussed in Chapter 5.] And from this warm, relaxed feeling place, you might want to give another invitation to that part of you that goes off the handle. . . . Maybe this is a safe enough place for it to come to awareness now. . . .

C: Yes . . . it's like this funny hard place in my chest . . . hard like a rock in there. . . .

143

T: You're sensing it there in your chest . . . hard like a rock. . . .
   Maybe it's okay to stay with that. . . .

C: [at first silent, then eyes open] My daughter says I need to
   think first, and I'm really trying to do that, but it's hard. . . .

It's not surprising that a client who needed some extra help to
slow down and bring awareness inward popped out of that inner
awareness after touching in there for a while. Some might call this
resistant, but my guess would be that this client found a slow mode
of inner contact quite strange, outside of her comfort zone. For such
a client, popping out is a natural movement that helps her feel safe
and comfortable. We naturally step back from new experiences, in a
move reminiscent of dipping a toe in the water and then coming out
for a while. The therapist needs to accept what happened, allow the
popping out, give empathy for what is being said, and wait for another opening to invite awareness inward again. The next time, the
client is likely to be able to stay in inner contact longer.

What the therapist should not do would be to say, immediately:
"Close your eyes, and go back to feeling your body." Such a suggestion goes against and disrespects the natural movement of the process.

"I Don't Want to Go There"

When a client expresses not wanting to "go in there" or "feel that"
or "touch in on that" or the like, we want to completely go along
with this "not wanting to." When the clinician can accept and respect the part of the person that is feeling the need to "not go there,"
and invite contact with the "not wanting to," the client's sense of
safety increases and the process is able to move forward.

C: I don't want to get into anything today. I'm tired of the whole
   thing.

T: Okay, we don't have to get into anything if you don't want to.
   Maybe just acknowledging that, that feeling of tired-of-the-
   whole-thing.

Gendlin recounts such an interaction:

C: I did not want to come today. I do not have anything more to
   talk about (laughs). Really, there is a level I do not want to

touch. I got there once before and I got into crying and I could not get out of it; I could not stop crying. . . .

T: You do not want to fall in there again that way.

C: Right. Usually, I believe in feelings and I think: If you feel it, it gets better. But on this, I don't know.

T: So we won't say: Just feel it. You did that and it was not better. Whatever we'll do here, you would like it to be in a different way . . .

C: Right. (And then there is a long silence.) I can feel it right there, just below where I am.

T: Let's stay here a long while, just relating to it down there, without going there.

C: (long silence) The way the whole thing feels is that I am no good, and I am helpless to do anything about it. And I cannot hardly touch that. (1990, p. 217)

Notice the levels of what is going on in this segment. First the therapist grasps what the client does not want to have happen: "You do not want to fall in there again that way." Not just once, but twice, the therapist emphasizes that he understands and agrees; just feeling it is not what we will do here, today. Supported by the safety of that assurance, the client takes time and reports, "I can feel it right there, just below where I am." This is a beautiful illustration of Self-in-Presence, the ability to be with an emergent felt experience without having to be it. The therapist emphasizes that he gets and supports what is happening, including himself by using the word "let's": "Let's stay here a long while, just relating to it down there, without going there." This is what he thinks the client is already doing, but by saying it, he supports and joins the process. The result is that the client is able to contact the place where there is a richness to her felt experience, a sense of more, in process. Although she says, "I cannot hardly touch that," she is touching it.

Blankness, Sleepiness, the Fog Rolls In

For a client to get sleepy in a therapy session might be an indication of nothing more than a warm room, a comfortable chair, a soothing voice, and possibly not enough sleep the night before. But there are times when we have a strong sense that sleepiness is coming for another reason, a reason that has to do with where the client is in the process at that moment.

> C: It feels like there's a well of pain there in my belly. . . . Something feels wounded in there . . . and it's a wound that can never heal . . . [head nods]. Wow, I just got really sleepy! I have no idea what I was just talking about.

As clients begin to be able to touch emotional experiences that connect to states previously dissociated, it is natural and common for the dissociative phenomena to reoccur, at least temporarily. One way to talk about this is to say that "parts" emerge that are terrified that contact with these emotions will be too much for the client to stand. They are worried that the client has now as few resources for handling overwhelming emotional experience as she had in the past when these emotions were first triggered. These parts are ready and able to, in essence, bring back the dissociation they had relied on for protection, in the form of sleepiness, blankness, spaciness, the inability to think or concentrate.

We can understand the coming of these dissociative phenomena as a signal that the current process feels unsafe to some part of the client, and we can hear it as a request, so to speak, for more safety. The process itself is saying that the therapist needs to be Self-in-Presence and appropriately close, supporting the client's Self-in-Presence. This will include acknowledging that a part worried about going too fast and too deep for comfort is present and has legitimate needs.

When a client begins to drop down and get close to emotional states that are described as "painful," "old," "wounded," and the like—and when we ourselves can feel, as we follow along at the bodily level, that the client is starting to touch in on something deep, old (i.e., "young"), and vulnerable—this is a time to stay close and go slowly. We will speak more frequently, not leaving the client alone, yet not pulling the client away from the deep contact. We may use the word "we" in our invitations (rather than "you") to convey the close company that we are offering. We'll use the language "you're sensing," and similar moves (see Chapter 5) to support Self-in-Presence in the client.

C: It feels like there's a well of pain there in my belly.

T: Yes . . . you're sensing it there in your belly . . . like there's a well of pain there. . . . Let's just be with that, you and me. Let it know that we are here with it.

C: Something feels wounded in there.

T: Ah, you're sensing that place feels wounded. It shows you—it feels wounded. You might let it know that we are with it.

C: I'm doing that.

T: Maybe you can check if it can tell, if it knows that we are with it.

C: Not so much, it's almost oblivious. It's in some kind of other time.

T: So you might sense what kind of contact it would like from *you* right now.

C: Now it's starting to know I'm here. . . .

It has been my experience that in a sequence like this, when the therapist is staying very close and confidently supporting the client's ability to be with his own felt experience, it is less likely that the fog will roll in.

If sleepiness or blankness does arrive, we can make a gentle guess that it may have come from a part that is reacting protectively against where the session was going. Then, as with all phenomena called resistance, we probably would invite the client to turn toward that part directly, and assure both the client and that part of her that there is no need to push ahead. We can just as productively be with what doesn't want to be with the original experience.

C: I just went blank. What was I saying?

T: That blankness came right when you were about to be with the scared part inside. Maybe there's something in you that doesn't want to be there. . . . Maybe you could check if that feels right. . . .

C: Yes, I don't want to get sucked into that.

T: Okay, so let's pull back from the scared part. Maybe just sense if it would be okay to be with something in you that doesn't want to get sucked into that. . . .

C: It's a tightness in my shoulders. . . .

Learning to Be Open to Feeling "Bad"

Sometimes a client seems to resist invitations to bring an open quality of attention to bodily felt states because he "doesn't believe in doing that sort of thing," saying such things as, "It's no good to dwell on what you cannot change." Fixed concepts like this are an example of how cultural patterns of disallowing emotional states can reinforce individual patterns of dissociation and protection from painful emotional states.

A client had persistent troubled feelings about his own mortality and asked for help with them. After a lead-in, he felt "something" in his stomach, and described it using words like "tight," "sore," and "painful."

The therapist said, "It sounds like that place could use some company. Maybe you could just be with that."

There was a pause. Then the client shifted decisively in his seat, opened his eyes, and announced, "I don't believe in spending time feeling bad about something I cannot do anything about."

Clearly, this client had become identified with a part of him that had been protecting him from painful feelings, a part that didn't know that feeling states can change. This seemed to be a part that believed that feelings can be managed and controlled, a point of view that suffers from the fact that it is never actually true. In some methods (such as IFS), the therapist might invite the client to ask this part to step back. Other methods (such as ACT) might use metaphorical stories to help the client experience the fruitlessness of trying to control emotions. Going in either of these directions could be compatible with a Focusing approach (see Chapter 9) if we check back with the client's felt sense after whatever we try.

Here's what this therapist actually did:

T: Wow, I sense how clear and determined you are about that! You don't want to spend any energy or time on something you cannot change.

C: That's right.

T: There's a kind of strength there, isn't there? I saw you sitting up straighter. . . . You might want to sense how that feels in your body, when you say no to spending time on feeling bad.

C: Yes, that feels like strength. I get stronger. There's no point in feeling weak.

T: Maybe you're feeling that in your body now, "I get stronger."

C: It's like my spine is made of something strong, like steel or oak. . . .

T: That sounds really strong. . . .

After a further time of supporting the client in having the feelings of strength in a bodily way, receiving them as a resource (see Chapter 6), the therapist invites a return to the feelings about mortality.

T: And there is *something in you* that you were sensing earlier, a place in your stomach that was feeling tight and sore and painful . . . something having a reaction to thoughts about your death. . . . Maybe the very strength you're feeling in your body now would allow you to turn toward that more sensitive place inside of you. Might that still be there?

C: Yes . . . I can feel it . . . something very sad in there. . . .

T: Ah! And *you* with your gentle strength can be a protector for that sad one in there . . . gently listening for whatever it needs to show you. . . .

C: It's sad about my kids losing me the way I lost my dad.

T: You might let it know you hear it. . . .

In the rest of the session, the client explored the loss of his father at age 15, and was able to give company to the evolving feeling states that emerged. At the end of the session, however, he said again to the therapist, "I don't see the point of dealing with feelings about things that can't change."

The therapist responded, "There are a number of things in life that can't change. The fact that we are all going to die is one of them. But feelings do change—as you actually experienced in this session. One of the great things about this work is that we are spending time with what *can* change, which is our feeling reactions to what life offers us. Does that make sense?"

THE EVALUATING CLIENT

It is extremely common for clients, when getting in touch with an inner experience, to immediately decide whether they like it— whether it is a good or worthy experience—and if not, to begin the process of exiling or marginalizing it. "This isn't a good feeling. I need to get past it. I just need to decide to let it go. . . ."

Sometimes the client will actually say, "I don't like it," but more often she will give it a label, and this label already begins the work of pushing it away: "It's scary." "It's ugly." "It's flawed/defective." "It's useless."

The first, obvious trap for a therapist in this situation is to join the evaluation, to implicitly or explicitly agree with the client that this inner experience is scary or ugly or flawed or useless. The other, more subtle, trap is to disagree, and try to talk the client out of the evaluation, saying something like, "You don't have to be scared of it," or "I'm sure it's not useless in every way."

From a Focusing perspective, a client in this situation is identified with an aspect of self that is disliking another aspect of self. As discussed in the previous section, this is likely to be an aspect of self that is trying to protect the person from painful feelings and the dysregulating experiences that accompany them, such as the flooding of boundaries and the helplessness it brings. This may also be an aspect of self that is doing the work of authority figures and societal norms, making sure that socially discordant emotional states (such as anger) are kept within bounds.

Here is what one could say to a client like this: "I can really understand that you are not liking that feeling of [use client's words]. Of course! It feels really unpleasant and it sounds like it's been getting in your way. And I feel pretty confident that our work is going to enable it to change, just as you're hoping. What I'm going to suggest, to start with, is that you consider approaching that feeling neutrally, not judging it good or bad. It is simply there, okay? I'll help you to bring attention to it, describing it just as it is. Let's try that, because I think you are going to find that that feels better already, and it will be the first step in the path to that feeling being able to change."

THE SELF-CRITICIZING CLIENT

Perhaps the most painful and debilitating instance of partial-self process is the client's experience of an inner critical voice. There are degrees of severity to a self-criticizing process, from a mild "You need to get it together" to a vicious voice harshly attacking the person's worth and undermining his or her very right to exist.

Some methods approach this "inner critic" experience by encouraging the client to disrespect the critical voice, such as having the client say to it, "I won't listen to you as long as you're talking to me in that tone of voice." Although this intervention—if the client is even able to do it—seems to enable the client to feel inwardly stronger, at least for a while, it has serious drawbacks. Pushing away an aspect of self is not an action that would come from Self-in-Presence. Encouraging a client to disrespect or push away an inner criticizer actually reinforces identification with another partial self, the one being criticized. In our view, this is not real progress, nor does it bring lasting change.

Many years of experience have borne out our view that the inner critic is an aspect of self that has a primitive protective function, trying to prevent the repetition of negative experiences (Cornell, 2005a; McGavin & Cornell, 2002). Disrespecting it or rejecting it does nothing to lessen its painful frequency. We'll simply see another layer of self-criticism added, as in, "I'm feeling tense because I'm trying not to criticize myself so much."

The recommended Focusing approach is to support the client in being Self-in-Presence in relation to the criticizing self-aspect. This isn't a simple move, however, because the experience of being inwardly criticized tends to throw the client into identification with a criticized one inside. Being Self-in-Presence with this whole experience will mean identifying neither with criticizing nor with being criticized. In addition to the usual ways of facilitating Self-in-Presence (see Chapter 5), there are some supportive invitations that can be used uniquely with a criticizing process.

The Inner Critic Is Worried

We start by assuming that any critical voice is from a part that is fearful or worried, even if it doesn't seem that way at first. In many cases we don't have to guess what the inner critic is worried about; it often states its worry quite clearly, as if it were already true. "You are going to look like a fool" is what it says if it is *worried* you will look like a fool. "You are a stupid idiot" is what it says when it is worried that the truth about you is that you are a stupid idiot.

This kind of negative prediction when worried is a typical human process. "We're going to be late," your spouse says when the traffic closes in. "You're going to fall!" calls the mother who is chasing her toddler through the store. We often state what we are worried about as if it were a fact. It would be more accurate, and kinder, to say, "I'm concerned that . . ."—although it wouldn't be as forceful. So we often skip that preliminary phrase—and so do the self-critical parts of us. Adding back phrases like "it is concerned that . . ." or "it is worried that . . ." increases the accuracy of what is being said, and cushions the reactions of other parts of us. Similarly, when the criticizing part insists on an action, as in, "You have to start going to the gym," we can assume that it is worried about what will happen if the action is not taken.

We want to support the client in disidentifying with the criticized aspect of self that experiences the criticizer as attacking, mean, angry, vicious, and so on. Supporting the client in turning toward an inner criticizing process with the assumption that it is worried will tend to do this. "It's worried" tends to bring the criticizing part down to a human size, deserving of compassion and empathy for its worry and of appreciation for its work on behalf of the person.

The idea of this part being worried can be brought smoothly into an empathic reflection.

C: I'm getting this voice saying this is useless—there's no point.
T: You're hearing something in you say that it is *worried* that this is useless and there's no point. You might let it know you hear its worry.

The idea of the criticizing part being worried can be brought in by the therapist directly rather than in a reflection.

C: Now I'm getting that familiar voice saying I'm going to fail at this too, so why bother?
T: Sounds like that part of you is worried about something.
C: Yes . . . it's worried I'm going to fail. . . . It doesn't want me to fail.
T: Maybe you could let it know you really hear that it doesn't want you to fail.

C: That's funny! I thought it wanted me to fail! It's actually on my side. . . .

Inner Criticism Is Not the "Mind" or the "Ego"

Some methods—and some clients—refer to this kind of criticizing voice as a kind of "thinking," or call it the "mind" (Harris, 2009). This is understandable, because there is indeed a kind of thinking going on, albeit of a rather primitive sort, like the thinking of a young child. But to call this aspect of self "the mind" is to remove the possibility of using the word "mind" for a larger, more integrated function. When a client calls this process "the mind," I unobtrusively rephrase it as "something in you." This opens up the possibility of a more compassionate connection with this "something" that is worried, a connection which a label like "mind" makes less likely.

C: Now my mind is coming in, saying that this is all pretty silly.
T: Something in you is calling this "pretty silly." Sounds like it is worried about something.
C: Yes . . . it's worried I'm wasting my time. . . .

Exactly the same is true of the term "ego." For whatever reason, some systems and some clients will call a criticizing voice "the ego." We can respect those systems while at the same time rephrasing such statements so that "something" substitutes for "ego." Every fixed conceptual system interferes with available-for-change, immediate experiencing if it is used without dipping freshly into the present moment (Cornell, 2009).

C: My ego is talking to me now, comparing me to other people, saying I'm not as good.
T: Ah, something in you is comparing you to others. Maybe it is worried about how you stack up.

Notice that rephrasing words such as "mind" and "ego" with "something in you" doesn't bring up a discussion about whether those terms are helpful. It simply offers an alternative phrase that the client is likely to find more helpful. So the client is not derailed from the present experience into a discussion of language and conceptual terminology, but can go smoothly forward.

Inner Criticism Is Reactive to Emotional States

The criticizing voice is rarely the first experience that a client is having. It typically comes in after (and because) a client is in touch with some emotional experience that the criticizing one finds worrisome.

C: There's also a sense of annoyance coming up.

T: You're sensing something in you is feeling annoyed.

C: Maybe even angry.

T: Ah, you're sensing it's maybe even angry. Maybe you could stay with the feel of this right now.

C: It's like it feels there's something unfair about this. . . . Ugh! Now another part is coming in, like choking it, saying, "You should be grateful for what you have."

T: Ah, this other part comes now, saying to the first one, "You should be grateful for what you have."

C: It makes me think of my parents, their messages to me, like I should be feeling like everything was my fault, even children starving in Africa. I knew that was odd, even then. . . . I'm thinking about my parents now, like how could they think that?

T: So you actually didn't believe you were responsible for everything. You thought it was strange that your parents seemed to think that.

C: That brings a relief . . . and also something is scared, doesn't want me to feel stronger. It's worried about something. . . .

T: Maybe you can stay with it, sense into its worry.

C: [pausing, sensing] Oh! It's worried I will disown my roots and lose my identity. . . . Wow, I didn't know that was there.

Inner Criticism Can Sound Like a Parent But Is Not That Parent

Inner criticizing voices can sound like a person's parents, claiming similar values and using similar phrases. This does not mean—as a client might assume—that this "is" the parent, living inside the person. When given compassionate attention, a part such as this reveals its own reasons for its protective guardianship, which can be different from the parent's reasons for being critical. The criticizer is not the parent inside us, but it is a part of us that learned its vocabulary and style from the way that a parent criticized, and that functions to protect the person from the parent's retribution.

In this chapter we've discussed some of the more challenging types of client process, instances when clients don't find it easy to move into a Focusing mode of awareness and get felt senses. In all such cases, the fundamental suggestion is to respect the client's process as how she needs to be at this moment, and to find ways to invite attention to the presently felt experience even if it is not what was expected.

Difficulties in connecting with felt senses in body awareness may be connected with trauma and the systems of protection that the organism created around traumatic experiences. In Chapter 8, we look at some ways of using Focusing types of attention with clients who have trauma, addictions, and depression.

Chapter 8

FOCUSING WITH TRAUMA, ADDICTIONS, DEPRESSION

The processes described in this book have been relatively content free. We've had examples from clinical sessions, but without diagnosis or client history, and without a classification of the type of issue the client was facing. This is a natural consequence of the fact that, in Focusing-oriented work, content is less important than manner of experiencing. However, readers may be interested in clinical examples of using the Focusing process with some of the more serious challenges that bring clients to therapy. For this chapter I chose the issues broadly defined as trauma, addictions, and depression, because they are so commonly found among clients who seek the support of psychotherapy. If a client is suffering serious disruptions in her ability to manage daily life and relationships, we can be sure that past trauma underlies that situation. Addiction and depression—often both together—are serious conditions associated with trauma and the attempt to survive it.

The Focusing process is an effective support to clinical work with trauma and with such trauma-related client issues as addiction and depression (Fleisch, 2008; Ikemi, 2010; McGavin & Cornell, 2008; Tidmarsh, 2010). Mary K. Armstrong, in her moving and inspiring book *Confessions of a Trauma Therapist*, states flatly: "The best approach I know for healing trauma is Focusing," and goes on to say:

Focusing teaches the client to be compassionate and accepting of any information that bubbles up from previously hidden levels of awareness. It works *around* resistance, which is understood as protection that was needed at one time in the person's life. . . . The client learns to be her own understanding therapist between sessions and after the therapy is over. (2010, p. 205)

Trauma, addiction, and depression are huge topics, and it's not my intention to cover them thoroughly. The intent here is simply to point to some of the ways that a Focusing awareness can combine with other methods to offer effective therapeutic support for clients with these types of challenges.

WHAT TRAUMA IS

The key point to make about trauma is that it is to be understood experientially—what happened was or was not traumatic for a particular person. Van der Kolk, van der Hart, and Marmar write, "What constitutes trauma is highly personal and depends on pre-existing mental schemata" (1996, p. 304). Clearly it also depends on the resources available—or not—in the person's environment at the time of the occurrence of the traumatic event or events and afterward.

From a Focusing point of view, trauma can be understood as the severe lack or opposite of the organism's implied life-forward movement, as defined and discussed in Chapter 1. The experiential body process "recognizes" trauma as the absence or opposite of what would have carried life forward at that moment.

When needed interactions are lacking or missing and implied sequences cannot occur, the body (experiential process) continues to imply (indicate/disclose/move toward) what is needed for moving forward. When clients are not on track with or relating to this bodily experiencing, therapist's interactions can reactivate the blocked process. Many avenues (including reflective listening) can facilitate this opportunity for stopped aspects of client's living to flow into further process. This sense of flow, of bodily energy coming alive, opening outward, is a key com-

157

ponent of allowing the body process to reduce stress and unwind trauma-based blockages. (Fleisch, 2009, personal communication)

Trauma results in stopped process (see Chapter 1), and behaviors such as dissociation and addiction arise, which are attempts by the organism to solve the problem that the stopped process presents, but which fail to actually carry life forward past the stoppage.

Working With Trauma in a Body-Oriented Way

There is increasing agreement that trauma must be worked with therapeutically in a way that includes the body. Bessel van der Kolk writes in the foreword to Ogden et al.:

> In the West, approaches that involve working with sensation and movement have been fragmented and have remained outside the mainstream of medical and psychological teaching. Nevertheless, working with sensation and movement has been extensively explored in such methods as *Focusing,* sensory awareness, Feldenkrais, Rolfing. . . . Traumatized individuals, first and foremost, need to learn that it is safe to have feelings and sensations. (2006, p. xxiii, italics mine)

Body is no longer seen as separable from mind and meaning. Babette Rothschild writes: "When healing trauma, it is crucial to give attention to both body and mind; you can't have one without the other" (2000, p. xiv). Daniel Stern writes:

> Historically, we, in the modern, scientifically-oriented West, have isolated the mind from the body, from nature, and from other minds. . . . We are now experiencing a revolution. . . . This new view assumes that the mind is always embodied in and made possible by the sensorimotor activity of the person, that it is interwoven with and cocreated by the physical environment that immediately surrounds it, and that it is constituted by way of its interactions with other minds. (2004, pp. 94–95)

It is a great advance that a bodily dimension is now commonly included and understood as interwoven with mind. Working somatically is not done instead of working by talking, but rather there is a sense that psychotherapy involves the whole person sitting there—body, emotion, and mind (if the three can even be separated)—being met by a whole person sitting here.

Focusing-oriented therapist Lauren Mari-Navarro told me, "There is no life issue for which I've found IRF [Inner Relationship Focusing] unsuitable. I still use other psychotherapeutic modalities as they are appropriate, but based on my understanding of so much of the recent research in neuroscience and trauma, it's the body-based methods that are finding the greatest efficacy for lasting change."

Rothschild (2000) describes how body awareness offers a resource for trauma therapy by offering the client an anchor in the present moment and a way to put on the brakes. Working with trauma especially requires us to include the body at some level, because trauma and the incomplete experiences that it implies are carried by the organism in a bodily way. Levine (2010) points out how clients' small movements may be cues to larger movements that need to happen because they were orienting movements arrested at the time of the trauma. His method, Somatic Experiencing, is a powerful way to work with trauma, and can be combined with Focusing (see Chapter 9).

> These [traumatized] children, who have become "stuck" at some point along a once meaningful and purposeful course of action, engage in habitually ineffective and often compulsive patterns of behavior. . . . Such memories are encoded not primarily in the neocortex but, instead, in the limbic system and brain stem. For this reason behaviors and memories cannot be changed by simply changing one's thoughts. One must also work with sensation and feeling—really with the totality of experience. (Levine, 2010, p. 138)

A Focusing way of working can empower clients dealing with trauma and the results of trauma by giving them a more solid sense of Self-in-Presence as a place from which to begin to have experiences that were implied and incomplete, in a safe environment. Using a Focusing type of awareness, clients know they can go slowly, and can more easily sense—and respect—inner signals of needing to go more slowly or take a break.

Grindler Katonah describes how the client's fresh contact with a felt sense allows integrated growth to occur.

Especially working with trauma, when clients are able to "be with the felt sense," rather than just re-experiencing a traumatic aspect, fresh expressions of meaning are free to emerge and integrate with their present life purpose. . . . This back and forth process enables an unworded body sense to become "known" through meaningful symbols that continue to resonate with the body, opening the whole organism for the possibility of integrated growth in the present. (in press, p. 4 in draft)

I'll start my presentation of working with trauma in a Focusing-oriented way by telling the tales of two clients.

Monica and the Twisted Aura

Monica started therapy because she felt a lot of suffering from what she termed "not having integrity as a person" and "not knowing my own wishes." She would be unable to make simple decisions such as which friend to invite to a social event. When friends expressed hurt feelings, Monica would feel terribly guilty and have a strong urge to "set things right," even if she was objectively not at fault.

Monica showed a strong ability to be able to hold Self-in-Presence for herself. Without many preliminaries, the therapist was able to invite her to get a "whole body feel" of "not having integrity." What came first was panic, which she described as electrical currents running through her body. The therapist was careful to make sure that Monica felt safe in the room and able to be with the panicky feelings. He did this by inviting her to check if she felt safe to continue, and inviting her to sense this sense of "safe to continue" in her body. At the same time he confirmed this with his own inner sense (see Chapter 10).

Next Monica described a feeling behind her neck, which she called an "aura." Sensing into the aura, she said it was as if the aura were twisting away, trying to turn away from the world. To Monica herself, the aura felt "twisted, wrong." The therapist helped Monica to acknowledge and accompany these feelings.

In the next session, inviting attention inwardly to what needed to come, again Monica brought up the issue of "not having integrity,"

160

and again the feeling was behind the neck, like a "twisted aura." She said it was like "not wanting to be here, not wanting to be in the world." After quite a while of attending and sensing, the therapist invited Monica: "Take time to invite this sense of being twisted away, what next step *it* would like to have, in order for you to have integrity." Tears came immediately, and then a body movement. Monica sensed the aura twisting as if it were turning toward something. She said that it was like being able to face the attacker, and take the shame in the face, and just feel the shame. These words came before either Monica or the therapist knew what "attacker" referred to, or what was "the shame" being talked about.

Then more came. As Monica described the feeling of facing the attacker, she began to talk about her mother. She remembered many times at 8, 9, 10 years old, waking up from sleep being beaten by her mother, then verbally abused. The verbal abuse would culminate in her mother announcing, "I will kill myself," making it sound like this was because Monica was such a bad kid. The mother would go into the kitchen and lock the door, and Monica would stand at the locked door begging for forgiveness for unknown transgressions. Her mother would stay silent or say, "It's too late. It's over. You are so disappointing."

These were not new memories, but the fact that they came up in this context, when Monica was able to be Self-in-Presence and be with her body's felt sense of "facing the attacker and taking the shame in the face," made these memories freshly relevant and able to function in a changed way of living. Previously, Monica had felt no connection between her traumatic history with her mother and her current experiences with friends. Now, she could feel how the terrible guilt that she felt when a friend had hurt feelings, and her irresistible urge to "set things right," was speaking directly to her of how it felt to stand at that locked kitchen door, afraid that her mother would commit suicide and it would be her fault. Acknowledging and allowing the feelings in the context of memory brought a relaxing in the panic and tension, and a new ability to distinguish present situations from the past. Being able to let the implied movement complete itself, from "twisted away" to "facing the attacker," allowed the stopped process to flow forward.

Although a great deal of relief came from the session with the "facing the attacker" movement, trauma healing is a big process that happens over many sessions, each one bringing steps of change. There is not one dramatic session of change. Rather, over time, what needed attention came up in Monica's sessions in new ways, each time slightly differently.

In a subsequent session, Monica brought up the question of decisions. Faced with two friends both wanting time with her, Monica didn't know how to tell what she herself wanted. This was a decision about going on a weeklong vacation when one guest was allowed, and there were two friends who both wanted to be invited to go with her. The therapist said, "I am going to say these two sentences slowly, and you notice what happens inside you with each one. 'I want to go with A on the vacation.' 'I want to go with B on the vacation.'" When the therapist said the second sentence, he could see Monica's face twist, but he waited for her to tell him what had happened.

C: The first one is right.

T: How can you tell? What happened inside?

C: The first sentence felt good and right. It's about A and me going there and both enjoying ourselves. The second sentence—I could tell—it's not about that at all. It brought an anxious feeling, like this is more about me proving I am her friend.

T: Maybe you're feeling that anxious feeling there now.

C: Yes, it's like I'm afraid I will lose somebody I don't want to lose. I have felt this before—it's familiar.

T: So you might ask it—what is the core of it, what it is *most* anxious about?

C: [pausing] The biggest fear is that I am guilty of provoking a reaction in someone else that I can no longer control. . . . Ah, and now I see my mother's face. I have this big feeling of guilt, like an inner pressure. I have to set it right.

T: There is something in you that feels guilty or that is guilty. . . .

C: That's not quite it. . . . Uh . . . more like, it feels forced to feel guilty.

T: Ah, it feels *forced* to feel guilty! Maybe check with it, if that is right, if that fits how it feels.

C: Yes, that feels a lot better. The feeling of pressure is a lot lighter.

Finding this different formulation brought relief that could be felt in the moment, and Monica was now able to make sense of the feelings of guilt and needing to "set things right" that were so common in her current relationships. She was able to make more differentiations between what was occurring in her present life and what needed attention in her traumatic history. Today Monica is finding it easier to find her own wishes and preferences in her relationships with others. Questions of her own sense of integrity still come up, but she is more able to turn toward her own feelings, acknowledge them, and move forward.

Isabel and the Wall of Shit

Isabel came to therapy because of serious burnout. She had switched jobs to a position with less pressure in the hope of getting some relief, but still felt depressed and exhausted. She also felt very stressed by her relationships with coworkers, which seemed to be always conflictual.

At the start of her work in therapy, Isabel did not have much experience of Self-in-Presence, so helping her to experience it became a key goal. Isabel came into her first sessions feeling that *she* was depressed, *she* was exhausted—merged with the problematic feeling states rather than able to give them attention with awareness. The emergent process described in this section took place over a number of sessions.

After a discussion that included the way they would work together and what Isabel wanted from therapy, the therapist took Isabel through a lead-in (see Chapter 7) designed to help her experience a stronger sense of being Self-in-Presence through embodied groundedness. When Isabel was able to do this, the therapist then invited her to sense her "whole body feel" about the burnout.

After a pause, Isabel said, "I feel like shit." The therapist waited, not sure at what level Isabel was speaking. It turned out, from what she said next, that she was speaking seriously and descriptively.

> C: It's like I am full of this gray matter. It's like shit, a wall of shit.
> T: Ah, that's what you're feeling there, like gray matter, like a wall of shit.

The therapist's tone of voice communicated calm acceptance and interest in what was there and what would come next.

C: I can never be myself.

Supported by the therapist, Isabel was able to be with this feeling of gray matter or wall of shit, and the sense of "I can never be myself."

C: [pausing a long time, then] There is something under it, under the shit.

T: You are sensing there is something under the shit.

People who have traumatic states often encounter "walls," barriers of some sort in themselves. The function of the wall is protective, and part of what it is protecting from is the state of overwhelm (activation) that is so often associated with trauma. Therefore, it would not be a good idea to imply in any way that we want to get past the wall. Notice that the therapist merely gives a reflection ("You are sensing there is something under the shit"). He does not ask what it is. Even such a simple question would be likely to be experienced as pressure to go past the wall, and might well dysregulate the process, bringing overwhelm or dissociation.

Isabel reported sensing something very sad, very disappointed, very hurt or injured, behind the wall of shit. She then began to talk again about conflicts with people at work. It was as if touching on the "something" behind the wall of shit was enough for now. The therapist respected this.

In a subsequent session, invited to sense in her body, Isabel began to describe feeling as if she was smaller than she really was, bent forward, as if she was making herself smaller. "I feel like I am inside a box which forces me to sit like this." The therapist could see Isabel's body actually bending forward, as she made the movement that matched the inner feeling. He invited her to sense if it would be okay to stay with this feeling. This invitation supported Isabel in being Self-in-Presence.

Next Isabel reported feeling an anxiety about not fitting in. "If I don't fit in, everyone can see it, and they will throw me out, and I will never fit anywhere." She made herself even smaller, and the therapist invited her to be with this, using an invitation that is a further support for Self-in-Presence.

T: Maybe *you*, the larger you, can be with this wanting-to-be-small place.

C: [pausing] It's like there's a wound, and I'm bent over, trying to protect this wound.

T: No wonder something is trying to protect it, if it feels like an open wound. . . . You might sense how it needs you to be with it.

C: It feels like this is important. I really need to stay here.

At this stage memories began to come forward, not new memories, but newly relevant, emerging now from her ability to be present to the bodily experience. She described being sexually bullied as a teen-ager at school, a repeated situation for which she got no help or rescue for a long time. Every day she tried to be invisible. It was bad enough and hopeless enough that she considered suicide. She said that ever since that time, she never again had a feeling of fitting in the world, belonging in society. The words that came were: "Other people really can do that to me. I can't feel at home anymore."

In addition to the school memories there were other memories, many occasions since the time at school, even up to the present day, when she felt that other people identified her as a "good victim." "There *are* bullies and they *can* identify me." The next realization was, "So I can't be like I am, or they can identify me." She sensed that connected to this was the question, "Am I guilty for what happened to me?" And this led to a memory of her mother, who was depressed, who forbade her to cry anywhere but in her own bedroom. Isabel would come home from school in the afternoon wondering if her mother had gotten out of bed yet, and whether there would be any food on the table. The atmosphere at home was gray, sad, depressive, with an underlying message of "it is your fault." Being able to acknowledge and "hear" these memories and the accompanying feelings brought noticeable relief.

Steps of change in therapy sessions lead to new ways of living in life situations. Isabel came to a later session and told her therapist about being at the dedication ceremony of a new site at her company. The building was gray and black, architecturally full of straight lines. Isabel reported finding the building "gruesome," as if it was full of sadness. This was a familiar experience for her, when something in the outside world would trigger her overwhelming sadness, pain, and helplessness, and it would feel as if the feelings were out there, in the world, rather than in her.

But now for the first time, because of her process in therapy, Isabel was able to stay with the pain at the dedication ceremony without identifying and without projecting, allowing it to be there without pushing it away and going numb. It felt like "a wave of sadness." It wasn't overwhelming. She was able to say, "I am sensing something in me is very sad." Being able to use presence language like this was a key for her. She was very pleased at her growing sense of being the strong holding presence for her own feeling states.

"I can feel there is more of a present 'I,' and that feels good, more stable." Her work in therapy continues to build on this strengthening foundation.

CHARACTERISTICS OF A FOCUSING PROCESS WITH TRAUMA

Essential to any psychotherapy involving Focusing, and even more centrally important when that psychotherapy involves trauma, is the strengthening of the aware sense of self that we are calling "Self-in-Presence (see Chapter 5). The therapist determined that Monica was able to be Self-in-Presence before he invited her to get a body felt sense of her presenting issue. In the case of Isabel, the therapist took her through a process that was designed to strengthen her experience of Self-in-Presence, before inviting her to get a felt sense.

In both cases, when the felt sense came, the first experience and description of it ("twisted aura," "wall of shit") did not necessarily make sense to client or therapist. Without requiring the felt experience to be understandable, the client was able to keep awareness with the felt experience and sense into it further. At a certain point in both processes, relevant memories emerged. These were not new memories, in the sense that the client already knew that those things had happened to her, but their emergence within the Focusing session had a relevance that allowed the memories to be processed along with a sense of what had been missing for the client in those experiences.

Another characteristic of a Focusing process with trauma is that realizations emerge in layers or stages, along with associated memories. When the client can be Self-in-Presence and in aware contact with a felt sense, supported by the therapist's holding presence, what emerges in the client's process tends not to be overwhelming to the point of triggering activation or dissociation. Instead, the client (supported by the therapist) spends time with each feeling state with associated memories and realizations until there is a readiness for the next feeling state to emerge. If activation does happen, this is a signal to slow down and attend to the establishing of safety again. It may appear as though the next layer had been underneath this one, waiting to be uncovered, but actually spending time with a felt sense allows something to form that has never formed before.

The trauma happened to someone. Because of the way trauma results in a kind of frozenness in time of the experience, the client may find inside himself the "someone" who is the traumatized one, still at the age when the trauma happened. Yet another characteristic of a Focusing process with trauma is for the client to have a relationship with that inner younger self, which can result in accessing the positive qualities that had previously been frozen. Grindler Katonah tells the story of a client who had been raped at age 11, and how her therapy progressed with the support of Focusing:

> Mary was able to develop an inner relationship of compassion with the "young girl" in her that was raped. She began to talk about this young girl inside who "died back then." Not only had she lost her "carefree innocence" but she was also "stuck in time," unable to grow up.

> T: I invite you to bring your attention inside with a quality of compassion and interest. How do you sense that young girl now? The girl in you that was traumatized and no one was there to comfort her. How is it inside now when you notice her?
> C: I can sense how scared she was. . . . It's like I'm saying to her . . . it's OK to feel scared . . . Mmmm. That feels good. . . . to talk to her like that. It's like I feel young again. . . . there is a little energy there . . . like I'm coming alive a little.
> T: So there is a new sense of feeling young again. . . . Maybe it fits to say: "I'm coming alive a little . . ." Check inside.
> C: Mmm . . . I'm coming alive a little! (deep breaths, shy smile). (Grindler Katonah, in press, p. 14 in draft)

A final and very important characteristic of a Focusing process with trauma is that the client is able to access an organismic "knowing" of "what should have happened" in a bodily felt way, resulting in a new resource of inner strength and resilience. "What should have happened" is related to Gendlin's concept of implying (see Chapter 1) in the sense that the person's bodily interactional process did not imply the traumatic events, but rather implied (for example) safety, bodily integrity, and wholeness.

The emergence of "what should have happened" often comes after a fair amount of processing of the trauma has already been done.

Characteristics of a Focusing Process With Trauma

- The therapist helps the client establish and maintain Self-in-Presence as a safe holding environment for traumatic material.
- Through pausing and forming a felt sense, the client can allow aware contact with the way the body holds the traumatic material now.
- Realizations, relevant memories, and new behavior possibilities emerge in layers or stages, allowing integration and a sense of safety before the next stage.
- The client forms a supportive relationship with the inner younger self who went through the trauma, resulting in accessing previously unavailable qualities.
- The therapist supports the client in having "what should have happened" as a bodily felt experience, resulting in a new resource of inner strength and resilience.

ADDICTIONS

The pattern of addictive behavior and substance abuse or "misuse" can be seen as one form of avoidance and dissociation from unbearable emotional pain and the absence of reparative relationships. Alan Tidmarsh is one Focusing-oriented therapist who has found strong links between addiction and severe trauma histories.

For some time now I have worked with clients who have difficulty with alcohol and substance misuse, either their own use or a family member. If I think of therapeutic health as coming from a being-with, then these clients seem to demonstrate a being-without in so many ways. . . . A significant proportion of my clients have suffered neglect, abuse or trauma in early life. Always when listening to these childhood stories I am struck by the painful ambivalence of relationships involved. During moments of neglect the child is torn between rejecting the wrong and desiring the contact, backwards and forwards, touching and withdrawing, neither being right. (Tidmarsh, 2010)

Tidmarsh recommends "foregrounding the relationship" as a way of doing Focusing-oriented therapy with clients who have addictive process. This means that he works very much in an interactive process with the client, face to face and with eyes open, engaging the client with a process that includes his own felt reactions, sensed and then shared, with an invitation to the client to check if this reaction also fits for her.

My own experience with working with addictions includes the assumption that "the part that wants to do the behavior" should have a turn to speak and communicate about what it has been trying to do for the person. It may take quite a while to arrive at the place where it is possible to have this conversation, because it is only the person as Self-in-Presence that the "addict" part will trust enough that it will speak honestly about its motives. Without real effort to achieve being Self-in-Presence, the person is far more likely to be identified with another part, the one who is horrified and terrified by the "out of control" behavior, and wishes to do anything to stop it. Part of the work of the therapy will be to help the client find his way to Self-in-Presence by sufficiently acknowledging the parts, so that the addict part can tell its story and show what it is protecting.

The following dialogue illustrates the typical movement of this type of process in an abbreviated version.

C: I have to stop going on those porn sites. It's ridiculous, it's childish, and I'm afraid it's going to hurt my marriage.

T: So if you like, we could have a conversation with the one in you who is signing on and going to the porn sites.

C: I just want it to stop. It has to stop.

The client is identified with the part that needs the behavior to end. However much this resonates with what will ultimately be a healthy outcome, being identified with it will interfere with the Focusing because as long as the Focuser is identified with the part that calls the other part "ridiculous" and "childish," the part we need to listen to will not feel safe enough to come out. Before anything else, the therapist makes sure that what was said is heard.

> T: Of course, I know you want it to stop, and you're feeling how something in you is afraid it will hurt your marriage.
>
> C: That, and I really don't have the time. It takes up time I can't afford.
>
> T: Really good reasons why you don't want to do it. Yet there is a part of you that does do it. And maybe it would be helpful to get curious about that one.
>
> C: It's a habit, that's all. A stupid, bad habit.
>
> T: Well, but there *is* something in you that is doing that behavior, after all. It might be good to get to know it directly. At least it might be worth a try.
>
> C: All right. How would I do that?
>
> T: Let's just have you pause right now. . . . Feel your body contacting the chair. . . . Feel the inner area of your body, throat, chest, stomach, belly. . . . And then inviting in there, the part of you that signs on, that goes on the porn sites. Inviting and waiting.
>
> C: [pausing] It's like this "gotta-gotta-gotta" feeling. I feel a grabbing in my belly and below.
>
> T: Yeah, let's let that be here. And you might ask it what it wants for you, from doing that. Going on the porn sites.
>
> C: Total immersion. Getting lost in that world. Nobody else's feelings to deal with.
>
> T: It's letting you know what it wants from you is total immersion, getting lost in that world, nobody else's feelings to deal with. Check with it if that's right.
>
> C: Like pushing everyone away, especially Katie. Like going off alone and slamming the door.
>
> T: You're sensing it's like pushing everyone away, your wife, everyone, and slamming the door. Let's just be with that, sense what comes.

C: Lonely . . . I'm getting this really sad feeling. There's a lonely kid in here.

T: Ah. And maybe you can be with him. Maybe you and I can be with him.

It needs to be clear to the client that this empathic listening to the emotional state of the "part that wants to do the action" is not an endorsement of doing the action.

Working With an Issue About
Addiction to Emotional Eating

A client has been discussing her concerns about her weight and health, wanting to lose weight, upset at herself for eating a lot of junk food and gaining weight. This is not the first time this issue has been discussed. This client is often overwhelmed and flooded with emotional reactions, in our terms, "identified" with emotional experience (see Chapter 5). In this segment, notice how she starts from the identified and overwhelmed position.

C: I don't know why I am eating so much junk food. Like just today, I bought this healthy lunch, but instead went out and ate a big bag of potato chips. [visibly upset] Why do I sabotage myself this way? Is it that I don't like myself, or I just don't care . . . ? I don't know what it is—and I hate that I've gained back some weight. ["I hate that . . ." is what we would call an identified position.]

T: So you're aware of something in you that wants to eat what it wants—and that something else in you is angry, upset at this part. . . . I wonder if you sense it this way. [The therapist uses the phrase "something in you" to help the client disidentify from both sides in this inner war, and then invites the client to check if this way of saying it fits.]

C: [pausing to sense] Yeah, it does feel like that, like I get this good food, then something else takes over and goes for whatever I want. [When the client can sense that "something" takes over, we are now in a position to invite the client to turn toward that something with interested curiosity.]

T: So you are sensing something in you that seems to "take over" and eat whatever it wants. I wonder if you are in touch with that in you right now. Perhaps if it helps, vividly imagining that incident from earlier today you mentioned. . . .

C: [pause, closes eyes] Yeah, I can feel it now. It's right here. [touches her abdominal area] It feels like a lot of energy there, something stirred up. [The client has been able to take this key step, sensing inwardly and describing how it feels there, with minimal instruction. The therapist will recognize this contact and support staying with it.]

T: Right now you are connecting with that place in you—with a lot of stirred-up energy. You might want to acknowledge that place—sort of like saying hello to it. . . .

C: It's hard to stay with it—because I'm so angry at that overeating. . . . [As in this case, we often see clients move back into the identified position, especially with long-term, emotionally charged issues. The therapist will use "something" language to invite her back to Self-in-Presence.]

T: Yes, you are also noticing something else there that is experiencing some anger toward this place. You can also acknowledge that. See if it wants some time right now, or maybe it's willing to wait while you stay with this other place in you.

C: Actually, when I check inside, it feels okay to be with this other place. I really want to get to the bottom of this pattern. . . .

T: Okay. So you want to stay with this other place—right in your stomach area. Maybe keeping that gentle hand right there, letting it know you're with it. When you stay there, you could notice how it feels in your body, what comes. . . . [The therapist reaffirms the area of the body—"stomach"—and verbally mirrors the client's hand, which he can still see touching that area. He gives a gentle invitation to notice how the experience there feels and what is emerging there.]

C: [sigh] Yeah—when I keep that hand there, it eases a little.

T: Yes, so right there, that inner place is receiving that gentle, accepting energy, and it eases. . . . Now, if it feels right, you might stay there, perhaps sensing what comes, or maybe asking it if it's willing to tell us something about this wanting to eat. . . . [Once there is enough inner contact, we can try introducing inquiries without as much risk they will take the person into preformed concepts.]

C: What is coming is an image of me as a kid, always being alone, and having to fend for myself. I had to take on so much re-sponsibility and take care of myself at an early age. . . . I'm tired of it! [welling up of tears, crying] That kid in me doesn't want to be so responsible, to have to plan meals, go to the gym, etc. She wants to be free, to just do what she wants . . . and be taken care of.

T: There's a lot of deep feeling coming from there—sensing how much that "kid" in there had to take on so much burden and self-responsibility, when she should have been taken care of . . . and you can sense how much energy is there to break free from constrictions, and responsibility. . . . You might let her know inside that you hear this. . . .

C: When I go back there, I could sense something tighten up in my chest. It's an anger at not being taken care of, and always having to make decisions and do the right thing all by herself. She doesn't want to listen to anybody. . . .

T: Yes, we might imagine that being left alone for so long, no wonder something in you is angry about that. No child can or should raise themselves—so you could also ask yourself, if you were going to be a better parent to this child than you had, maybe sense how you would be. . . .

C: What I get is some type of discipline, a loving but firm struc-ture. I guess I haven't been a very good parent to her—and when I sense myself being that caring parent, that feels right. I sense a loosening in my chest area.

This was explored a little more. The client felt this realization was an important step and commented that her whole body felt calmer, more centered. The next day the therapist received an e-mail from the client: "What if I were my own parent today? What would I do to ensure my child's success and happiness?" followed by several very deep and thoughtful ways she would interact and work with this child. (This vignette is adapted with permission from one pre-sented by Glenn Fleisch [Cornell & Fleisch, 2007].)

DEPRESSION

As with trauma and addictions, we won't try to give a complete pic-ture of how to work with depression, but only to offer some examples to show some ways that a Focusing orientation might play out with a client who has symptoms of depression.

The first case is recounted at some length by Akira Ikemi in his article, "An Explication of Focusing-Oriented Therapy From a Therapy Case." It's a beautiful example of a Focusing-oriented, experiential, relational way of working, over a series of eight sessions.

> The client showed typical symptoms of depression. He had depressive mood, sleep disturbance, either loss of appetite or tendency to overeat, nightmares, lowered motivations and concentration. He also had anxiety about leaving his home, or more specifically, leaving his son, to go to work. The client said that his condition was "progressively getting worse." He visited a psychiatrist who prescribed him antidepressants (SSRIs) but he did not take the medication. He felt that medicines were not the answer to his condition. (Ikemi, 2010, p. 109)

Ikemi took a history, and learned that the client's daughter had died of a long illness at the age of 5, 2 and a half years before. Initially the client had taken a 3-month leave from work, but then had gone back to work and worked harder than ever. His depression had a gradual onset. Toward the end of the first session, Ikemi invited him to sense his "weather inside." This is a type of Focusing invitation developed by a colleague, Shoji Tsuchie. The client seemed delighted to be asked.

> To my invitation to sense his weather inside, the client smiled and said, "Wow, that's a great question! I love this kind of question. You know, nobody would ask me about that anywhere else. . . . In the clinics they ask about symptoms but not about this! . . . Yes, it's cloudy inside. Lousy rain, too. It's been like that for quite a while.

In the second session, the client brought up the question of the inner weather, and said that today it was cloudy inside. Ikemi invited him to stay with the cloudy feeling. This allowed the client to sense more specifically: He felt a fog in the chest and a cloud in the back of his neck. Describing the cloud further, he said it gave him "low visibility" and said he had been feeling low visibility ever since his daughter's death. By the end of the session, the cloud in the back of his neck had lifted, and he felt better.

In the third session, the client declared his need to take a leave of absence from work. He had "no motivation for work" and said, "all the work is stuck." Ikemi explained to him the procedure for getting leave. The client then sensed how his body was feeling now.

"Foggy in my chest—it's like old cotton in a futon. [And let's see, what is the old cotton telling you?] Wow, that's an important question! I need these questions that nobody would ask me anywhere else! . . . I don't know what it's telling me . . . but I feel it has something to say."

Between the third and fourth sessions, the client took a trip to the United States to visit the physician who treated his daughter. He had been drawn to this doctor, and they had developed a friendship. At the start of the fourth session, he reported that he had gotten his month's leave from work, but felt little relief since he still thought about work all the time.

"[And how do you feel inside today?] The old cotton is still there. It has less color now. I wish it wasn't there. [Let's be friendly to it.] . . . Oh, yes, as you say that, I was thinking that maybe the old cotton has been here a long time now. I just didn't recognize it. . . . It's saying, 'Do you recognize what I'm saying?' And I'm listening, but I can't hear."

Near the end of that session, Ikemi found himself saying to the client, "I feel you are in the process of change." The client responded, "Ah, yes. You feel that too! Yes. Whenever I come here, I feel like I'm evolving. So getting better is not getting back to where I started. There is no point of return, because even that point keeps changing."

Interview 5—"The weather inside has been lousy. Cloudy with lightning and thunder. . . . I feel uneasy in the center of my spine . . . maybe the old cotton has changed its shape . . . I went to the library to read about depression. I found a book that said: *it's time you accept yourself.* That really resonated with me. [How?] I don't know." (Time up.)

In the sixth session, the client reported that his leave from work had been extended for another month, and he was feeling more relaxed and comfortable at home. Invited by the therapist, he sensed inwardly and found, again, the old cotton. "It's like I'm in a sound-proof room, and it absorbs sound, heat, humidity. . . . I can't enjoy things . . . no motivation for anything. . . . It's quiet and comfort-able, but dangerous."

At the start of the seventh session, which took place about a month later, the client reported that his leave from work had been extended again. Some of his depressive symptoms had improved: His sleep was better, and his appetite had increased. But the "weather inside" didn't show much change. "It's stuffy and hot inside. I used to be active. I like traveling overseas. Now I can't seem to plan any-thing." The client described some past instances of taking his family on trips to experience living in a different culture, but said that didn't interest him now. Reflecting on this session, Ikemi wrote:

> I was impressed by the client's dedication to education and cross-cultural experiences, and by his respect for health care services and its providers. I was also a little puzzled, since it did not match my image of someone striving up the Japanese cor-porate ladder. The client's depressive symptoms improved to a certain extent, but only, it seemed, because he had time off from work. How he felt inside did not change much. As com-pared to the early stages of this therapy, the movement in his experiencing seemed somewhat stagnant.

But things were about to change dramatically. When Ikemi opened the door to the client for the eighth session, which turned out to be the final one, the client looked really different: bright and energetic. He announced that all his depressive symptoms were gone, and he was going back to work.

> "Even the foggy cotton went away, I feel all clear. Now, as I look back, *it was a message* to me, that my daughter died at age five and now she was sending me this message *"Daddy, do some-thing to help others, don't go on like this."* It was my *heart's message.* I didn't read your book [*Listening to the Heart's Message*, by Akira Ikemi, in Japanese]. I bought it and kept it on top of my stereo, but just looking at the cover of the book one night, it clicked!
>
> "I had always thought about that, but living a corporate life was so different, the opposite direction. There wasn't even time

to be with my family and in the little time I had, I would get upset with them because I was worn out. *This self-contradiction was the disorder.* Now, as I say it, it's even more clear. So even though I return to work, I'll quit, as soon as I find another job. I want a job helping others, especially children. I respect the nurses and the doctors who helped my daughter. I want to live like them. Now I have the courage. My daughter gave me the courage. When she died, it was like all the blood in my body changed. All my values changed. I used to be so competitive and on the run. Now my values have changed completely!"[1]

As the client spoke, new aspects of his experiencing kept emerging. Ikemi felt he was in the presence of someone at the highest level on the Experiencing Scale (see Chapter 1), "where new facets of experiencing keep getting explicated, as in a continuous felt shift." He could perceive no trace of depression; he sensed his client as full of life and energy. A few months later he heard that the client, after having returned to work, had quit the corporate job to work with children. He continued to be energetic and grateful for therapy, with no trace of depression.

In reflecting on this client and his change, Ikemi points to Gendlin's idea (1973) that psychopathology is not "bad contents inside" but a way of living.

---

1. In the introduction to the journal issue where Ikemi's article appeared, Campbell Purton comments from a Focusing-oriented perspective on what happened for Ikemi's client:

> How should we think about what is happening here? We could connect various theoretical schemes—religious, psychological, philosophical—to such experiences, and thereby "explain" them. However, the focusing-oriented approach stays with the *experiencing,* and with the client's own words—in this case, "She was sending me this message." . . . It is an example of what Gendlin (1991) called *naked saying,* the sort of saying that is characteristic of poetry, where one could *miss* the meaning by raising questions about whether the child "really" sent the message. The meaning can be there in what is said, without the need for an external scheme into which to fit it. As in the person-centered approach generally, the focusing-oriented approach does not commit us to *any* particular scheme; it allows the client's meaning to form in whatever way it will, through providing an environment that facilitates the coming (or forming) of what needs to come (or form) (2010, p. 92).

> A person changes by *living differently*. [Focusing-oriented ther-
> apy] does not look for bad contents inside, but creates the oc-
> casion for a person to live differently. . . . In this case it turned
> out that the client chose to live differently at the end of ther-
> apy. The living differently, however, came not only at the end
> of therapy. Taking a leave from work was a choice that the
> client made to live differently, although its meaning was not
> explicit until the end of therapy. Moreover, a different way of
> living began at the very first interview. The client's excitement
> about my asking him about the *weather inside* . . . had already
> initiated in him a different living—a different mode of relating
> to himself. (Ikemi, 2010, p. 113)

Ikemi modestly doesn't say much about how his own way of
being impacted this client's process. Reading between the lines, we
have the impression of a curious, warm, friendly but nonintrusive
presence, who often shares the client's puzzlement rather than
knowing what should happen, yet who keeps returning attention to
how it feels inside: "How is the inner weather?" He didn't give advice to the client, other than his process-oriented encouragement to
stay with the feel of the old cotton and ask what it wanted to say. Yet
the title of a book he wrote (not the book but simply the title) turns
out to be one of the clues that the client draws on, in the search to
unlock the puzzle of what will bring his life alive again.

It's clear to me that the client's attention to his own process happened within an environment of therapy in which the relationship
between client and therapist was a key element. As a Focusing-
oriented therapist, Ikemi remained interested in and open to what
the client's own process would reveal. The word "reveal" isn't quite
right, though, because this kind of therapeutic movement isn't a
discovery of something long hidden so much as a creative emergence of something implied but never before lived.

Reading a case like this, or experiencing this kind of process in
our clients, may make us wonder about seeing depression as a kind
of stopped process where the person has gotten onto the wrong road
and doesn't know how to find the "right" one. Of course I would
never want to oversimplify the complexity and seriousness of depression, and we know that many factors may be involved. But I
have now seen many examples like this one, where a client's curi-

ous, nonjudgmental attending to what is bodily felt, supported by an attentive, accepting therapist, creates a road out of a depressive state and into a life with new possibilities.

Listening for Life Energy in Depressive States

Depressed states are often connected to the attempt to not feel, as if the feeling that would come is too much and cannot be allowed. The person seems to sink more and more into a state of numbness, apathy, lack of feeling. In psychotherapy, a combination of the genuine contact with the therapist, and the possibility of inner contact with present experiencing just as it is, allows for a gradual process of allowing feeling to emerge.

Focusing-oriented therapist Glenn Fleisch (2009) says that the principle in working with depressed states is to connect with even the tiniest bit of life energy that might be there. What we mean by life energy would be any little bit of movement in the direction of life (see Chapter 6). If you ask people to describe their situation, often the life energy will reveal itself to you. We are not suggesting to ask people if they feel some sense of life energy. Part of what it means to be depressed is that the person is not able to get in touch with the life energy that is there. If we listen in a relaxed way and stay connected with what the client is saying, there is often a glimmer of life that can be noticed, although the client might be ready to go right past it. We might need to call for a pause so that what has life in it doesn't get overlooked.

Fleisch describes a client who said he had been in a major depression for years, which had recently gotten worse. "You could see it even in a postural sense, in his slumping down. So I checked with him: 'Like something in you is carrying a heavy burden? Something like that?'" The client said yes, and went on to discuss his sense of his family having high expectations of him.

After a period of empathic listening, Fleisch asked the client, "What kind of things do you do? What do you like to do?" The client replied, "I like to drive in my car, alone."

T: Maybe we can sense what that's like.
C: When I'm in my car, nobody expects anything of me. I like to drive in the country, with the scenery.

T: Notice if you have a sense what that whole thing might feel like. . . .

The client reported feeling a sense of warmth and relaxation in his chest, and his shoulders moved back and up, into a more relaxed stance. Fleisch invited him to stay with the enjoyable feelings and let them be there fully. Over time this client was able to use the positive feelings, from driving in his car alone, to create inner safety for exploring the issues behind his depression. He was also able to expand the activities in his life that felt enjoyable to him, and eventually was able to start working again.

In an even more dramatic story, Fleisch tells of a client who found life-forward energy in the desire to go under the covers. This was a woman who had attempted suicide and had been alcoholic. She described herself as "not really present in the world." She mentioned something about a painful wound inside but said that she didn't want to go there.

C: All I really want to do is go to bed and pull the covers over my head.
T: Of course I understand that overall, in the long run, you'd really like to be able to get up and live life. But let's just sense . . . maybe there is something in that pulling the covers over. Would it be okay maybe, to just sense into that?
C: Okay.

When she let herself imagine playing out the desire to go to bed and pull the covers over her head, she had an image of being a little girl in a room with her mother and father. Apparently she had been abandoned when she was very young.

T: Maybe just sense what that feels like.
C: It feels secure, warm . . . [bursts into deep sobbing] You mean it's okay that I go under the covers?
T: Not only okay, but something in you knew more than we did about what it needed.

The client had been fighting with her desire to go under the covers. Now she could sense the life energy in that pattern, and the life energy was already moving forward.

How One Person Shifted Depression
With Self-Awareness

As I was in the process of writing this book, I heard from a woman who pulled herself out of depression in one remarkable day of self-witnessing. I was so inspired by what she wrote that I asked permission to share it here. Here is her story in her own words.

> I used to suffer from depression and would have days where I felt overwhelmed by life, debilitated by it, staying in bed crying and fighting feelings of being bodily toxic, as if I were literally creeping out of my skin. For a long time my reaction to this was to turn what I was experiencing into self-hatred and loathing.
>
> One day, for some reason, I found that I was able to be present to myself and what was occurring. I didn't leave my room, but I didn't go back to bed either. Instead I started to become curious about what was going on. I remember even looking at my face in the mirror and witnessing the anxiety, tears and distress and thinking, "Wow, how extraordinary I look, how bodily real these feelings that are affecting me." I still suffered all day but my experience of it was different. I was more expanded and aware. The next day I felt quite healed and integrated.
>
> I have never experienced the same loss of myself when becoming overwhelmed since. The way I would say it to my friends was: "I am much more the captain of my ship."

This was a woman who found a way to shift her experience of debilitating depression on her own, through close attention to exactly how she was feeling. Of course such a story is not meant to deny the seriousness of clinical depression and the likelihood that professional support will be needed in most cases. But I tell this story because it illustrates the power of bringing attention to exactly what one is experiencing here and now, that it can make a difference, even in the most serious cases. If we can support our clients in bringing this kind of attention to what they are experiencing, their possibilities for change expand, and this is what we want.

In this chapter on working with trauma, addictions, and depressions, it has been made clear that Focusing can combine with ways of working with clients that come from a variety of modalities. In Chapter 9 we explore more specifically how Focusing can blend with and enhance various ways of working, and can complement what you are already doing with clients.

Chapter 9

BLENDING FOCUSING
WITH DIFFERENT
THERAPEUTIC MODALITIES

By this point, it should be clear that Focusing can blend with and support what you are already doing with clients. Because Focusing is a natural process of change, it finds its way into every clinical setting. By becoming conscious of this, we can enhance this process of change even further. Clinicians who are already using one of the methods discussed in this chapter or other similar methods may appreciate suggestions on how to combine Focusing with them if desired.

I've chosen the 10 methodologies discussed in this chapter with the intention of offering a representative sample of types of psychotherapy being done today; even so, much has been left out, both from my abbreviated pictures of the methodologies I discuss and in terms of other important methodologies not discussed. I hope that the brief ideas presented here will give you an idea of how to combine Focusing with whatever methods you are using.

In discussing how Focusing can be blended with other modalities, I do not mean to suggest that those other modalities are lacking or incomplete. Each modality discussed in this chapter is one I respect and that is practiced successfully and helpfully. Yet there are always clients who need something more, and it's possible that facilitating

Focusing awareness would be a supportive adjunct to the ways you already have for meeting therapeutic goals.

A NOTE ON PSYCHOTHERAPY INTEGRATION

There was a time when it was assumed that doing one modality of psychotherapy excluded all others, and whatever method you were using needed to be tightly adhered to. Since at least the 1980s this is no longer the case. Eclecticism is common today, as is both shown and supported by the flourishing of such organizations as the Society for the Exploration of Psychotherapy Integration (SEPI). Marvin Goldfried (2001) edited a fascinating collection of memoirs by psychotherapists who discovered in the course of their careers that they needed to expand their way of working from the discipline they first learned. In almost every case the result is a psychotherapist with a more eclectic approach rather than someone who has switched allegiances from one fortress to another.

> It is not at all atypical for practicing clinicians to encounter instances in which they find their theoretical approach to be lacking, where they then decide to borrow methods from other orientations. And perhaps in more philosophical moments, it is also likely that they might consider the possibility that the complexity of human functioning and the therapeutic change process cannot be captured adequately by their particular school of thought. (Goldfried, 2001, p. 4)

Rothschild (2000) points out the importance of adapting the therapy to the client rather than the other way around. Because of this, it is important for a psychotherapist to be familiar with a number of treatment models.

From the very start of my work with Gene Gendlin, he emphasized that Focusing did not belong by itself but needed to be combined with other avenues. He is a great believer in responding to the person as the person needs to be responded to, and therefore it is best if the clinician is familiar with as many modalities as possible.

> All orientations and procedures interfere with psychotherapy insofar as they are held to tightly. Priority must always be

given to the person and to the therapist's ongoing connection with the person. Like procedures, all theories can be destructive, if we think that a person is what a theory says. A person is a who, not a what. . . . The person is always freshly there again, always more than ideas and procedures. (Gendlin, 1996, p. 172)

Focusing is not itself a modality of therapy but can be seen as a kind of metamodality, a way of working that can underlie and connect any kind of work we do. When we bring Focusing into our work, we are bringing not a technique but a view of the nature of human life, how our bodies imply positive growth in the direction of fuller life.

[Focusing] lends itself to being crossed (Gendlin's term for a kind of cross-fertilization process) with almost any theory or approach. This integration process is quite complex, however, because Focusing isn't something simply added on like another technique. It is an underpinning that informs the way a therapist experiences the nature of human life and the process of growth. It includes assumptions such as: a. Every bit of human experience has a further step of movement implicit in it. b. Our bodies are not self contained machines, but open receptive environments registering vast knowledge of the situations in which we live. c. We are capable of tapping into this "bodily knowing." (Preston, 2005, p. 4)

COGNITIVE-BEHAVIORAL THERAPY

Cognitive-Behavioral Therapy (CBT), one of the most widely used therapeutic modalities today, began in the 1950s as "part of the movement away from seeing emotional problems as a sickness or abnormality. . . . Instead, behavior therapists viewed emotional problems as maladaptive learning" (Fodor, 2001, p.131). Learning theory principles were brought to the conceptualization, assessment, and treatment of mental disorders. In the 1980s, behavioral approaches were joined by cognitive therapy approaches that viewed disorders as arising from faulty thinking. The resulting confluence of behavioral and cognitive approaches is not as unified as the name "Cognitive-Behavioral Therapy" would suggest, but is a broad tent within which practitioners may be more behavioral or more cognitive, yet share an emphasis on client-therapist collaboration in creating and implementing treatment plans, and on teaching clients skills of both self-soothing and self-observation (Craske, 2010).

In the interviews that I did for this book, I encountered many psychotherapists combining CBT methods with a Focusing perspective. For example, clients dealing with anxiety or phobias might ask the therapist if there were a way to clear or release the symptoms, and the therapist would then offer graduated steps of exposure to the fear stimulus as in CBT. The client would then use Focusing to check inwardly if something about the issue remained to be dealt with, and might move back to the Focusing process to deal with the remaining aspects. Clients who need support in handling anxiety symptoms between sessions can be offered self-care processes from Focusing such as "let a gentle hand go there" and "let it know you hear how scared it is" (see Chapter 5).

Another typical aspect of CBT is goal setting and treatment planning in collaboration with the client. A Focusing mode of sensing can be used with goal setting so that the client can sense if the goal feels right, or if it needs to be adjusted a bit to make it more likely to happen. A therapist using CBT might listen for a while to a client to elicit the client's goals, and then ask, perhaps, "Shall we make that a goal?" (Beck, 2011). Blending in a Focusing approach, a therapist might then invite the client to get a felt sense of the goal, check the present wording, and sense if it felt like a "good fit."

T: How about finishing and handing in just one of the papers? Shall we make that a goal?

C: Uh, sure, I guess so.

T: How about if you take a moment to pause and get the whole of how that idea sits with you? [Notice how a felt sense can be invited without using the words "feeling" or "body" if those words are not compatible with the clinician's orientation.]

C: I guess I'm . . . there's a little uneasiness there.

T: Take some time to let that come out a bit more.

C: It's about . . . I'm not sure I'm even in the right program at school.

T: Okay, how about if the first goal is for you to get clear what is the right program for you?

C: [deep breath] Yes!

Clients who are facilitated to get a felt sense during goal setting and treatment planning are more likely to be engaged and motivated to carry out the homework and stay with the treatment plan. This same kind of inward checking can be implemented when treatment strategies are being evaluated and reassessed.

SELF PSYCHOLOGY

Self Psychology, founded by psychoanalyst Heinz Kohut (1984), is a flourishing movement with many practitioners and branches within psychoanalysis today (Lessem, 2005; Stolorow & Atwood, 1992), bringing a strong emphasis on the potential for the relationship between therapist and client to fill in deficits in the client's developmental experiences of relationships that should have been nurturing. Self Psychology is one of the branches of psychodynamic psychotherapy, which deals with the unconscious and interpretation of transference as key psychotherapeutic concepts.

One of the primary modes of therapeutic process in self psychology is a kind of attunement that Rowe and MacIsaac call "expanding attunement":

This is not only a matter of hearing the content of what the patient says, but is also an attunement to *how* the patient experiences what he or she says. . . . Expanding attunement is an intersubjective process whereby the analyst attempts as closely as possible to experience what the patient is experiencing, which includes the patient's simultaneous experience of the analyst. (1991, p. 137)

This kind of attunement is profoundly compatible with a Focusing process. Indeed, it is hard for me to imagine how a clinician could even follow this advice without doing some form of felt inner awareness.

I'll give one example of how a Focusing orientation might support a self-psychological way of working. Rowe and MacIsaac offer a lengthy and helpful discussion of a case with "Ms. O," a 26-year-old woman who was highly anxious and suffered from a number of physical symptoms. This segment is from a session in the seventh month of treatment:

> Ms. O walked slowly to the couch and lay down. She was silent for some time. She said, "I don't know what to say. My mind seems blank." She was silent for several minutes, apparently struggling with her thoughts. I said, "It's hard to get started today." The communication of my understanding of her experience seemed to ease her tension. (1991, p. 166)

The author points to the aim of this response as being an expression of "my thinking and feeling my way into Ms. O's experience." As such, of course, this response is complete and does exactly what it was supposed to do within the therapeutic context.

If, however, there had been a wish to bring a more consciously Focusing-oriented way of being into this setting, one can imagine the therapist phrasing his response this way: "You are sensing it's hard to get started today." Or even: "You are sensing something in you finding it hard to get started today." Such a therapist response constitutes an invitation to the client to sense and accompany her own feeling state. If one wanted to combine a Focusing approach into a self-psychological framework, this would be one way to begin.

INTERNAL FAMILY SYSTEMS THERAPY

The Internal Family Systems (IFS) model of psychotherapy is an empowering method of understanding human problems, as well as an innovative and enriching philosophy of practice that invites both therapist and client to enter into a transformational relationship in which healing can occur. IFS was developed by Richard Schwartz when the inner parts encountered by his bulimic clients called forth his training in family systems therapy. Although many methodologies address multiple ego states and work with parts, Schwartz developed a unique approach centered on the strength and clarity of his concept of "Self leadership." The client is assumed to be capable of being Self, a noncoercive, collaborative inner leader (Schwartz, 1995).

IFS forms a natural partnership with Focusing for many reasons. IFS and Focusing share an emphasis on empowering the client while viewing the client's issues in a nonpathologizing way. Clients are assumed to have the resources they need for healing and transformative change. There is a strong similarity between the IFS concept of Self and the Focusing concept of Self-in-Presence.

As an IFS therapist helps a client get in touch with a part, the part is often experienced as an image, in a process called by Schwartz "insight": "'Seeing' is not always the proper term for this process, because while for some clients it is like watching a Technicolor movie, for others it is less a vision than a kind of sense that these things are happening" (1995, p. 113).

From watching demonstrations of IFS therapy, and reading accounts of the process, I have become convinced that felt senses often emerge naturally as inner parts are contacted. IFS practitioners even use the term "felt sense," and the description, starting with something vague that gradually reveals itself, certainly sounds like a felt sense to me.

> Sometimes a part is not clear at first. It starts out as a vague image or felt sense—for example, "folded over on itself." You get to know a part like this by staying with your experience in a patient and curious way. Don't push for clarity prematurely. If you are open and interested, the part will know that it is welcome, and the nature of it will become clearer in the course of a few minutes. For example, "folded over on itself" might gradually reveal itself as a part that is curled up to protect itself from attack. (Earley, 2012, p. 116)

Bringing a Focusing way of working into IFS might include inviting this felt sense of a part more deliberately, even in the cases when the experience doesn't come in this way at first.

> C: I see an old woman—she looks like a witch and she's frowning at me.
>
> T: You might take some time to sense if you have the feel of that old woman, in an embodied way.
>
> C: Like a clenching tightness across my shoulders.
>
> T: And let's have you stay aware of that clenching tightness as you ask inside if it is okay to have a talk with that old woman.

One thing we might expect is that bodily changes will reflect changes in the process, as the parts reveal what they have been trying to protect the person from or guard against. IFS practitioners already invite body awareness frequently. As I said, the two methods are quite compatible, and with a conscious awareness of bringing Focusing into IFS and IFS into Focusing, this compatibility can serve both even more.

ACCELERATED EXPERIENTIAL-DYNAMIC PSYCHOTHERAPY

AEDP (Accelerated Experiential-Dynamic Psychotherapy) was created by Diana Fosha, who states the central philosophy behind her work:

> To live a full and connected life in the face of difficulty and even tragedy requires the capacity to feel and make use of our emotional experience. So much of the alienation from and fraying of family and social life that lead individuals to seek therapy can be traced to the terror of affect. . . . If affect-laden experiences can be made less frightening in the therapeutic environment—that is, if patients can be helped to be safe enough to feel—then they can reap profound benefits, for within core affective states are powerful adaptive forces and processes with tremendous therapeutic potential. (2000, p. 13)

From the elegant simplicity of this fundamental premise, Fosha has built a complex and detailed methodology that is profoundly relational and rests on carefully worked-out theoretical foundations. The importance of affect as a "wired-in, adaptive, expressive, communicative aspect of human experience" is related to the secure attachment process for human infants, which leads to resilience in the face of trauma.

Fosha refers to a "core state" that seems quite similar to our Self-in-Presence, and says that fostering an internal secure attachment through self-to-self relatedness is a key aspect of her work. In terms of its similarity to Focusing, Fosha states that "such a huge part of AEDP is about exploring in detail and with no expectations the person's textured experiences" (personal communication, 2012).

Fosha's definition of "core affect" could well include felt senses, and is quite compatible with a Focusing awareness:

The term *core affect* has been chosen simply to refer to that which is vital and spontaneous and comes to the fore when efforts to inhibit spontaneity (i.e., defensive strategies) are not in operation. . . . *Core affect*, or more precisely, *core affective experience*, refers to our emotional responses when we do not try to mask, block, distort, or severely mute them. (2000, p. 15, italics in original)

To illustrate how a more specific use of Focusing might integrate with AEDP, I picked a vignette from Fosha (2000) that illustrates a process of supporting a patient experiencing a freshly felt energy arising after a powerful mourning process. I chose this vignette because it strikes me as very similar to the Focusing emphasis on listening for the life-forward direction (see Chapter 6).

> PATIENT: I woke up on Monday and I was comforted by this thought . . . "I have to find this out and we might be together again someday but this has to happen first. . . . So let's go."
> THERAPIST: Hmmm.
> PATIENT: And I woke up on Monday and I said "Let's go" (big full smile). And I've been checking with this feeling and asking, "Is it a defense?" And it isn't. It's just "Let's go."
> THERAPIST: Let's go. . . . That's wonderful.
> *(Later in the session.)*
> THERAPIST: I am so taken with this "Let's go." It's very deep.
> PATIENT: It feels very good. (Fosha, 2000, p. 168)

Without in any way suggesting that Fosha's way of working with this client was not complete in itself, I will take the opportunity to suggest what I might have done if I had been this therapist. I hope I would have been just as taken with the feeling of life energy in the "Let's go" of the client after a long mourning process. I probably would have been "feeling along" with this in my own body—as I'm sure Fosha was. (See Chapter 10 for the therapist's use of her own felt process.) At some point I might have said, "Yes! Let's really have this 'Let's go,' have it here. Maybe you have a feel for how your body is now, now that you have this 'Let's go.'"

The client can both "have" the fresh, life-moving-forward feeling and sense into it, sense the ways that it contains more that hasn't quite been put into words yet.

DIALECTICAL BEHAVIORAL THERAPY

Dialectical Behavioral Therapy (DBT), developed by Marsha Linehan especially for working with clients diagnosed with Borderline Personality Disorder, combines cognitive-behavioral principles with methods of mindful awareness drawn from Buddhist practice and an emphasis on a climate of unconditional acceptance in the therapeutic alliance (Linehan, 1993).

As set forth by Linehan, a dialectical view on the nature of reality and human behavior has three primary characteristics: the principle of "interrelatedness and wholeness," the notion that reality is "comprised of internal opposing forces (thesis and antithesis)," and the assumption that the "nature of reality leads to a wholeness continually in the process of change" (Linehan, 1993, pp. 31–33). These principles, especially the first and the third, are completely consistent with the philosophical view underlying Focusing. So are the fundamental assumptions that "patients are doing the best they can," and "patients want to improve" (Linehan, 1993, p. 106).

A key aspect of DBT is what is called "structured skills training" (Linehan, 1993, p. 103). Patients generally work in small groups in addition to being seen in individual therapy. The skills trained include: core mindfulness skills, distress tolerance skills, and emotion regulation skills. Focusing would be a helpful process to teach in DBT groups, as it offers resources in all three of these areas.

DBT and Focusing are clearly compatible and combinable. After all, the mindfulness practices of DBT already involve sensing the body exactly as it is. To bring in Focusing, one could add invitations to the client to pause and allow the "whole feel" of a current issue to come into awareness, and then to describe and acknowledge what comes.

SOMATIC EXPERIENCING

Somatic Experiencing (SE) is the process psychotherapy created by Peter Levine (1997, 2010), based on an understanding of how the natural process of organismic resiliency in the face of trauma can get interrupted and shut down, and can also be facilitated to resume. Levine's research and work reveal the key role of the body in healing from trauma. The concept of survival-oriented body movements needing to complete in order for trauma to release is a powerful one, and very much in harmony with the Focusing idea of stopped process implying what it needs to carry forward. In creating Somatic Experiencing, Levine incorporated a Focusing awareness. His way of working with clients includes asking them to sense both challenging and resourceful experiences in the body. Both Focusing and Somatic Experiencing place an emphasis on the body's natural healing processes and look for resources of strength and resiliency in the client's bodily felt experience.

In Levine's accounts of processes with clients, it's not hard to see moments when Focusing is probably happening. For example, in this segment with "Miriam," Levine asks his client to repeat a gesture slowly, and then notice how her arms feel when she makes the movement. Miriam's response at first has the characteristic hesitation and self-correction of a Focusing process:

> "It feels like I'm pushing something away . . . no, more like holding something away . . . I need more space, that's what it's really like." She sweeps her arms from in front of her and off to both sides, creating a 180-degree range of free motion. She lets out a deep and spontaneous breath: "I don't feel as suffocated, and my belly isn't hurting like it was when we started." (Levine, 2010, p. 161, ellipses in original)

From the vantage point of Focusing, it is an unusual feature of the session with Miriam that a felt sense is expressed as a movement. Unusual, but not unheard-of. Focusing-oriented therapist Glenn Fleisch (2008) has done a great deal of work with client gestures as implicit leads, and his way of working includes inviting clients to repeat movements slowly and sense how that feels.

Levine's account continues:

> She extends her arms, flexing her wrists again. This time she holds them out for several seconds, almost at arm's length. "It's the same problem . . . at work and with my husband, too." She now places her hands gently on her thighs. "It's so hard for me, I don't know why but . . . I don't feel like I have a right to do this . . . like I don't have a right to my own space." (2010, p. 161, ellipses in original)

Levine asks her if this is more of a feeling or a thought, and Miriam replies that it is really a thought. This is a fascinating session that goes on much longer in Levine's account, and is obviously of great value to the client. Without in any way suggesting that something else should have happened, we can imagine how it could have gone differently with Focusing.

> C: It's so hard for me, I don't know why but . . . I don't feel like I have a right to do this . . . like I don't have a right to my own space.
>
> T: You are sensing *something in you* that feels like you don't have a right to your own space. . . . Maybe you could sense, how and where you feel that *something* that feels you don't have a right to your own space.

The distinction between feelings and thoughts becomes less relevant if any thought can become a felt sense, a "something" given attention from Self-in-Presence, which can then open and move forward.

I interviewed a number of psychotherapists who combine Somatic Experiencing with Focusing, and they all mentioned that adding support for Self-in-Presence through the conscious use of presence language ("You are sensing something in you feels . . .") has been a helpful addition to working with SE. Clients supported to be Self-in-Presence can receive even more of the benefits Levine refers to when he says: "Helping clients cultivate and regulate the capacity for tolerating extreme sensations, through reflective self-awareness, while supporting self-acceptance, allows them to modulate their uncomfortable sensations and feelings" (2010, p. 137).

SENSORIMOTOR PSYCHOTHERAPY

Sensorimotor Psychotherapy was developed by Pat Ogden, drawing from the Hakomi method of body-centered psychotherapy of Ron Kurtz (1997), and intended as a synthesis of methodologies for working with body sensation and movement but without the use of touch (Ogden et al., 2006). Working purely in a sensorimotor way is not yet a Focusing-oriented process, because sensorimotor psychotherapy as such is concerned with body responses defined as "instinctual and nonconscious" (Ogden et al., 2006, p. 5). As we have seen, Focusing brings in a dimension of body awareness that is blended and integrated with felt meaning; a felt sense is not an instinctual and nonconscious experience, but one that is deliberately invited and contains an intricate mesh of connections with life meaning and implied forward steps.

However, sensorimotor psychotherapy and Focusing can be combined productively, as a number of therapists I spoke with are doing. As one illustration of how they can be combined, I'll point to a client story told in Ogden et al.:

> One client who presented with visible tension across her shoulders was directed to notice this tension and explore it for meaning. She reported that it felt like the tension was holding back anger—an insight gleaned from awareness of her body rather than from cognition. This insight led to the realization of an erroneous belief that she had no right to be angry at her abusive father. Working with the anger through the tension itself (slowly executing the movement the tension "wanted" to make, processing the associated memories, beliefs, and emotions, and learning to relax the tension) assisted this client on her road to fuller self-expression and resolution of the emotions related to her past traumatic events. (2006, pp. 12–13)

I was struck when I read this passage that this client sensed that the tension was holding back anger using "awareness of her body rather than . . . cognition." This could very well have been a place where the client was getting a felt sense, especially since it led to an insight about an erroneous belief. The sensorimotor therapist had the client work with the anger "through the tension itself" by inviting missing movements and learning to relax the tension. Had this been a place where a therapist wanted to bring in some Focusing, we can imagine that the session might have gone like this:

T: You might let it know you hear how angry it is.

C: Yes, it's angry . . . and there's some feeling like . . . it's not okay to be angry. I have no right to be angry at my dad.

T: Ah, you're sensing something in you feeling like it's not okay to be angry at your father. So you have the angry feeling . . . and you have something in you saying it's not okay to be angry

> . . . and both are there. . . . You might want to say to the tension, "No wonder it's so tense, if there's both an angry feeling and it's not okay to be angry."
>
> C: That's right, yes. That brings some relief. Not okay to be angry—I'm letting it know I hear. . . . Now it's relaxing. My shoulders are relaxing.

A therapist who has both sensorimotor work and Focusing at hand can choose, based on the needs and style of the client, whether to use purely sensorimotor methods of executing movements and relaxing tensions, or whether to facilitate an inner empathic contact with what those tensions have been trying to do. The two processes can be combined by moving from one to the other within a single session.

EMDR

Eye Movement Desensitization and Reprocessing (EMDR), developed by Francine Shapiro (2002), is a psychotherapy approach that includes eight phases of treatment, containing elements of many effective psychotherapies in structured protocols. At the heart of the treatment, the therapist facilitates the client's eye movement across his or her field of vision. There is a mindfulness component of open awareness, in that the client is instructed to "just notice what happens."

Armstrong (1998) writes about combining Focusing and EMDR in treating trauma, describing her own practice with adults recovering from the effects of childhood trauma, particularly child sexual abuse. Sitting with the traumatic material in the company of someone who provides closeness without intrusion, as in a Focusing approach, is a profoundly remediative experience. In Armstrong's view, EMDR adds the ability to "jump start" the traumatically held material (1998, p. 28).

Mary C. Howard, a psychotherapist who was already trained in EMDR when she began learning Focusing, told me how she now combines Focusing and EMDR.

> Focusing has given me a new way to help clients regulate their nervous systems as well as teach them how to self-regulate. I

especially like the Inner Relationship idea of helping the client be Self-in-Presence. Whatever is there for the client needs to be honored and acknowledged. Acknowledgment is the best way to be present, because you validate in a nonjudgmental way. I love the Focusing because it is so gentle and their bodies are always in charge. From EMDR I use the bilateral stimulation for times when people are just looping, stuck in their heads, having a hard time settling into their bodies and becoming quiet enough to tap into and stay with their felt senses.

Bilateral stimulation can be done through eye tracking of the fingers, or auditorially using prepared recordings, or through tapping on both sides of the body. This therapist finds that bilateral stimulation, an EMDR technique, has a calming effect that enables her clients to quiet their minds and move into their bodies. Once they calm and go into the body, slowing down from the distracting chatter in their heads, they are able to be available to what is really needing their attention, in a Focusing way.

Another way that EMDR and Focusing can be combined is that clients who are familiar with the effects of EMDR might ask for it when their psychotherapy session reaches a certain point. "This feels like a place for EMDR." Therapist and client can move into an EMDR style of processing, and then afterward use a Focusing type of sensing as a further way to process and integrate what came.

> With some clients I'll set aside a block of sessions for EMDR. With others, a single session may get things moving. Still others who are familiar with EMDR . . . will ask for just enough eye movement during a session to get the trauma moving, so that the felt sense can be carried forward. (Armstrong, 1998, p. 29)

PERSON-CENTERED AND EXPERIENTIAL PSYCHOTHERAPY

Focusing emerged from the research collaboration between Eugene Gendlin and Carl Rogers, informed by Gendlin's philosophical perspective. In the work of Rogers, this stream flowed forward into Person-Centered Therapy (Rogers, 1961), a flourishing methodology in many areas of the world of psychotherapy (Mearns & Thorne, 2007; Warner, 1998). Experiential psychotherapy was established by Gendlin (1973) and has been joined today by many strands of practice (Purton, 2010), all sharing the perspective that the essence of change is in the client's experiencing process.

There is no need to write about the integration of Focusing into experiential psychotherapy, since this is the mode of therapy in which Focusing is already most at home. Focusing can also be brought smoothly into Person-Centered Therapy through the emphasis on grasping the client's frame of reference (Purton, 2004), to which can be added an attentiveness to what is forming within the client's experiencing (Gendlin, 1968).

> C: "I would like to change my insensitivity. It's one reason I'm coming into therapy. . . . I've come a long way though. When I was young I didn't know anything about feelings."
>
> T: "When you look back you feel pretty good about how far you've come."
>
> C: "I've also made it to my present job, which is near the top, and I'm not known to be a hard person."
>
> T: "You've done it without being a bad person."
>
> C: (cries) "I'll be damned. I don't know why I'm crying. That's dumb."
>
> T: "Something wells up in you that says, 'I'm not a bad person!'"
>
> C: "Is that what it is?" (Gendlin, 1996, p. 22)

In their excellent guide to Person-Centered Counseling, Dave Mearns and Brian Thorne (2007) show how an awareness of Focusing can join with and enhance the emphasis on close empathy that is already a key element of a person-centered way of working. "Simply focusing on the known surface feelings may only be going over old ground, whereas focusing on 'the edge' (the felt sense) can be the door to the unknown" (p. 48).

EMOTIONALLY FOCUSED THERAPY

This book has been about doing individual therapy, not couples therapy. But our chapter on combining Focusing with other methods would not be complete without discussing Sue Johnson's Emotionally Focused Therapy, because it is a way of working with couples that is eminently combinable with Focusing.

When I was reading Sue's book *Hold Me Tight: Seven Conversations for a Lifetime of Love*, I was struck by her ability to listen for and facilitate felt senses in her clients.

> As James's eyes close for a moment, I hear the emotional down elevator begin to ding. "It's like Vincent looks distracted. He doesn't focus on me at all," James says, tearing up. If we quietly stay with our emotions, they often just develop, like a fuzzy image gradually getting clearer. James continues, "So I get this lump in my throat . . ." (Johnson, 2008, p. 116)

I was so intrigued that I asked Sue to chat with me about whether she was consciously incorporating Focusing with her clients. She said no, not as such—although a remarkable Focusing session she once received helped her make important life changes. Her approach to therapy is experiential, a category within which Focusing falls. "There is a sort of generic process where you slow things down, use empathy, use imagery—and this gets people into their emotions." I asked her whether her definition of "emotion" would include body awareness and meaningful connections as well as the categorical emotions such as anger and sadness, and she replied,

> The way I think of emotion is, it has all these elements in it— body, thoughts, etc. We still call it emotion because it has an action tendency. If a client says "Right now I'm shattered," I don't try to change that into some categorical emotion like fear or despair. I say, "What's it like to feel that?" or "What's it like in the body, feeling shattered like that?"

That kind of facilitation is no different from what I would do when facilitating Focusing, so I would put Emotionally Focused Therapy on a list of methods that not only can be combined with Focusing, but that essentially already do incorporate Focusing.

HOW TO COMBINE FOCUSING WITH ANYTHING

There are many more ways of combining Focusing with different methodologies than I can mention in this chapter. To name a few more, briefly: There is an excellent book on the topic of combining Focusing with Solution-Oriented Therapy by Bala Jaison (2004). There is a movement of Focusing-Oriented Art Therapy (see Rappaport, 2009). Emotion-Focused Therapy for Individuals, formerly known as Process-Experiential Psychotherapy, incorporates Focusing as one of its integrated methods (Elliott et al., 2004). Friedman (2007) describes combining Focusing with Hakomi therapy. Ecker, Ticic, and Hulley (2012) describe a method for "memory reconsolidation" and note that it can be facilitated by Focusing.

The way to combine Focusing with anything else is to always come back to connecting with the client's experiencing, no matter what else we do. Whatever we suggest, whatever we invite the client to say or do, whatever we offer as an interpretation, if we then check with the client—and most important, invite the client to check with himself—how that felt, what impact it made, what experience is here now, then any methodology can be enhanced with the life-forward process of the client's own experiencing process.

There is one more key factor in bringing Focusing into clinical settings, perhaps the most important of all: the clinician's own ability to be inwardly present and aware of felt senses. In Chapter 10 we explore the power of the clinician's own Focusing in the therapeutic process.

Chapter 10

FOCUSING FOR THE THERAPIST

My client arrives in my office at the end of a long day, my last session of the evening. The way she comes into the room, the set of her shoulders as she closes the door, her quick sideways glance at me— all this has already impacted me by the time I choose to become aware of my felt sense of being here with her right now. I might not make that choice. I might do a whole session "on rote," slightly out of touch with myself, depending on my techniques to carry me through. But I have learned that those are not the good sessions, not for my clients and not for me.

My felt sense of here and now will include my own tiredness, will include the reverberation of the previous sessions with other clients, the meeting with my staff in the morning, the chat with my sweetie at lunchtime. All those situations I am still living in as I sit down with this client, here and now. I have learned that if I try to push my own felt living away and make myself a blank, I am actually less available for this person in front of me now. So I don't do that. But I'm also not immersed in or preoccupied with what I am carrying from other times.

I have learned that it helps a lot to inwardly acknowledge what is here for me now. When I acknowledge what I feel, it seems to lessen its grip on me. It backs off, as it were, allowing me to attend to what needs my attention now, without pushing any aspect of me away. "Tired . . . especially in the shoulders . . . a little anxious about what Joe's doctor said . . . excited about how the writing is going." All that is here, and I inwardly sense it and say hello to it, even as I am sitting down and meeting my client's eyes. The tiredness eases a little. The other feelings fade into the background. I am here.

Within myself now I am sensing the quality of my being with this client, which is impacted by and emerges from how she is with me and with herself, as well as our history from past sessions that we both carry. It would take hours to detail all of that, and still we couldn't capture it all—but it is all here in the felt experience of now, which we both hold implicitly. There is a difference between this level of experiencing that is always present and the awareness of it. The client may not be directly sensing it yet—or ever—but I certainly need to be.

During our session, my felt awareness of "me" and "us" will be a resource for me and for my client. It will make it more likely that my client will feel me as genuinely present with her. It will be a source for those intuitive moments when I offer something that might turn out to be actually helpful. It will be a place to go and check if something happens that needs for me to articulate my own reaction.

The fact that I am in touch with my own felt experiencing, and I am calmly able to be present, primarily for my client and also for myself, can be a model for my client. This ability to be Self-in-Presence, aware and in touch with felt experience, yet from a larger perspective, will serve my client well if she can move into it more and more for herself. Perhaps I will be offering facilitative prompts to support her in doing this, but none of them will have much effect if I am not coming from that place myself. And even without any overt prompts, my own felt contact as Self-in-Presence communicates to her. It both holds her process respectfully and safely, and shows how she can give that safe holding to herself, even without an explicit word being spoken about it.

If our interpersonal process gets bumpy, if I fail to understand her as she wants to be understood or if there is some other kind of rupture, if irritation or anger flares between us or there is a shutting down from a loss of trust, then my own felt experiencing will be a source of guidance, as I feel my way forward into what needs to be spoken in order to resolve, repair, and grow from what broke down between us for a while.

Later, when the session is over and my client has gone, I still have my felt sense of our interaction to tap into if I need to and if it needs me to. If there is something about our work together that troubles or puzzles me, that I need to take to consultation or just work through by myself, I will start with my own felt sense of this client and how we were, feeling into the implicit knowing of what's not quite right and what is needed.

In all of these ways, a clinician's contact with her own felt experiencing supports, informs, and carries forward the living process of therapy for her clients and for herself. In the rest of this chapter, we'll look more thoroughly at the various ways that the therapist's Focusing process facilitates psychotherapy.

WHEN THERAPISTS KNOW FOCUSING

Clinicians tend to want to learn new methods and processes in order to offer them to their clients. "How can I facilitate Focusing in my clients?" is the natural first question. Surprisingly, however, it might be even more important for the outcome of therapy for you to be Focusing during the therapy hour than for the client to be Focusing. In research reported in Hendricks (2001), there was a high correlation between therapists knowing Focusing and clients having positive therapy outcomes.

Lynn Preston writes: "In order to have a focusing oriented therapy, it is necessary for the therapist to know focusing—not the client" (2005, p. 4).

Capacities—such as the capacity for Focusing—develop in an intersubjective context. When what is being invited in the other is a quality of attention, the first requirement is that we ourselves have that quality of attention. For example, you cannot very effectively help another person to be calm if you yourself are not calm. The ability to know what we feel and think—and know that other feelings and thoughts are possible and may be held by other people— seems to develop only in a relational context (Fonagy et al., 2002). The same is true of the capacity to pause awareness and allow felt senses to form, the process called Focusing. Focusing ability is inherently relational.

A therapist who is grounded in his or her compassionate Self-in-Presence and in contact with his or her own felt senses during therapy is:

- Supported in preparing for sessions and debriefing after sessions—whether going on to another client or going home
- More available to the client as a genuine person, even without explicit self-disclosure
- More able to access embodied, situational, felt knowledge about what the client might need
- Modeling and demonstrating the Focusing process without having to teach it
- Able to access genuine felt process when needed to repair ruptures that have occurred
- Able to work through reactions to "difficult" clients

You might be wondering: How can I feel myself at the same time as I attend to my client? If you're like me when I started out, feeling yourself and attending to another person might seem like nearly opposite activities.

Learning to have contact with how I felt at the same time that I was attending to another person was not an easy skill for me to develop. In my family of origin, the "right" thing to do was always to pay attention to the other person, never to one's own self. That's how I ended up in my 20s without a clue how to tell what I was feeling. When I learned to do Focusing, I slowly managed to find my own inner sense. But when another person had the floor, or when the conversational ball was bouncing back and forth, my sense of myself vanished. When I was learning to do psychotherapy in my 30s, and my supervisors advised me that my own feeling state when I was with a client should be part of my field of awareness, I felt like I was being asked to rub my stomach and pat my head at the same time—while whistling "Dixie." I didn't even know how to begin to feel myself while I was supposed to be attending to someone else.

But it happened. Practice, and intention, lots of practice, and lots of intention—and now my felt experience is available any time, whether I am with a client, with a friend, speaking to a group, attending a meeting, or right now, as I sit here writing. Usually it's not saying much. It's just a quiet hum. But if something in there needed attention, I would know it.

Focusing-oriented therapists know that feeling their own felt experiencing during therapy is part of what they do.

As I sit across from a client, my intention is to be with them as they explore their life experience. To do this, I let my attention fall down into my body. There I can hover with a physically felt sense that includes a present feeling of the other person, how we are together, my present mood, what I understand about therapy . . . in fact, many aspects of the situation all at once without grasping onto anything in particular. In this non-attached state, I can be with another person without trying to figure them out or fix them. It is "being" rather than "doing" and is what I recognize as an essential aspect of existential-phenomenological therapy. (Madison, 2001, p. 3)

Akiko Doi and Akira Ikemi describe how this "continuous attending" to both self and other is woven into the fabric of a Focusing-oriented or person-centered psychotherapy:

Therapists cannot expect the client to get in touch with feelings and talk from those feelings without attending to their own feelings. Self-disclosure, genuine responses and sharing on the part of the therapist are tips of the icebergs. Underneath these apparent responses is the continuous attending to the client's feelings as well as to the therapists' own feelings. Underneath there is a respect for whatever contents that emerge from both the experiences of the client and of the therapist. Through this process of referencing, persons emerge newly, and both client and therapist become "congruent" or genuine. (2003, p. 99)

Am I always aware of my client and myself equally? No, it doesn't feel that way. The quiet hum inside me usually doesn't need much of my attention. Awareness is not always equally divided between me and my client, nor is it always 80% client and 20% me. It flows between us as needed. If something happens that needs me to pay attention to myself, I can do that. I'm never, or rarely, out of touch with my own felt experience, but it usually doesn't occupy very much of my attention—until it needs to.

A mentor once said to me, "You can't take another person to a place that you haven't gone yourself." To give an obvious example, if I want my client to be relaxed and comfortable, it cannot help but matter whether I myself am relaxed and comfortable. If I hope that my client will have the courage to face what feel like inner demons, then I need to have faced some of my own. And I need to be continuing in the process of self-exploration and self-care, which is not one that ever is finished and over with, but is ongoing.

> Your commitment to doing your own emotional work means that no matter how harrowing your client's memories, how intense her fear or rage, or how bone-wearying her depression, you're there for it all. If you start to feel overwhelmed, you take care of yourself so that you won't abandon her or disappear. (DeYoung, 2003, p. 56)

How you are in the therapy room is not just a matter of what you know or what you think. Surely your values, attitudes, beliefs, and concepts do make a difference. Everything you have learned, both from classrooms and from experience, is there with you and your client in the therapy relationship. But this is not just "head" knowledge. What you know and what you have gone through is part of your lived experience here with your client. How you feel, what you believe, and what you value are here, too. Your client can feel your presence, how you are, even without being aware of feeling it. "A person can sense another person's manner of attending," psychotherapist Joan Lavender said to me.

That our clients can feel us, feel how we are with them, is a good thing. "Our authentic personal involvement, emotional responsiveness, and unavoidable subjectivity, far from interfering, are essential features of every successful psychotherapy" (Wallin, 2007, p. 171). However, it matters enormously how aware I am of what I am bringing into the room and into the relationship.

Lynn Preston writes of a student who did not realize that her own anxiety about anger was impacting a client's progress. A class exercise about how a therapist's "deep seated nonconscious relational fears and expectations" can impact therapy led to a realization for this student, that Preston describes in this way:

> Mary . . . confided to the class that she felt anxious about the emergence of anger in her work. She flashed on a patient whose brother had committed suicide. The therapy with this client had gone well while the feelings of mourning centered around sadness and loss. But when the patient began to feel angry at his brother, Mary became anxious. Just that morning

he had ended his therapy session by saying that he was think-ing of stopping—that he felt therapy wasn't helping him any more. Mary came to class feeling troubled and bewildered about what had gone wrong. As a result of the class discussion something seemed to click into place for her. She felt enlivened as she glimpsed a new aspect of what might be going on be-tween her and her client. She realized that perhaps she had subtly dissuaded him from bringing his angry feelings to her. "How does this help her?" another student asked. "She is still going to have trouble dealing with her client's anger."

"It has already helped me," Mary said. "I feel less confused and helpless. This larger way of looking at it has shifted some-thing inside me. I am imagining that I can ask my client if he is experiencing me as discouraging his angry feelings. It seems possible now to have a different kind of conversation about it." (Preston, 2005, p. 20)

There is no doubt that "how we are" impacts our clients in many ways, and the more we can develop further, carrying forward our own stopped processes, the more we can be available for our cli-ents.

Focusing-oriented therapist Carol Sutherland Nickerson writes:

Because of the effects of my own Focusing practice, my clients are now sitting with a therapist who has a more integrated brain; one whose emotional, mental and physiological regulat-ing systems are working better and better all the time. Profes-sionally, I listen better, conceptualize a client's needs faster and respond to transference and counter-transference issues with faster recognition, more ease, and clarity. (2009, p. 9)

DEBRIEFING AFTER A CLIENT, PREPARING FOR THE NEXT CLIENT

Often a clinician sees many clients, one after another, throughout a working day. What we would most like is to be present to each cli-ent, not still carrying with us our thoughts and feelings about earlier clients in a way that interferes with our being present to the person in front of us. Of course we have such thoughts and feelings; we're not immune to them, and the fact that we carry our clients with us in some way between their sessions is a key part of the relational process that is psychotherapy (DeYoung, 2003). But when I am with this client, I want my reactions to my previous clients to be acknowledged and contained, over on the side, not in between us.

Focusing can be used after one session and while preparing for the next, as a way to sense and acknowledge any reactions that have come in me and are still lingering, in response to the client just past. I can even do this while writing notes, so that the process of writing case notes is not only an intellectual exercise, but one in which I take time to sense my felt experience of what happened for the client—and me—in the session. I might ask myself a question such as, "Where in the session did I feel the most interested and alert? Where in the session did I sense the client's process felt most alive?" I might also ask myself, "What am I still carrying? What feels like a concern? Did something in me get triggered?" It's unlikely I'll have time to go fully into these issues in the short time between clients, but by sensing and acknowledging them I can set them down. I can come back later. I don't need to carry them into the next session.

If another client is on the way in, I can prepare for his arrival by acknowledging whatever I am feeling, and strengthening my sense of Self-in-Presence. Glenn Fleisch (2009) describes a grounding exercise that can be done in a few minutes, before a client comes in: "I feel my feet on the ground. I envision my body solid in my space. I envision being neutral and flexible, so I can go whichever way the client goes. I become aware if I have any agendas for this session, personal or professional. If I do, I acknowledge them."

BEING MORE AVAILABLE TO YOUR CLIENT AS A GENUINE PERSON

In 1990 Gene Gendlin spoke movingly to a group of psychotherapists about what is essential, on the side of the therapist, for the process of psychotherapy to happen. In his view, it was "to be present as a living being." He went on to say, with a characteristic twinkle, "And that is lucky, because if we had to be smart, or good, or mature, or wise, then we would probably be in trouble." He didn't mean, of course, present in the sense of merely taking up space.

Someone who is checking e-mail on a smartphone is "present"—but not very available. Gendlin meant we need to be present in the sense that we are available, both to the other person and to ourselves—and because we are available to ourselves, we are more available to the other person.

> Then I am just here, with my eyes, and there is this other being. If they happen to look into my eyes, they will see that I am just a shaky being. I have to tolerate that. They may not look. But if they do, they will see that. They will see the slightly shy, slightly withdrawing, insecure existence that I am. I have learned that that is okay. I do not need to be emotionally secure and firmly present. I just need to be present. (Gendlin, 1990, p. 205)

"Being available" does not necessarily mean self-disclosing. In most cases, it simply means that I am present, the client can feel me as being present, and if he looks me in the eyes, he can feel that there is someone real over here. Of course I have no control over what my client actually feels. On the other hand, it is absolutely clear that how I am has impact, not simply what I say. If I am in touch with myself, present to my own felt experience, and at the same time attentive to the client and ready to take in what she says and feels, this has an impact on the client.

A client who can feel the therapist as genuinely present is more likely to feel trust in the therapist and in the therapy setting. He is more likely to have access to his own emotional states in a safe inner holding environment (Self-in-Presence), and the work of therapy is more likely to go forward. The therapist in touch with himself creates an "experiential environment" (a phrase I first heard Joan Lavender use) within which client change in the client's own direction can occur.

Being in touch with myself during a session with a client means that I'm aware of the intricate mesh of my own feeling state. This is usually a background awareness, because my attention puts the client in the foreground. But sometimes my own feeling states come forward, and I have learned that this is an essential part of the process of supporting a client. I have learned that I am less present when I am trying to wipe my own feelings off the board, than when I have my feelings.

In my early years of working with clients, I was embarrassed by my own emotional reactions, and thought I was being unprofessional when they came up during a session. Now, I let them be here. When a client spoke of losing his cat, who had been with him for 17 years, I could feel in my own body what it might be like to lose a friend who had been woven into one's life for so long. My eyes filled with tears, and my voice naturally contained my own feeling. His eyes met mine, and we met there, each with our own feelings, yet woven together by how we each felt. In another case, a client was talking on, but I could feel a word that he had spoken earlier still resonating in my felt awareness. When he paused, looking to me for some input, I said, "I'm still with that word you said earlier—'honesty'—I'm not sure why but . . . it sounded important." His eyes filled with tears. "That's the most important thing of all," he said softly.

> It is of little importance how good, wise, strong or healthy the therapist is or seems. What matters is that the therapist is another human person who responds, and every therapist can be confident that he can always be that. To be that, however, the therapist must be a person whose actual reactions are visible so that the client's experiencing can be carried further by them, so the client can react to them. Only a responsive and real human can provide that. No mere verbal wisdom can. (Gendlin, 1968, p. 217)

Even self-disclosure is not ruled out, as long as it is for the purpose of enhancing the client's process in some way, and as long as one makes sure to come immediately back to contact with the client. Neil Friedman describes this in his book on doing Focusing-oriented therapy:

> I am a very human therapist. I express my feelings when my client is stuck—going nowhere, externalizing, intellectualizing, making small talk, not engaging me and therapy. I do so also when clients are with their feelings, I have feelings related to theirs, and expressing mine will probably move us forward. Sometimes it doesn't. But so long as I quickly check in with my client after an expression of my feeling, no harm is done. *Checking-in is crucial. This means following-up a self-*

disclosure with a return to listening. That way if I'm off the track, we get back on it. And if my client doesn't want to hear from me, he tells me, and I respect his choice. (2007, p. 117, italics in original)

ACCESSING INTUITIVE MOMENTS

Therapists who know how to do Focusing themselves, and who are in touch with their own felt senses during a therapy session, have access to "embodied situational knowing" in the relational field, which includes what is going on for the therapist, what is going on for the client, and what is going on between them, moment by moment.

> When I look inside myself, I don't find some pure pristine "me." I find "a me-with-you." My experience of myself is facilitated, shaped and delimited by this "me-with-you." . . . There is always an us. There cannot be an "I" without an "us." (Preston, 2005, p. 7)

Focusing-oriented therapist Glenn Fleisch (2009) describes a kind of "felt imagination," such as with a client who said, "My wife asks me how I feel, she's frustrated with me because I don't share my feelings. I don't get her problem! I'm happy to tell her what I think!" Fleisch paused, sensing in his own body, and said to the client, "Some place in you is annoyed maybe? Or irritated?"

Neil Friedman (2007) also describes this kind of responding, which he calls "empathetic imagining":

> I feel my way into my clients' worlds to sense where they are at this very minute. I say or express what I imagine to be there. . . .
>
> The client mumbles something about loneliness. Then he sits silently for a few minutes. I don't want him to be lonely here too.
>
> T: (softly) I imagine you are feeling quite sad . . . maybe cut off . . . [no response] . . . maybe, isolated—
> C: Yeah. [He starts to cry and goes on to bring up vivid experiences of first loneliness, then sadness, then anger. He be-

comes quiet again. but it feels like a different kind of quiet.
Five minutes or so pass.]

T: I imagine it feels . . . *good* to share all that with someone—

C: Finally.

T: Finally.

C: Yes it does. I've held it back a long time. I do feel better now.
(Friedman 2007, pp. 122–123, ellipses and italics in original)

Bundschuh-Müller describes a kind of "Presence" that includes
the therapist's bodily experiencing:

By means of an enhanced sensitivity/receptivity for the client's
experiencing, therapists can use their Self as a tool for understanding and responding to the client. In the same way they
can sense how their responses influence the client. When he
or she is therapeutically present, the therapist's bodily experiencing is a reflection of an inner synthesis of the experience
the client expresses and feels plus the therapist's own experiencing plus her professional expertise. In therapeutic presence
the therapist's body is a receptor and a guiding factor in the
process. . . . The body is an instrument; it is "tuned in" and
develops a resonance—consonant or dissonant—to whatever
is being communicated to it. (2004)

We are not always guided by sureness. Sometimes—often—it is
unsureness that is our guide. A sense of a client's affect not fitting
with her words may bring a sense of puzzlement in us, not being
sure what is happening, or not knowing how to be facilitative. We
may be unsure what to do with this "not knowing," and we may
keep it with us for many minutes while continuing to attend to the
client. What we eventually say to the client may emerge from this
unsureness rather than from any kind of clarity, and this also can
bring the client's process forward.

Focusing-oriented therapist Akiko Doi tells the story of a case like
this, and I'll let her tell it in her own words:

The client was a man in his mid-20's, and had just begun
working in a research facility of a major corporation. His problem was that he felt his current job as an engineer was not
suited for him. When the therapist first met him, he took a
leave of absence from his office because of sleep disorder, de-

pression and anxiety, and was eager to switch to a different job that really suited him.

During the first five sessions, the client repeatedly insisted that his current job was not right for him because he didn't have the capabilities that were demanded by his job in engineering R&D. The client was very talkative; however, he did not seem to touch down inside. . . . The therapist asked the client to feel inside for his felt sense of the situation, and she also reflected the feelings the client expressed. However, the client kept repeating that he had "no capability." He was going around in circles. Whenever the therapist asked him how he felt about the whole thing, he answered, "It's difficult to explain," and did not go much further. The therapy seemed blocked.

In the relationship with this client, the therapist was unable to understand what was really annoying for the client, even after five sessions. The therapist had been trying to find out what was it that made him so upset that he should consider leaving his job. In other words, the therapist felt incongruent, which made her uneasy.

In the sixth session, the client again remarked that he did not want to return to the same office because he might re-member the bad feelings and bad atmosphere.

T: What was it about the atmosphere that made you feel bad? [Long silence]

C: It's difficult to explain . . . Maybe I don't have the right capability, or the job is not right for me. [This was the answer that had been repeated many times. The therapist still did not under-stand.]

T: You said you might remember the bad atmosphere. What kind of atmosphere was that?

C: Bad atmosphere . . . maybe others don't find it so bad.

T: [Persistently] But it was bad for you, wasn't it? Can you let me understand what the atmosphere was that made you feel bad? [Silence again] Was it too quiet?

C: No, it was not like that.

T: Were other people too absorbed with their work?

C: Absorbed in work . . . Well, it wasn't easy for me to ask silly questions.

Here was a whole new view of the problem! It wasn't that he had no "capability." He felt foolish to ask questions and didn't want to bother others with "silly" questions. Despite this, however, the company gave him difficult research objectives and he felt overloaded and isolated. The therapist finally understood what was so tough about the job for him.

After the sixth session, the therapy process was changed. Instead of the blocked process in the first five sessions where the client did not touch down inside, the client gradually expressed his feelings, and the topic was changed from the persistent topic of "not having capability" to how to "communicate with others." . . . From there on, the client gradually began to speak from the situation as he felt it. His intellectual evaluation that he "had no capability" diminished. He gradually started to work on how tense he felt about asking questions and how he felt "trenched in" from the attacks coming from his boss. He was "getting in touch with" his feelings, referring to them and explicating from there. (Doi & Ikemi, 2003, pp. 96–98, ellipses in dialogue in original)

MODELING AND DEMONSTRATING FOCUSING WITHOUT HAVING TO TEACH IT

There are always potential complications in trying to teach a skill to a client, or even in subtly facilitating a different way of being, no matter how respectfully. The Focusing moves of pausing and inwardly sensing, being respectful and accepting of what is presently felt, may be modeled by the therapist in her way of being with the client. This modeling can serve as a transmission of the Focusing skills and attitudes in a way that is embedded in the therapeutic relationship, and doesn't carry with it the complications that could arise from the explicit teaching of a skill within psychotherapy.

When the therapist says to the client, genuinely, "I need a moment to take in what you are saying" (see Chapter 4), this communicates to the client on a number of levels. The therapist cares enough about what the client is saying to ask for time to take it in. The concept of needing time to take something in, and the behavior of asking for that time, now have permission and validation within the relationship. The client can do this time-taking too, with his own process.

Ideally, as we've said, the therapist is in contact with his own felt experiencing during the session. This is a source of much of what the therapist says and does, as well as being likely to be experienced by the client as genuine presence. Usually the therapist will not explicitly refer to his own felt sense when speaking to the client, but sometimes there is reason to do so, and then this too becomes a kind of modeling and demonstrating of a Focusing way of being.

> T: While you were talking about your daughter, I started to feel this little aching in my heart. [gestures toward chest] It's something like . . . a feeling of missing something. . . . I get the image of a little girl who is getting ignored. I don't know if that fits at all for you, it's just what comes.
>
> C: [eyes fill with tears] I don't know why I'm crying. . . . I get so caught up in my daughter. . . . I think sometimes that is a way I have of ignoring myself. I have needs too.

MY SELF-IN-PRESENCE HOLDS AND MIRRORS YOURS

What I hope to support in my clients is an inner relationship of caring, compassion, and interested curiosity. In this inner environment, felt senses can form and receive the attention that allows life-forward steps to emerge from them. (See Chapter 5 for a fuller discussion of this inner relationship and some ways to facilitate it.)

There are two other relationships that enable and make possible the quality of the client's nurturing inner relationship: my relationship with the client, and my relationship with myself. In my relationship with my client, I embody qualities of acceptance and interested curiosity, openness to what is not yet articulated, and respect and compassion for what is emerging. I am able to offer these qualities most of the time because they are also embodied in my own inner relationship, because I have been able to turn with acceptance and curiosity toward my own emergent feelings. Having done so, I am more clear, more available in my attention, more flexible about understanding points of view and ways of being other than my own.

What I can give to myself, in the way that I give it to myself, I can also give to you.

Internal Family Systems Therapy has a very similar approach to Focusing in terms of supporting the client's identification with a strong Self from which to be a holding and healing presence for wounded aspects or parts. In a powerful and moving chapter, Schwartz writes about the "parallel process" in which the way that the therapist can be with the client becomes a support for how the client can be with himself.

> Many psychotherapies know that deep healing takes place when a client who expects to be humiliated or rejected experiences the therapist's acceptance and love instead. . . . After disclosing or manifesting their most shameful parts, clients are profoundly relieved to be met with compassion and the words, "It's just a part of you—not who you are—and even that part isn't what it seems to be." This is the parallel process. When the therapist responds to the client's extreme parts from Self, the client does also. Compassion and acceptance are contagious and can seep through the cracks into all levels of the internal system. (2013, p. 5)

As Schwartz points out, the therapist's trust that the client has a strong Self available, which can be accessed and acted from, enables the client to grow in trust in her own ability to be that Self. Most of all, though, it is our own ability to be Self-in-Presence, and to return to it when we lose it for a time, that makes an environment of nurturance and support for the client's growing ability to be Self-in-Presence for herself.

A FOCUSING-ORIENTED THERAPY IS A RELATIONAL THERAPY

The process of change in psychotherapy happens in a relationship in which both people, therapist and client, participate. Therapies that recognize the truth of this can be called "relational," and surely Focusing sits well in a relational therapy. The theory that underlies Focusing, as we saw in Chapter 1, views the life of a living organism as inextricable from its environment. "We feel our life events because our bodies are a continuous experiencing of the whole situation that we are living. . . . The whole body is interaction with its environment in an intricate way" (Madison & Gendlin, 2012, p. 82). And of course, our environment is above all other people.

It is unthinkable that a person could form a felt sense outside a relational context. Even if no other person is in the room at the time that you get a felt sense, you are living in an embedded mesh of relationship, without which you would not even be alive. Within psychotherapy, the therapist-client relational matrix is a space in which felt sensing can have its greatest potential to bring change.

Lynn Preston writes about how client and therapist can get a felt sense of the relational process itself, and how that enhances and amplifies the process of change.

> As we stand on the unclear edge of the ocean of "us-ness," and sense into the "intersubjective field," what comes is newly constituted relational truth. And even if it's a problematic truth, it brings "opening," "give," "freedom," and "groundedness." As the sense of the "us" gets thicker, more complex, more meaningful and precise, the individuals become more their unique, particular selves. (2005, p. 16)

TURBULENCE IN THE INTERPERSONAL SPACE

When things don't go smoothly in the relationship between client and therapist, we need contact with our own felt experience as a resource for the genuine contact with our own feelings and empathy for the feelings of the client that the working through of the trouble calls for. In a sensitive, thoughtful article exploring changes in her own Focusing process related to aging, Joan Lavender (2010) describes a session with a client who was furious with her for a breach of trust and had come in for a last session before quitting therapy. Lavender was able to sense and speak from her present moment experiencing, which resulted in a shift for the client, who decided to remain in therapy.

> While I had failed Terry in the incident preceding this session, in the session cited I was able to manage my feelings enough

to be able to use Focusing as a way to carry forward my and then her (our) experiencing. (2010, p. 32)

When something that occurs interpersonally sets off issues of trust for the client, a combination of empathy for the client's process and aware contact with what we ourselves are feeling can be called on, to support a mutual staying-in-the-moment with what happened, how it felt, and what could emerge from it. Failures and breakdowns in relational interaction are at the heart of almost all—if not all—pathologies, and thus the therapist-client relationship has an exciting potential to be a place where a kind of living forward can happen that, until now, was only implied.

> Whatever is being defeated in the client's usual behavior and interaction pattern must not be defeated here, in this interaction with the therapist. It must instead be carried further and beyond the usual self-defeating pattern. It must succeed here, whereas it usually fails elsewhere. (Gendlin, 1968, p. 220)

The fact that the client can live in the therapeutic relationship in a new way is one level; the client's embodied felt experience of living in that new way, in a shared felt understanding with the therapist, takes the whole experience to another level.

WORKING THROUGH REACTIONS TO CLIENTS

Whether you work within a tradition in which your own reactions to clients are understood as "countertransference," or whether you see your feelings in response to your client as a "relational event" (DeYoung, 2003), or understand them in some other way, there is no question that your own emotional reactions to your clients need attention as a part of the psychotherapy process. And there is no question that there is a world of difference between having those reactions without awareness, versus bringing them to awareness.

Focusing can be a powerfully effective way to bring to awareness and work through reactions to clients that might otherwise block your ability to be present in the way you would like to be. Lauren Mari-Navarro told me:

What I find myself doing if I experience getting activated by a client's content that may overlap with issues in my own life, is that I use the Focusing moves of acknowledging and saying hello to that feeling or part that just got triggered. Learning to focus has made me very quick at recalibrating so that I can bring myself back with full and complete attention to my client, even with intensely activating material. In what seems to be just a matter of milliseconds, I give myself a mini Focusing session, silently saying, "Oh, hello to that place that remembers feeling just that way. I'm acknowledging that that is there in me. I'm letting it know I will come back to that in my own session later, or even just doing some focusing alone after I'm done with this session." I really like feeling I can come back to being fully present for the client no matter how activating that experience may have initially been. My client is who I am there for in this moment, and later I can take care of listening to those places in me that may need more attention. I happen to also be thankful for the opportunity to notice what is left undone in my own emotional life without it impacting the quality of my therapeutic work with clients.

Focusing-oriented therapist Carol Sutherland Nickerson (2009) describes a time when she felt irritated with a client with "borderline" features and was considering telling the client to find another therapist. In a Focusing session facilitated by a colleague, Nickerson acknowledged her own feelings from a place of Self-in-Presence, and invited a felt sense about her reaction to the client. The process brought Nickerson memories of her childhood relationship with her sister. Bodily felt realizations about what was missing in that early relationship brought a sense of relief, and a return to feelings of caring about the client.

> I resumed my work with this client as scheduled and noticed a major shift in my own presence with the client. I no longer felt I needed to be hypervigilant about maintaining composure as I listened to the client. I felt openness inside, like I was listening with new, fresh ears and a renewed commitment to providing optimal clinical treatment. This shift continued and the client's ability to self-regulate and observe her own experience

was evident in her progress over many more months of treatment. (Nickerson, 2009)

Focusing can help you discover whether reactions to clients are "just you"—as seemed to be the case in Nickerson's example—or are somehow coming as a part of the client's process in therapy and need to be brought up there. Gendlin discusses how important it is for the therapist to be aware of uncomfortable reactions in a relationship with a client and then allow them to live in the therapeutic relationship in a new way.

> The therapist keeps a special lookout for reactions of his own that are uncomfortable (feeling "on the spot," embarrassed, impatient, or otherwise troubled). Almost always the therapist will discover these reactions in himself at a time when he has already behaved so as to cover them up, cope with them, suppress them, or try to get away from them. It is natural that we tend to "control" such reactions, and usually they are slight enough to make control very easy. Nevertheless, they contain important information about what is just then happening in the interaction.
>
> It is natural for a therapist to feel a little incompetent or maladjusted himself when he has these reactions. Certainly such reactions will often involve whatever is incompetent or maladjusted in him, and no human lives without such aspects. But to see only this is to miss an essential aspect of psychotherapy: If the client is a troubled person, he cannot possibly fail to rouse difficulties in another person who relates closely with him. He cannot possibly have his troubles all by himself while interacting closely with the therapist. Necessarily, the therapist will experience his own version of the difficulties, twists, and hang-ups which the interaction must have. And only if these do occur can the interaction move beyond them and be therapeutic for the client. . . . Somehow, with the therapist, the patient doesn't only repeat; he gets beyond the repeating. He doesn't only relive; he lives further, if he resolves problems experientially. . . . Thus, feelings of difficulty, stuckness, embarrassment, being manipulated into a spot, resentment, etc., are essential opportunities for the relationship to become therapeutic. But this cannot happen if the therapist

knows only how to "control" these feelings in himself (i.e., force them down). Of course he can control them, since usually they are not very strong. On the contrary, the therapist must make an extra effort to sense them in himself. Certainly he must (and usually can easily) stay in control of such feelings and not be undone or unduly upset by them; but he must also see them as his valuable concrete sense of the now-ongoing difficulty, the now-manifest hang-up of the interaction and of the client's experiencing process. (Gendlin, 1968, p. 218)

Focusing—being Self-in-Presence and sensing what one is feeling from a perspective of curiosity and getting to know it better—allows uncomfortable reactions to be acknowledged, felt, and brought up in therapy with a compassionate awareness, so that the ways in which the client has encountered stopped and stuck interactions in the past can now be lived differently; not avoided, but completed. The therapist's ability to sense his own reactive feelings in the presence of the client and neither push them away ("control") them, nor get caught up in them and thereby react from them without awareness, is absolutely key to this relational process of therapeutic healing.

SELF-CARE

Working with clients, however rewarding, can also be hard on us. Like all caregivers, we can burn out, giving more energy than we have, getting into a cycle of ending each day more drained than fulfilled, and starting the next day without having truly replenished ourselves. Our clients can demand enormous attention, energy, and care with boundaries. In addition, the stories of our clients, some horrific, can lead to an effect now known as "vicarious trauma." (Rothschild, 2002)

Having a process like Focusing can greatly support us in the essential self-care that we need in order to recover our own resiliency in the face of sometimes emotionally and physically draining—and potentially traumatizing—work with our clients.

One clinician said to me, "I myself have low energy and depression and it can be challenging to work with people who have low energy and depression. I can feel my own aliveness being drained. I hear someone talking about the world pressing in like a heavy weight, and all I'm aware of is, I feel like that too." She brings Focusing into her sessions with clients first of all by being aware of her own body, her own reactions. She would be having the reactions anyway, but with Focusing, she is able to be Self-in-Presence with her reactions so they don't interfere with her attention to her clients. She acknowledges the part of her that somehow feels she is supposed to be farther along than her clients. With Focusing, she is not nearly so drained, and is more able to access her strong self with a nurturing quality of self-attention.

Another clinician told me about working with clients who have eating disorders in the severe range. She is especially aware of the seriousness of this potentially life-threatening issue, and she is grateful to have Focusing with her as she works with this type of client. "I sense how important it is for *me* to stay present, with something like anorexia. Because it's a scary illness. So I am Focusing, in contact with how I am, even if I am only taking information. I want to be sure to be very present, and to do that, I want to be sure to be very much in contact with myself."

Using Focusing for self-care may mean Focusing during sessions, acknowledging and inwardly attending to what is coming up for us there. Just as with working through reactions to clients, we may also bring feelings of being drained, overwhelmed, or vicariously traumatized into a Focusing-oriented supervision (Madison, 2004) or peer supervision where we can have the full attention of another person while we spend time with something in us that needs attention. The result is an ability to return to client sessions refreshed and renewed, able to bring our full selves again to the work that our clients do with our company and support.

As clinicians, our own process of being inwardly connected to experiencing from moment to moment in the therapy setting and also before and after we see our clients is crucial and determinative for how much we can facilitate Focusing in our clients. Our own Focusing process is a source of our genuine presence and our ability to respond to our clients in a way that interacts with and supports their own "carrying forward." Our being in touch with ourselves at an experiential level can offer us the emotional presence we need to go through difficult relational times with our clients. We can use Focusing to feel complete-for-now with one client and be ready for the next person through the door, and we can bring our more persistent challenging reactions to clients into Focusing sessions with peers or supervisors so that our own needed steps of change can occur, and clear the way for us to be fully present with our clients.

The Focusing process can support us at the same time that it provides us with a way to support our clients. We and our clients both can be in contact with the fresh edge of experiencing, the emergent process in the moment that is the essence of change.

Appendix

A ONE-PAGER TO SUPPORT CLIENTS IN USING PRESENCE LANGUAGE AT HOME

Overwhelmed? Sometimes we get identified with how we are feeling at a given moment. Our minds and bodies are carrying stress, upsetting events, choices we might be struggling to make, and so on. Maybe we can't think well and feel on the verge of tears, on edge, or like we might lose our temper at any moment. When we are identified with "a part of ourselves," we can experience great difficulty bringing ourselves to the present moment, where we might otherwise feel calmer, clearer, and able to function at a more optimal level. The following is from Inner Relationship Focusing, a mind-body relational process, created by Ann Weiser Cornell, PhD, and Barbara McGavin.

Presence Language

Notice the differences between these sentences:

1. I feel so frustrated by what she did.
2. Something in me feels so frustrated by what she did.
3. I am sensing something in me that feels so frustrated by what she did.

Do you feel a difference?

Your turn:

1. I feel _____.
2. Something in me feels _____.
3. I am sensing something in me that feels _____.

After you shift your language, notice what difference it made.

Adapted from a client handout created by Carol Nickerson, LCSW.

SELF-FOCUSING CUE CARD

Coming In

- "I'm taking time to sense into my body, first the outer areas, then throat, chest, belly, and so on."
- "What wants my awareness now [about that issue]?"

Making Contact

- "I'm sensing something . . ."
- "I'm acknowledging this something."
- "I'm sensing how it would like me to be with it."
- "I'm finding the best way to **describe** it."
- "I'm **checking** the description with my body."

Deepening Contact

- "I'm sensing if it's okay to just **be with** this."
- "I'm sitting with it, with **interested curiosity.**"
- "I'm sensing how *it* **feels** from **its point of view.**"
- "I'm sensing if it has its own **emotion** or mood."
- "I'm letting it know I hear it."
- "I'm open to any more it wants to let me know."

Coming Out

- "I'm letting it know it's time to stop soon."
- "I'm letting it know I'm willing to be back."
- "I'm thanking my body and my body's process."

From the Focusing Training Program, Focusing Resources Inc., http://www
.focusingresources.com.

References

Ainsworth, Mary. (1969). Object relations, dependency and attachment: A theoretical review of the infant-mother relationship. *Child Development*, 40.

Amodeo, John. (2007). A focusing-oriented approach to couples therapy. *Person-Centered and Experiential Psychotherapies*, 6(3), 169–182.

Armstrong, Mary K. (1998). Treating trauma with focusing and EMDR. *The Folio: A Journal for Focusing and Experiential Therapy*, 17(1), 25–30.

Armstrong, Mary K. (2010). *Confessions of a trauma therapist.* Toronto: BPS Books.

Bärlocher, Daniel. (1999). Motivating latent coping resources: Focusing as part of treatment for chronic headaches. *The Folio: A Journal for Focusing and Experiential Therapy*, 18(1), 127–128.

Beck, Judith S. (2011). *Cognitive therapy for challenging problems: What to do when the basics don't work.* New York: Guilford.

Bion, Wilfred. (1967). Notes on memory and desire. *Psychoanalytic Forum*, 2(3), 271–280.

Boukydis, Zack. (2012). *Collaborative consultation with parents and infants in the perinatal period.* Baltimore, MD: Brookes.

Bowlby, John. (1988). *A secure base: Parent-child attachment and healthy human development.* New York: Basic Books.

Brenner, Helene. (2012, January–February). Bringing the heart of focusing-oriented therapy into your practice. Phone seminar offered through Focusing Resources Inc.

Bundschuh-Müller, Karin. (2004). "It is what it is, says love . . . ": Mindfulness and acceptance in person-centred and experiential psychotherapy (Elisabeth Zinschitz, Trans.). In Thomas Heidenreich & Johannes Michalak (Eds.), *Achtsamkeit und Akzeptanz in der Psychotherapie* (pp. 405–456). Tübingen: DGVT-Verlag. English translation: http://www.focusing.org/fot/fot_articles.html

Burns, David D. (1980). *Feeling good: The new mood therapy.* New York: Morrow.

Cornell, Ann Weiser. (1993). Teaching focusing with five steps and four skills. In David Brazier (Ed.), *Beyond Carl Rogers*. London: Constable.

Cornell, Ann Weiser. (1996). *The power of focusing*. Oakland, CA: New Harbinger.

Cornell, Ann Weiser. (2004). How I met Focusing. *Focusing Connection Newsletter*.

Cornell, Ann Weiser. (2005a). *The radical acceptance of everything: Living a focusing life*. Berkeley, CA: Calluna Press.

Cornell, Ann Weiser. (2005b, November–December). An invitation to presence. *Psychotherapy Networker*, 56–61.

Cornell, Ann Weiser. (2008). *The focusing teacher's manual*. Focusing Resources, http://www.focusingresources.com

Cornell, Ann Weiser. (2009). Presence meets ego. *Focusing Connection Newsletter*.

Cornell, Ann Weiser. (2012). Get bigger than what's bugging you. E-course, Focusing Resources, http://www.focusingresources.com/get bigger.htm

Cornell, Ann Weiser, & Fleisch, Glenn. (2007, August 15). Inner relationship focusing in therapy. Presented at American Psychological Association, Division 32.

Cornell, Ann Weiser, & McGavin, Barbara. (2002). *The focusing student's and companion's manual, part one*. Berkeley, CA: Calluna Press.

Cornell, Ann Weiser, & McGavin, Barbara. (2008). Inner relationship focusing. *The Folio: A Journal for Focusing and Experiential Therapy*, *21*(1), 21–33.

Cozolino, Louis. (2002). *The neuroscience of psychotherapy: Building and rebuilding the human brain*. New York: W. W. Norton.

Craske, Michelle. (2010). *Cognitive-behavioral therapy*. Washington, DC: American Psychological Association.

Damasio, Antonio. (1994). *Descartes' error*. New York: Penguin.

Damasio, Antonio. (1999). *The feeling of what happens: Body and emotion in the making of consciousness*. San Diego: Harcourt.

Depestele, Frans. (2004). Space differentiation in experiential psychotherapy. *Person-Centered and Experiential Psychotherapies*, *3*(2), 129–139.

DeYoung, Patricia A. (2003). *Relational psychotherapy*. New York: Routledge.

Doi, A., & Ikemi, A. (2003). How getting in touch with feelings happens: The process of referencing. *Journal of Humanistic Psychology*, *43*(4), 87–101.

Earley, Jay. (2012). *Self-therapy: A step-by-step guide to creating wholeness and healing your inner child using IFS*. Larkspur, CA: Pattern System Books.

Ecker, Bruce, Ticic, Robin, & Hulley, Laurel. (2012). *Unlocking the emotional brain: Eliminating symptoms at their roots using memory reconsolidation.* New York: Routledge.

Elliott, Robert, Davis, Kenneth L., & Slatick, Emil. (1998). Process-experiential therapy for posttraumatic stress disorders. In Leslie S. Greenberg, Jeanne C. Watson, and Germain Lietaer (Eds.), *Handbook of Experiential Psychotherapy.* New York: Guilford.

Elliott, Robert, & Greenberg, Leslie. (1997). Multiple voices in process-experiential therapy: Dialogues between aspects of the self. *Journal of Psychotherapy Integration, 7,* 225–239.

Elliott, Robert, Watson, Jeanne C., Goldman, Rhonda N., & Greenberg, Leslie S. (2004). *Learning emotion-focused therapy: The process-experiential approach to change.* Washington, DC: American Psychological Association.

Fisher, Andy. (2002). *Radical ecopsychology: Psychology in the service of life.* Albany: State University of New York Press.

Fleisch, G. (2008). Right in their hands: How gestures imply the body's next steps in focusing-oriented therapy. *Person-Centered and Experiential Psychotherapies, 8*(3), 173–188.

Fleisch, Glenn. (2009). Personal communication. Training program in Focusing-oriented therapy, lectures and course handouts.

Fodor, Iris. (2001). Making meaning of therapy: A personal narrative of change over four decades. In Marvin R. Goldfried (Ed.), *How therapists change: Personal and professional reflections.* Washington, DC: American Psychological Association.

Fonagy, Peter, Gergely, Gyorgy, Jurist, Elliot, & Target, Mary. (2002). *Affect regulation, mentalization, and the development of the self.* New York: Other Press.

Fosha, Diana. (2000). *The transforming power of affect.* New York: Basic Books.

Fosha, Diana. (2008). Transformance, recognition of self by self, and effective action. In Kirk J. Schneider (Ed.), *Existential-integrative psychotherapy: Guideposts to the core of practice* (pp. 290–320). New York: Routledge.

Fosha, Diana, Siegel, Daniel J., & Solomon, Marion. (Eds.). (2009). *The healing power of emotion: Affective neuroscience, development, and clinical practice.* New York: W. W. Norton.

Frezza, Elena. (2008). Focusing and chronic pain. *The Folio: A Journal for Focusing and Experiential Therapy, 21*(1), 328–337.

Friedman, Neil. (1982). *Experiential therapy and focusing.* New York: Half Court Press.

Friedman, Neil. (1987). *Therapeutic essays.* New York: Half Court Press.

Friedman, Neil. (2007). *Focusing-oriented therapy (FOT).* Lincoln, NE: iUniverse.

Geiser, Christiane. (2010). Moments of movement: Carrying forward structure-bound processes in work with clients suffering from chronic pain. *Person-Centered and Experiential Psychotherapies, 9*(2).

Gendlin, Eugene. (1961). Experiencing: A variable in the process of therapeutic change. *American Journal of Psychotherapy, 15*(2), 233–245.

Gendlin, Eugene. (1964). A theory of personality change. In Philip Worchel & Donn Byrne (Eds.), *Personality change* (pp. 100148). New York: John Wiley and Sons.

Gendlin, Eugene. (1968). The experiential response. In Emanuel Frederick Hammer (Ed.), *Use of interpretation in treatment* (pp. 208–227). New York: Grune and Stratton.

Gendlin, Eugene. (1973). Experiential psychotherapy. In Raymond J. Corsini (Ed.), *Current psychotherapies* (pp. 317–352). Itasca, IL: Peacock.

Gendlin, Eugene. (1978). The body's releasing steps in experiential process. In James L. Fosshage & Paul Olsen (Eds.), *Healing: Implications for psychotherapy* (pp. 323–349). New York: Human Sciences Press.

Gendlin, Eugene. (1981). *Focusing.* New York: Bantam.

Gendlin, Eugene. (1984). The client's client. In Ronald L. Levant & John M. Shlien (Eds.), *Client-centered therapy and the person-centered approach.* New York: Praeger.

Gendlin, Eugene. (1990). The small steps of the therapy process: How they come and how to help them come. In Germain Lietaer, Jan Rombauts, & Richard Van Balen (Eds.), *Client-centered and experiential psychotherapy in the nineties* (pp. 205–224). Leuven: Leuven University Press.

Gendlin, Eugene. (1991). On emotion in therapy. In Jeremy D. Safran & Leslie S. Greenberg (Eds.), *Emotion, psychotherapy and change* (pp. 255–279). New York: Guilford.

Gendlin, Eugene. (1993). Three assertions about the body. *The Folio: A Journal for Focusing and Experiential Therapy, 12*(1), 21–33. .

Gendlin, Eugene. (1996). *Focusing-oriented psychotherapy.* New York: Guilford.

Gendlin, Eugene. (1999). Implicit entry and focusing. *Humanistic Psychologist, 27*(1), 80–88.

Gendlin, Eugene. (2004a). The new phenomenology of carrying forward. *Continental Philosophy Review, 37*(1), 127–151.

Gendlin, Eugene. (2004b). Five philosophical talking points to communicate with colleagues who don't yet know focusing. *Staying in Focus, 4*(1), 5–8.

Gendlin, Eugene. (2007). Focusing: The body speaks from the inside. Presented at the 18th Annual International Trauma Conference, Boston, MA. Transcript available from the Focusing Institute.

Gendlin, Eugene. (2011). Focusing, psychotherapy, and the implicit. Recorded phone seminar, available from http://www.focusingresources .com

Gendlin, Eugene, Beebe, John, Cassens, James, Klein, Marjorie H., & Oberlander, Mark. (1968). Focusing ability in psychotherapy, personality and creativity. In John M. Shlien (Ed.), *Research in psychotherapy* (vol. III, pp. 217–241). Washington, DC: American Psychological Association. http://www.focusing.org/gendlin/docs/gol_2049.html

Gendlin, Eugene., & Lietaer, Germain. (1983). On client-centered and experiential psychotherapy: An interview with Eugene Gendlin. In Wolf-Rudiger Minsel & Wolfgang Herff (Eds.), *Research on psychotherapeutic approaches: Proceedings of the 1st European conference on psychotherapy research, Trier, 1981* (vol. 2, pp. 77–104). Frankfurt am Main: Peter Lang. http://www.focusing.org/gendlin/docs/gol_2102.html

Gendlin, Eugene., & Zimring, Fred. (1955). The qualities or dimensions of experiencing and their change. Counseling Center Discussion Paper, *1*(3). Chicago: University of Chicago Library.

Germer, Christopher K., Siegel, Ronald D., & Fulton, Paul R. (2005). *Mindfulness and psychotherapy*. New York: Guilford.

Goldfried, Marvin R. (Ed.). (2001). *How therapists change: Personal and professional reflections*. Washington, DC: American Psychological Association.

Grindler Katonah, Doralee. (In press). Focusing-oriented psychotherapy: A contemplative approach to healing trauma. In Victoria Follette, Deborah Rozelle, Jim Hopper, David Rome, & John Briere (Eds.), *Contemplative methods in trauma treatment: Integrating mindfulness and other approaches*. New York: Guilford.

Harris, Russ. (2009). *ACT made simple*. Oakland, CA: New Harbinger.

Hendricks, Marion N. (1986). Experiencing level as a therapeutic variable. *Person-Centered Review, 1*(2), 141–162.

Hendricks, Marion N. (2001). Focusing-oriented/experiential psychotherapy. In David Cain & Jules Seeman (Eds.), *Humanistic psychotherapies: Handbook of research and practice*. Washington, DC: American Psychological Association.

Hendricks-Gendlin, Mary. (2003). Focusing as a force for peace: The revolutionary pause. Keynote address to the Fifteenth Focusing International Conference 2003 in Germany, available at http://www .focusing.org/social_issues/hendricks_peace.html

Hinterkopf, Elfie. (2004). The experiential focusing approach. In Len Sperry & Edward P. Shafranske (Eds.), *Spiritually oriented psychotherapy*. Washington, DC: American Psychological Association.

Ikemi, Akira. (2007). Focusing/listening training program in business corporations: A personal account of its development in Japan. http:// www.focusing.org/business/japan.htm

Ikemi, Akira. (2010). An explication of focusing-oriented therapy from a therapy case. *Person-Centered and Experiential Psychotherapies, 9*(2).

Jaison, Bala. (2004). *Integrating experiential and brief therapy: How to do deep therapy—briefly and how to do brief therapy—deeply.* Toronto: Focusing for Creative Living.

Johnson, Sue. (2008). *Hold me tight: Seven conversations for a lifetime of love.* New York: Little, Brown.

Kabat-Zinn, Jon. (2005). *Coming to our senses.* New York: Hyperion.

Klagsbrun, Joan. (1999). Focusing, illness, and health care. *The Folio: A Journal for Focusing and Experiential Therapy, 18*(1), 162–170.

Klagsbrun, Joan. (2001). Integrating focusing with health care. *Staying in Focus, 1*(1).

Klein, Marjorie H., Mathieu, Philippa L., Gendlin, Eugene T., & Kiesler, Donald J. (1969). *The experiencing scale: A research and training manual* (vol. 1). Madison: Wisconsin Psychiatric Institute.

Kohut, Heinz. (1984). *How does analysis cure?* Chicago: University of Chicago Press.

Korbei, Lore. (2007). Eugene Gendlin. (Elisabeth Zinchitz, Trans.). Unpublished manuscript. (Original work published 1994.) From http://www.focusing.org/gendlin/docs/gol_2181.html

Kurtz, Ron. (1997). *Body-centered psychotherapy: The Hakomi method.* Mendocino, CA: LifeRhythm.

Lavender, Joan. (2010). Some thoughts about focusing and aging: Losses and gains. In *The Folio: A Journal for Focusing and Experiential Therapy, 22*(1), 26–35.

Leijssen, Mia. (2007). Coping with fear in short-term experiential psychotherapy. *The Folio: A Journal for Focusing and Experiential Therapy, 20*(1), 25–35.

Lessem, Peter A. (2005). *Self psychology: An introduction.* Lanham, MD: Jason Aronson.

Levine, Peter. (1997). *Waking the tiger.* Berkeley, CA: North Atlantic Books.

Levine, Peter. (2010). *In an unspoken voice: How the body releases trauma and restores goodness.* Berkeley, CA: North Atlantic Books.

Linehan, Marsha M. (1993). *Cognitive behavioral treatment of borderline personality disorder.* New York: Guilford.

Madison, Greg. (2001). Focusing, intersubjectivity, and therapeutic intersubjectivity. *Review of Existential Psychology and Psychiatry, 26*(1), 3–16.

Madison, Greg. (2004). Focusing-oriented supervision. In Keith Tudor & Mike Worrall (Eds.), *Freedom to practice.* London: PCCS Books.

Madison, Greg. (2011). Let your body be your coach. In Emmy van Deurzen & Monica Hanaway (Eds.), *Existential coaching* (pp. 117–127). London: Palgrave.

Madison, Greg, & Gendlin, Eugene. (2012). Palpable existentialism: An interview with Eugene Gendlin. In Laura Barnett & Greg Madison (Eds.), *Existential therapy: Legacy, vibrancy and dialogue* (pp. 81–96). New York: Routledge.

Main, M. (1999). Epilogue. Attachment theory: Eighteen points with suggestions for future studies. In Jude Cassidy & Phillip R. Shaver (Eds.), *Handbook of attachment: Theory, research, and clinical applications.* New York: Guilford.

McGavin, Barbara. (1994, September). The victim, the critic, and the inner relationship: Focusing with the part that wants to die. *Focusing Connection.*

McGavin, Barbara, & Cornell, Ann Weiser. (2002). *The focusing student's and companion's manual, part two.* Berkeley, CA: Calluna Press.

McGavin, Barbara, & Cornell, Ann Weiser. (2008). Treasure maps to the soul. *The Folio: A Journal for Focusing and Experiential Therapy, 21*(1), 41–60.

Mearns, Dave, & Thorne, Brian. (2007). *Person-centred counselling in action.* Thousand Oaks, CA: Sage.

Millan, Cesar. (2007). *Be the pack leader.* New York: Harmony Books.

Müller, Dieter, & Feuerstein, Heinz-Joachim. (1999). Chronic physical pain: Your body knows the answer. *The Folio: A Journal for Focusing and Experiential Therapy, 18*(1), 96–107.

Nickerson, Carol J. Sutherland. (2009). Inner relationship focusing: Strengthening attachment and interpersonal neurobiological integration. Focusing Resources, http://www.focusingresources.com/articles/strengthening_attachment.htm

Nickerson, Carol J. Sutherland. (2012). Attachment and neuroscience: The benefits of being a focusing oriented professional. *The Folio: A Journal for Focusing and Experiential Therapy, 23*(1), 47–57.

Ogden, Pat, Minton, Kekuni, & Pain, Claire. (2006). *Trauma and the body: A sensorimotor approach to psychotherapy.* New York: W. W. Norton.

Omidian, Pat, & Lawrence, Nina Joy. (2007). A community based approach to focusing: The Islam and focusing project of Afghanistan. *The Folio: A Journal for Focusing and Experiential Therapy, 20*(1), 152–160.

Parker, Rob. (2007). Making peace from the inside. *The Folio: A Journal for Focusing and Experiential Therapy, 20*(1), 36–47.

Perls, Fritz, Hefferline, Ralph F., & Goodman, Paul. (1951). *Gestalt therapy.* New York: Julian Press.

Preston, Lynn. (2005). Two interwoven miracles: The relational dimension of focusing-oriented therapy. Focusing Institute, www.focusing.org/fot/fot_articles.html

Preston, Lynn. (2008). The edge of awareness. *International Journal of Psychoanalytic Self Psychology, 3*(4).

Purton, Campbell. (2004). *Person-centred therapy: The focusing-oriented approach*. London: Palgrave-Macmillan.

Purton, Campbell. (2007). *The focusing-oriented counselling primer*. Ross-on-Wye, UK: PCCS Books.

Purton, Campbell. (2010). Introduction to the special issue on focusing-oriented therapy. *Person-Centered and Experiential Psychotherapies, 9*(2).

Rappaport, Laury. (2009). *Focusing-oriented art therapy: Accessing the body's wisdom and creative intelligence*. London: Jessica Kingsley.

Rogers, Carl. (1958). A process conception of psychotherapy. *American Psychologist, 13*(4), 142–149.

Rogers, Carl. (1961). *On becoming a person*. Boston: Houghton-Mifflin.

Rogers, Carl. (1986a). Reflection of feelings. *Person-Centered Review, 1*(4). (Reprinted in *The Carl Rogers Reader*. Boston: Houghton Mifflin, 1989.)

Rogers, Carl. (1986b). Client-centered approach to therapy. In Irwin L. Kutash & Alexander Wolf (Eds.), *Psychotherapist's casebook: Theory and technique in practice* (pp. 197–208). San Francisco: Jossey Bass.

Rogers, Carl. (1994). *Freedom to learn* (3rd ed.). New York: Prentice Hall.

Rothschild, Babette. (2000). *The body remembers: The psychophysiology of trauma and trauma treatment*. New York: W. W. Norton.

Rothschild, Babette. (2002, July–August). Understanding dangers of empathy. *Psychotherapy Networker*.

Rowe, Crayton E., Jr., & MacIsaac, David S. (1991). *Empathic attunement*. Oxford: Rowman and Littlefield.

Scaer, Robert C. (2001). *The body bears the burden: Trauma, dissociation, and disease*. Binghamton, NY: Haworth.

Schegloff, Emanuel A. (1968). Sequencing in conversational opening. *American Anthropologist, 70*, 1075–1095.

Schore, Allan N. (2003). *Affect regulation and the repair of the self*. New York: W. W. Norton.

Schwartz, Richard C. (1995). *Internal family systems therapy*. New York: Guilford.

Schwartz, Richard C. (2013). The therapist-client relationship in internal family systems therapy. In Martha Sweezy & Ellen Ziskind (Eds.), *Internal family systems therapy: New dimensions*. New York: Routledge.

Shapiro, Francine. (2002). *EMDR as an integrative psychotherapy approach: Experts of diverse orientations explore the paradigm prism*. Washington, DC: American Psychological Association Books.

Siegel, Daniel J. (2007). *The mindful brain: Reflection and attunement in the cultivation of well-being*. New York: W. W. Norton.

Siegel, Daniel J. (2010). *The mindful therapist*. New York: W. W. Norton.

Stapert, Marta, & Verliefde, Erik. (2008). *Focusing with children*. Ross-on-Wye, UK: PCCS Books.

Stern, Daniel N. (2004). *The present moment in psychotherapy and everyday life*. New York: W. W. Norton.

Stolorow, Robert, & Atwood, George. (1992). *Contexts of being: The intersubjective foundations of psychological life*. Hillsdale, NJ: Analytic Press.

Stone, Hal, & Stone, Sidra. (1993). *Embracing your inner critic*. San Francisco: HarperSanFrancisco.

Suetake, Yasuhiro. (2010). The clinical significance of Gendlin's process model. *Person-Centered and Experiential Psychotherapies, 9*(2).

Summerville, Mary Ellen. (1999). Listening from the heart to people living with cancer. *The Folio: A Journal for Focusing and Experiential Therapy, 18*(1), 42–46.

Tidmarsh, Alan. (2010, May 5–9). Being-with the being-without: Relational focusing with substance misusers. Presented at the 22nd International Focusing Conference, Hohenwart Forum, Germany.

Vanaerschot, Greet. (2004). It takes two to tango: On empathy with fragile processes. *Psychotherapy: Theory, Research, Practice, Training, 41*(2), 112–124.

Van der Kolk, Bessel A., van der Hart, Onno, & Marmar, Charles R. (1996). Dissociation and information processing in posttraumatic stress disorder. In Bessel A. Van der Kolk, Alexander C. McFarlane, and Lars Weisaeth (Eds.), *Traumatic stress*. New York: Guilford.

Wachtel, Paul L. (2008). *Relational theory and the practice of psychotherapy*. New York: Guilford.

Wallin, David J. (2007). *Attachment in psychotherapy*. New York: Guilford.

Warner, Margaret S. (1998). A client-centered approach to therapeutic work with dissociated and fragile process. In Leslie S. Greenberg, Jeanne C. Watson, & Germain Lietaer (Eds.), *Handbook of experiential psychotherapy*. New York: Guilford.

Warner, Margaret S. (2000). Person-centred therapy at the difficult edge: A developmentally based model of fragile and dissociated process. In Dave Mearns & Brian Thorne (Eds.), *Person-centred therapy today: New frontiers in theory and practice*. Thousand Oaks, CA: Sage.

Yalom, Irvin. (2002). *The gift of therapy*. New York: HarperCollins.

Yalom, Victor, & Yalom, Marie-Helene. (2010). Peter Levine on somatic experiencing. Psychotherapy.net, http://www.psychotherapy.net/interview/interview-peter-levine

INDEX

Index

empathic reflection, worried inner
    critic and, 152
empathy, xxii–xxiv, 7, 21, 135, 199
    inner, 113
    maintaining inner relationship of,
        100
    for not-wanting-to-happen of a
        part, 121
    Self-in-Presence and, 101
    turbulence in the interpersonal
        space and, 217
    working with forms and, 35
empowerment, 55
enjoyable feelings
    encouraging, 129, 130, 132, 133,
        143, 180
    as resource for Self-in-Presence,
        102–3
evaluating client, 149–50
evaluating feelings, being with vs.,
    114
existential-phenomenological therapy,
    "being" vs. "doing" and, 205
expanding attunement, as intersubjec-
    tive process, 187
expectations, mutual responsibilities
    and, 35–36
experienced body, 47
"experience-near"
    empathy in therapist-client rela-
        tionship and, 7
    first session with new client and, 32
experiencing, xvi
    change and, xxii
    clients referring directly to, xvii
    implicit dimension of, 47
    manner of, 9
    mindfulness and, 86
Experiencing Scale, xv, 9–11, 177
experiential change step, 14
experiential environment, 31
experiential guesses, offering, 36
experiential psychotherapy, Focusing
    and, 197–198
"Explication of Focusing-Oriented
    Therapy From a Therapy Case,
    An" (Ikemi), 174
explicit invitations, 56
eye contact, 31
Eye Movement Desensitization and
    Reprocessing (EMDR), Focusing
    combined with, 196–97
facilitative language, 57, 77
fear
    deeper layer of "not wanting some-
        thing to happen" and, 120

disidentifying from, 80
feelings
    current, inviting, 71
    feeling about, 103–5
    not wanted, 120–22
    wanted, 122–23
feeling state, being identified with, 92
felt experience
    attending to contact with, 100–101
    using words "it" and "something"
        for, 98
felt sense(s), xvi–xvii, 40, 87
    adjectives and, 76
    being open to feeling "bad" and,
        148–49
    change after formation of, 22–24,
        25
    client's inward checking of words
        and, 59–61
    clinician's own ability to be aware
        of, 200
    defining, 45–46
    delicacy of, 55
    describing, 21–22, 58–59
    distinguishing from emotions, 48–51
    as doorway into implicit dimension,
        60
    as doorway to fresh possibilities,
        111
    Emotionally Focused Therapy and,
        199
    experiences that are not felt senses,
        44–45
    explaining to client, 38
    explaining to others, 39
    expressing as a movement, 193
    Focusing for the therapist and, 201
    forming of, 4–5, 42, 61, 90, 97, 98,
        109, 112
    going beyond frozen structures and,
        19–21
    helping client to move toward, 113
    IFS therapy and, 189
    ignoring, temptation with, 52–53
    immediate, returning to, 69–70
    inner environment and, 215
    inviting directly, 67–68, 186
    "more than words can say" quality
        to, 43
    new awareness and, 22
    new conception of "body" and,
        47–48
    on not telling your clients about,
        61–62, 105
    "parts" vs., 109
    pausing, slowing down and, 63–68